PRACT █████████████ SO-BLN-396

# Scholastic
# Aptitude
# Tests

Complete Preparation for the
Scholastic Aptitude Test
Preliminary Scholastic Aptitude Test
and the
National Merit Scholarship
Qualifying Test

AN
ARCO
BOOK
**ARCO PUBLISHING, INC.**
219 PARK AVENUE SOUTH, NEW YORK, N.Y. 10003

An Arc Book
Published by Arco Publishing, Inc.
219 Park Avenue South, New York, N.Y. 10003

Third Edition, Fourth Printing, 1979

**Library of Congress Cataloging in Publication Data**

Main entry under title:

Practice for scholastic aptitude tests.

  Editions of 1963 and 1965 by E. C. Gruber.
  1. Scholastic aptitude test.   I. Gruber, Edward C.
Practice for scholastic aptitude tests.   II. Arco
Publishing, New York.

LB2367.G78      1977      378.1′6′64      77-3325
ISBN 0-668-04303-2 (Paper Edition)

Printed in the United States of America

# HOW THIS BOOK IS ARRANGED

This book is designed to help you achieve a higher mark on the Scholastic Aptitude Test. If you study the book diligently you will be able to answer the College Board questions much more easily.

PART I contains information that will familiarize you with the various aspects of the College Board Entrance Examination program—the nature of the test, how to prepare for it, etc.

PART II consists of a "College Board Vocabulary List" of more than 1,600 words. For a better score on the SAT, it is most important that you study this list and master it.

PART III gives a complete sample Scholastic Aptitude Test based upon the actual SAT.

PART IV, "Pinpoint Practice to Raise Your Mark," is really the heart of the book. Here is a thorough treatment of each phase of the SAT. Test after test is given in every type of question so that you may readily pinpoint and eliminate your weaknesses. An answer key follows each test.

PART V, "Parting Words of Advice," offers numerous helpful tips on preparing for the exam.

## THIS BOOK WILL HELP YOU

This book is designed to guide you in your study so that you will SCORE HIGH ON THE SCHOLASTIC APTITUDE TEST. This claim—that you will get a higher rating if you use this book properly—has both *educational and psychological validity for these reasons:*

1. YOU WILL KNOW WHAT TO STUDY—A candidate will do better on a test if he knows what to study. The Sample Test and SAT-type questions in this book will tell you what to study.

**2. YOU WILL SPOTLIGHT YOUR WEAKNESSES—** In using this book, you will discover where your weaknesses lie. The self-diagnosis will provide you with a systematic procedure of study whereby you will spend the greater part of your time where it will do you the most good.

**3. YOU WILL GET THE "FEEL" OF THE EXAM—** It is important to get the "feel" of the entire examination. Gestalt (meaning *configuration* or *pattern*) psychology stresses that true learning results in a grasp of the *entire situation*. Gestaltists also tell us that we learn by "insight." One of the salient facets of this type of learning is that we succeed in "seeing through" a problem as a consequence of experiencing *previous similar situations*. This book contains hundreds and hundreds of "similar situations"—so you will discover when you take the actual examination.

**4. YOU WILL GAIN CONFIDENCE—** While preparing for the exam, you will build up confidence, and you will retain this confidence when you enter the exam room. This feeling of confidence will be a natural consequence of reason "3" above (getting the "feel" of the exam).

**5. YOU WILL ADD TO YOUR KNOWLEDGE—** "The learned become more learned." In going over the practice questions in this book, you will not—if you use this book properly—be satisfied merely with the answer to a particular question. You will want to do additional research on the other choices of the same questions. In this way, you will broaden your background to be adequately prepared for the exam to come, since it is quite possible that a question on the exam which you are going to take may require your knowing the meaning of one of these other choices. Thorndike's principle of "identical elements" explains this important phase of learning—particularly as it applies to examination preparation.

# Contents

## Part One

### ESSENTIAL INFORMATION CONCERNING THE SCHOLASTIC APTITUDE TEST

# CONTENTS

## Part Two

## SCHOLASTIC APTITUDE TEST WORD LIST

## Part Three

## SCHOLASTIC APTITUDE TEST (SAMPLE)

# CONTENTS

## Part Four

## PINPOINT PRACTICE TO RAISE YOUR MARK

# CONTENTS

## Part Five

# PARTING WORDS OF ADVICE

# PART ONE
# ESSENTIAL INFORMATION CONCERNING
# THE SCHOLASTIC APTITUDE TEST

# All About the S.A.T.

## WHAT IS THE SAT?

The SAT is a three-hour multiple-choice examination offered by the Educational Testing Service on behalf of the College Entrance Examination Board as part of the Admissions Testing Program.

The SAT is designed to measure the verbal and mathematical abilities important for success in college. SAT scores give colleges a standard for evaluating the scholastic aptitudes of candidates from many different secondary schools. These scores, along with high school grades, recommendations, and interview reports, provide the basis for selection of students.

The SAT also measures the ability to use standard written English. However, this score is used for placement rather than selection purposes.

### Who Takes the Exam

With the steady increase of student enrollment in colleges throughout the country, some of these institutions are now "bursting at the seams." These schools of advanced learning are, accordingly, becoming more and more selective in student admission. Since secondary schools have varying standards of grading, it is understandable that high school marks alone will not suffice in the effort

11

to appraise objectively the ability of an undergraduate to do college work. An "A" in a course of English in High School X, may be worth a "C" in High School Y. Moreover, it is an accepted fact that even the teachers within a high school may differ among themselves in grading techniques. The SAT is highly objective. Consequently, it has become a sine qua non for many college admissions officers in order to predict success or lack of success for applicants.

The college interprets the SAT results as it (the school) sees it. A college that specializes in journalism, for example, will probably place more emphasis on the Verbal part of the Aptitude Test than on the Mathematical part. The stress may likely be reversed for admission to a college that gears its curricula about the sciences.

Applicants to well over 2000 colleges and universities in the United States and Canada are required to take the SAT as part of the application process. Application information supplied by each college specifies which examinations are required and the dates on which they should be taken. If you have not yet chosen among colleges, you should take the SAT in early winter of your senior year in order to meet the deadlines of whichever colleges you might choose.

## How Questions Are to Be Answered

The following will help you become familiar with the way in which answers are to be recorded.

30. Chicago is a
    (A) state (B) city (C) country (D) town (E) village

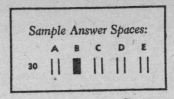

Note that the letters of the suggested answers appear on the answer sheet and that *you are to blacken the space beneath the letter of the answer you wish to give.*

## How to Prepare for the Scholastic Aptitude Test

Let us sound a warning at the very start of this discussion of "How to Prepare for the Scholastic Aptitude Test." Don't wait till a week or even a month before the examination, in starting your preparation for it. Cramming will do little for you. Be systematic. First, take the sample SAT that begins on page 69. Analyze the results. You should, thereby, get a fairly good idea of your areas of strength and your areas of weakness. Then concentrate on fortifying yourself where you are weak. Work hard with questions in those fields where the sample Test has spotlighted initial "softness." Work, work, work in these areas. You will fare considerably better on the SAT by following this simple procedure.

## How to Take the Scholastic Aptitude Test

There is no reason to become disturbed if you find that you are unable to answer a number of questions in a test or if you are unable to finish. No one is expected to get a perfect score, and there are no established "passing" or "failing" grades. Your score compares your performance with that of other candidates taking the test, and the report to the college shows the relation of your score to the scores obtained by other candidates.

Although the tests stress accuracy more than speed, it is important for you to use your time as economically as possible. Work steadily and as rapidly as you can without becoming careless. Take the questions in order, but do not waste time in pondering over questions which, for you, contain extremely difficult or unfamiliar material.

## Format of the Examination

The SAT is divided into six parts of thirty minutes each. In every form of the examination, two parts test verbal ability and two parts test mathematical ability. How well you do on these four parts determines the scores that will be reported to the schools you have designated.

A fifth part of the exam tests your ability to use standard written English. This part is scored separately and the score is used for placement only.

The remaining part may be either another verbal section or another mathematical section. In either case, the questions tend to be experimental in content, form, or timing, and the results are used by the testmakers for writing future tests. It may be quite clear to you which are the experimental questions, or the variations may be very subtle. In any case, it is to your advantage to do well on all six parts of the exam.

## What Subjects Are Covered

The SAT is a test of general intellectual ability, not an achievement test. Its purpose is to assess your future learning potential on the basis of how you have developed intellectually to this point.

There are four types of Verbal Questions on the SAT—two test Reading Comprehension, and two test Vocabulary. The Reading Comprehension questions include Sentence Completions to probe both your understanding of what you read and your ability to think logically, and Reading Interpretation to test your ability to analyze and evaluate reading material. The Vocabulary questions include Opposites to test the extent of your vocabulary and Analogies to measure your understanding of word relationships.

The Mathematical Questions cover arithmetic, algebra, and geometry through what is typically taught in ninth grade. You are not expected to memorize formulas. The formulas you need will be given to you along with the instructions. While the content of the questions is limited to basic math, the form of the questions may be quite unusual and require understanding of principles and flexibility of thought.

The questions testing your ability to use Standard Written English are of two types: a Usage test which requires you to locate an error within a sentence, and a Correction test which requires you to choose the most correct version of a given sentence.

## Verbal Part of the SAT

You will find a complete treatment of the Verbal Ability part of the Scholastic Aptitude Test in Part Four of this book. In these pages, you will get an explanation of each type of verbal question given. You will also be shown how to analyze each type. In addition, you will be provided with practice questions and answers for each type.

The Verbal section in the book includes adequate reference to the following classifications:

1. Vocabulary
   A. Synonyms
   B. Opposites
   C. Sentence Completions
2. Analogies
3. Reading Comprehension

Samples of each of the above types are illustrated here.


## SYNONYMS

*Directions:* Select the word (or words) in each group nearest in meaning to the word in capitals. Then, on the answer sheet, blacken the space beneath the letter corresponding to the letter of the answer you have chosen.

1. ABNEGATION
   (A) renunciation (B) failure to conform to rule (C) utter humiliation (D) sudden departure (E) confirmation

2. CLAUSTROPHOBIC
   (A) susceptible to disease (B) opposed to gambling (C) dreading closed places (D) hating or fearful of dogs (E) philosophic

3. SPUME
   (A) flood (B) froth (C) fountain (D) spillway in a dam (E) fume


## OPPOSITES

*Directions:* Select the word (or words) in each group opposite in meaning to the word in capitals. Then on the answer sheet, blacken the space beneath the letter corresponding to the letter of the answer you have chosen.

4. MUTATION
   (A) factotum (B) expiation (C) continuance (D) megalomania (E) numismatist

5. DIFFIDENCE
   (A) imbroglio (B) temerity (C) cognomen (D) effervescence (E) monopoly

6. AMALGAMATE
   (A) recriminate (B) procrastinate (C) scintillate (D) segregate (E) recuperate

## SENTENCE COMPLETIONS

*Directions:* Each of the sentences below has one or more blank spaces, each blank indicating that a word has been omitted. Beneath the sentence are five lettered words or sets of words. You are to choose the one word or set of words which, when inserted in the sentence, *best* fits in with the meaning of the sentence as a whole. Then, on the answer sheet, blacken the space beneath the letter corresponding to the letter of the answer you have chosen.

7. Andrew Jackson believed that wars were inevitable, and to him the length and irregularity of our coast presented a _____ that called for a more than merely passive navy.
   (A) defense (B) barrier (C) provocation (D) vulnerability (E) dispute

8. The progressive yearly _____ of the land, caused by the depositing of mud from the river, makes it possible to estimate the age of excavated remains by

noting the depth at which they are found below the present level of the valley.
(A) erosion (B) elevation (C) improvement (D) irrigation (E) displacement

9. It is a mistake to _____ the beliefs of an entire people from the _____ of a few representatives.
(A) deduce–actions (B) influence–appointment (C) question–success (D) glorify–failures (E) criticize–abilities

## ANALOGIES

*Directions:* Each of these questions consists of two words which have a certain relationship to each other, followed by five lettered pairs of related words. Choose the lettered pair of words which are related to each other in the *same* way as the words of the original pair are related to each other. Then, on the answer sheet, blacken the space beneath the letter corresponding to the letter of the pair you have chosen.

10. LAMP : LIGHT ::
(A) speech : applause (B) school : students (C) radiator : heat (D) typewriter : key (E) knowledge : life

11. BOAST : BRAGGART ::
(A) hope : optimist (B) happiness : idealist (C) admiration : hero (D) promise : friend (E) pride : prude

12. GRIEVANCE : REDRESS ::
(A) loss : compensation (B) reprisal : restitution (C) will : settlement (D) sorrow : pleasure (E) crime : punishment

## READING COMPREHENSION

*Directions:* Following the passage below, you will find three incomplete statements about the passage. Each statement is followed by five words or expressions. Select the word or expression that most satisfactorily completes each statement in accordance with the meaning of the passage. Then, on the answer sheet, blacken the space beneath the letter corresponding to the letter of the answer you have chosen.

The teacher lives in what has happened to the minds of his students, and in what they remember of things infinitely greater than themselves or than himself. They will remember, perhaps, that once in a while, in the midst of the routine of the classroom, it was something not himself that spoke, something not themselves that listened. The teacher may well be content to be otherwise forgotten, or to live in something grown to ripeness in his students that he, however minutely, helped bring to birth. There are many students thus come to fruition whom I should be proud to have say: "He was my teacher." There is no other immortality a teacher can have.

13. The title below that best expresses the ideas of this passage is:
    (A) moments of genius (B) the forgotten teacher (C) artist in the classroom (D) infinity in education (E) immortality for the teacher

14. A teacher is best known by
    (A) his jokes (B) what he quotes (C) his absent-mindedness (D) what his pupils achieve (E) his ability to manage class routine

15. The writer probably taught
    (A) first grade (B) mature adults (C) nursery school

(D) in ancient times (E) high school or college students

### Answer Key to Sample Verbal Questions

| | | | | |
|---|---|---|---|---|
| 1. A | 4. C | 7. D | 10. C | 13. E |
| 2. C | 5. B | 8. B | 11. A | 14. D |
| 3. B | 6. D | 9. A | 12. A | 15. E |

## Mathematics Part of the SAT

The Mathematics section of the Scholastic Aptitude Test is given at the same sitting during which you take the Verbal part (three hours altogether).

The Mathematics part tests your understanding of basic quantitative concepts such as the following:

Fractions
Conversion of Units
Ratio and Proportion
Averages
Interest and Percent
Time and Work
Rate, Time, and Distance
Series
Decimals
Algebra
Geometry
Graphs, Charts, and Tables

You will be asked to demonstrate your understanding of the above concepts by applying your knowledge to such problems as you have had in secondary school and, possibly, in elementary school. The Mathematical Ability Test is not a test of Advanced Mathematics. There are no problems in Advanced Algebra, Solid Geometry, Trigonometry, and such fields of advanced mathematical study.

Pages 277–293 will give you considerable practice for the Mathematics part of the Scholastic Aptitude Test. Samples of each type of mathematical concept are given below:

## Mathematical Ability

Samples of each of the foregoing mathematical types are illustrated below.

*Directions:* Each of the questions in this section is followed by five possible answers lettered A through E. Select the correct answer to each question and mark the corresponding space on the answer sheet.

### FRACTIONS

1. The fractional equivalent of .0625 is
   (A) 1/16 (B) 1/15 (C) 1/14 (D) 1/13 (E) 1/6

### CONVERSION OF UNITS

2. A boy picked one bushel of huckleberries and sold 24 quarts. How many quarts were left?
   (A) 4 (B) 8 (C) 12 (D) 16 (E) 20

### RATIO AND PROPORTION

3. In a certain city 12% of the elementary school teachers are men, 40% of the high school teachers are men,

and 20% of all the teachers in the elementary and high schools combined are men. What is the ratio of the number of elementary school teachers to the number of high school teachers?

(A) $\frac{13}{50}$  (B) $\frac{1}{2}$  (C) $\frac{5}{2}$  (D) $\frac{13}{5}$  (E) $\frac{10}{3}$

## AVERAGES

4. The salary for a group of executives was listed as follows: 18 at $5,000; 10 at $6,000; 8 at $7,500; 2 at $9,000; 2 at $10,000. The average salary was
(A) $5,400 (B) $6,000 (C) $6,200 (D) $6,400 (E) $7,000

## INTEREST AND PERCENT

5. A man's income is $25,000 per annum; his expenses per annum are $15,000. What per cent of his income does he save?
(A) 30% (B) 40% (C) 37½% (D) 60% (E) none of these

## TIME AND WORK

6. A laborer in Japan worked 30 days. He paid 2/5 of his earnings for board and room and had $81 left. What was his daily wage?

(A) $4.50 (B) $5.75 (C) $6.75 (D) $7.25 (E) $8.00

## RATE, TIME, AND DISTANCE

7. A man traveling 100 miles at $r$ miles per hour arrived at his destination 2 hours late. How many miles an hour should he have traveled to arrive on time?

(A) $\dfrac{50 - r}{50r}$  (B) $\dfrac{50r}{50 + r}$  (C) $\dfrac{100 - 2r}{r}$

(D) $\dfrac{50r}{50 - r}$  (E) $\dfrac{50r + 1}{50}$

## SERIES

8. In the series .04, .2, 5, _____ the number that follows logically is
   (A) 10 (B) 20 (C) 25 (D) 50 (E) 100

## DECIMALS

9. When 5.1 is divided by 0.017 the quotient is
   (A) 30 (B) 300 (C) 3,000 (D) 30,000

## ALGEBRA

10. A man was $r$ years old $m$ years ago. His age $b$ years from now would be expressed by
    (A) $r + m + b$ (B) $r - m + b$ (C) $m + r - b$
    (D) $b + m - 4$

## GEOMETRY

11. In the figure to the right, the
    length of diagonal AC is
    (A) 10 inches (B) 14 inches
    (C) 18 inches (D) 48 inches
    (E) 96 inches

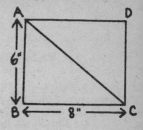

## GRAPHS, CHARTS, AND TABLES

Answer question 12 from the table below.

Distribution of the Total Population of the United States by Age Groups, 1940:

| Age Group | Per Cent |
|---|---|
| Under 15 | 25.00 |
| 15 to 34 | 34.50 |
| 35 to 54 | 25.62 |
| 55 to 74 | 12.90 |
| 75 and over | 1.98 |
| | 100.00 |

12. If, in the United States in 1940, 30 million persons were under 15 years of age, how many million persons (to the nearest 0.1 million) were in the 75 and over age group?
    (A) 1.7 (B) 2.0 (C) 2.4 (D) 23.8 (E) 37.9

### Answer Key to Sample Mathematical Questions

| | | | | | |
|---|---|---|---|---|---|
| 1. A | 3. E | 5. B | 7. D | 9. B | 11. A |
| 2. B | 4. C | 6. A | 8. C | 10. A | 12. C |

## Sample Problem:

*Directions:* For each of the following questions two quantities are given ... one in Column A; and one in Column B. Compare the two quantities and mark your answer sheet with the correct, lettered conclusion. These are your options:

A: if the quantity in Column A is the greater;
B: if the quantity in Column B is the greater;
C: if the two quantities are equal;
D: if the relationship cannot be determined from the information given.

| Item | Column A | Column B |
|------|----------|----------|
| $A * B = \dfrac{1}{A^2} + \dfrac{B}{2}$ | $\frac{2}{3} * \frac{1}{4}$ | $\frac{1}{4} * \frac{2}{3}$ |

## SOLUTION TO SAMPLE PROBLEM

(B) The value of Column A is $2\frac{3}{8}$, while the value of Column B is $16\frac{1}{3}$. Therefore, $B > A$.

## When and Where the Examination Is Given

The SAT is administered on six Saturday mornings at various regional test centers located in every state. The exam is not offered at each center on each date. When you write for the application form, you will receive the necessary information about time and place. The Student Bulletin which will be sent to you along with your application form will also give instructions for "exceptions" to routine administration circumstances.

## Important Information and Helpful Hints

**1. About skipping questions.** There is no penalty for skipping a question. While the questions are arranged in approximate order of difficulty, you may find some earlier questions more difficult than some later ones. Do not waste time puzzling over a difficult question. If there is time left, you can go back to it when you have finished the questions in that part which you find easier.

**2. About guessing.** You will be penalized one-fourth of a point for every wrong answer. Therefore, an educated, reasoned guess is probably worthwhile, but random guessing can work against you.

**3. About directions.** Reading and interpreting directions for each part of the exam must be done within the given time limits. The instructions in this ARCO Test Tutor are very similar to those on the examination. If you understand them thoroughly, you will save valuable time on exam day. Of course, you must still read all the instructions in your test booklet. There is always the possibility of a new type of question or an unusual twist to a familiar looking instruction. So—don't let your guard down.

No books, slide rules, compasses, rulers, dictionaries, or papers of any kind may be taken into the examination room; you are urged not to bring them to the center at all. Supervisors will not permit anyone found to have such materials with him to continue a test. Anyone giving or receiving any kind of assistance during a test will be asked to leave the room. His testbook and answer sheet will be taken from him and returned to CEEB, the answer sheet will not be scored, and the incident will be reported to the institutions named to receive the score report.

Scratch work may be done in the margins of the test-books. Scratch paper is not permitted.

You must turn in all testbooks and answer sheets at the

close of the examination period. No test materials, documents, or memoranda of any sort are to be taken from the room. Disregard of this rule will be considered as serious an offense as cheating.

If you wish to leave the room during a rest period or during a test, you must secure permission from the supervisor.

The examinations will be held only on the day and at the time scheduled. Be on time. Under no circumstances will supervisors honor requests for a change in schedule. You will not be permitted to continue a test or any part of it beyond the established time limit. You should bring a watch.

Do not be alarmed if, after the actual test, you discover that the test booklet of another applicant included questions which you did not have in your test. Every SAT has what we may call some "experimental questions." You may have experimental questions which are different from those of your neighbor test-taker. Don't worry about these experimental questions as far as the rating is concerned. The experimental questions do not count. However, since you have no way of knowing which questions on your test are experimental, do your best on every question in the test.

## Scoring and Reporting of Scores

Regardless of the number of questions on the examinations, SAT scores are scaled and reported on a scale of 200 to 800. The following scores are reported:
1. Overall Score
2. Mathematical Score
3. Verbal Score (Separate subscores are reported for Reading Comprehension and Vocabulary.)

The Test of Standard Written English is not scored as part of the overall score, since it is not meant to be a selection tool. The score on this test is reported on a scale of 20 to 80.

Five or six weeks after you take the exam, your scores will be reported to each college designated on your application form, to your high school and to you.

### Where to Get Student Information Bulletins and Application Forms

Your High School Guidance Officer may be able to supply you with information booklets and examination application forms. If not, you may write for this free information to:

College Board
Box 592
Princeton, New Jersey 08540
                or
College Board
Box 1025
Berkeley, California 94701

# Let's Talk About Achievement Tests

## WHAT ARE ACHIEVEMENT TESTS?

Achievement Tests are one-hour multiple-choice examinations designed to measure what you have learned in specific subjects. There are fifteen Achievement Tests administered by the College Board Admissions Testing Program.

The Achievement Test scores are reported on a scale from 200 to 800, in the same manner as SAT scores.

### Who Takes Achievement Tests

About one-third of the colleges that require applicants to take the SAT also require two or three Achievement Tests. You must check individual college catalogs to learn which Achievement Tests are required. The Achievement Tests are administered on three Saturday mornings at various test centers throughout the country. The information bulletin gives the details.

### What Subjects Are Covered

Achievement Tests are offered in the following subjects:

| | |
|---|---|
| English Composition | French |
| Literature | German |
| American History & Social Studies | Spanish |
| European History & World Cultures | Hebrew |

Mathematics Level I          Biology
Mathematics Level II         Chemistry
Latin                        Physics
Russian

## Correspondence Addresses

For a free copy of the Achievement Tests Information Bulletin write to:

College Board
Box 592
Princeton, New Jersey 08540
            or
Box 1025
Berkeley, California 94701

# A Bird's-Eye View of the P.S.A.T.

## WHAT IS THE PSAT?

The Preliminary Scholastic Aptitude Test is a two-hour multiple-choice type test offered by the Educational Testing Service on behalf of the College Entrance Examination Board and the National Merit Scholarship Corporation.

### Who Takes the Examination

Any high school junior who expects to go on to college can profit by taking the PSAT. It provides a chance to gain familiarity with the type of test you will face when taking the College Board Scholastic Aptitude Test (SAT) and an estimate of your ability to do satisfactory work at the college level.

### What Subjects Are Covered

The PSAT is a short version of the SAT. The Verbal Section and the Mathematical Section both contain questions similar in style and content to those found in the SAT. There is no Test of Standard Written English.

### Correspondence Addresses

Additional inquiries concerning the PSAT may be addressed to:

Box 589
Princeton, New Jersey 08540
                or
Box 1025
Berkeley, California 94701

# PART TWO
## SCHOLASTIC APTITUDE TEST
## WORD LIST

# Scholastic Aptitude Test Word List

It is very important that you study this list. A great many of these words have appeared time and again on previous College Entrance Tests—and may well appear on the test that you are going to take. The definitions given here are deliberately brief; this should help you to master the word meanings much more easily.

There are over 1600 words in this College Entrance Word List. Here is a workable plan to add these 1600 words to your vocabulary and, thus, score a much higher mark on the Verbal Part of your SAT. Learn 20 words each day and in less than three months you will have mastered this entire College Entrance Word List. What a difference it will make in your SAT score!

### NOW, PLEASE GET TO WORK!

1. **abase**—to degrade
2. **abash**—to embarrass
3. **abate**—to decrease
4. **abdicate**—to relinquish
5. **aberration**—variation
6. **abet**—to aid
7. **abeyance**—temporary suspension
8. **abhor**—to detest
9. **abject**—miserable
10. **abjure**—to renounce
11. **ablution**—cleansing
12. **abnegate**—to reject
13. **abominate**—to abhor
14. **abortive**—futile
15. **abrade**—to rub off
16. **abridge**—to shorten
17. **abrogate**—to abolish
18. **abscond**—to disappear
19. **absolution**—forgiveness
20. **abstain**—to refrain
21. **abstemious**—sparing in diet
22. **abstruse**—obscure in meaning
23. **abut**—to adjoin
24. **accede**—to consent
25. **acclimate**—to get used to
26. **acclivity**—upward slope

27. **accolade**—praise
28. **acerbity**—bitterness
29. **acme**—high point
30. **acolyte**—assistant
31. **actuary**—insurance computer
32. **actuate**—to incite
33. **acumen**—sharpness of mind
34. **adage**—proverb
35. **adamant**—inflexible
36. **adduce**—to propose
37. **adept**—skilled
38. **adhere**—to stick to
39. **adipose**—fatty
40. **adjunct**—attachment
41. **adjure**—to demand, request
42. **admonish**—to warn
43. **adroit**—skillful
44. **adulation**—praise
45. **adumbration**—omen, warning
46. **advent**—coming
47. **adventitious**—accidentally acquired
48. **adverse**—contrary
49. **adversity**—misfortune
50. **advocate**—to support
51. **aesthetic**—beautiful
52. **affected**—assumed artificially
53. **affidavit**—sworn statement in writing
54. **affinity**—relationship
55. **affirmation**—positive statement
56. **affluent**—plentiful
57. **agenda**—things to be done
58. **agglomerate**—to gather into one mass
59. **aggregate**—total
60. **agitate**—to stir up
61. **agnostic**—doubter
62. **agrarian**—rural
63. **akimbo**—position with hand on hip
64. **alacrity**—speed
65. **albino**—white
66. **alchemy**—medieval chemistry
67. **alienate**—to estrange
68. **alienist**—psychiatrist
69. **allay**—to calm
70. **allude**—to refer
71. **alluvial**—left by departing water
72. **alms**—charity
73. **altercate**—to quarrel
74. **altruism**—unselfishness
75. **amalgamate**—unite
76. **amatory**—loving
77. **ambidextrous**—versatile, skillful
78. **ambiguous**—indefinite
79. **ambrosia**—food for ancient gods
80. **ambulant**—able to walk
81. **ameliorate**—to improve
82. **amenable**—submissive
83. **amenity**—pleasing manner
84. **analgesic**—pain-reliever
85. **analogous**—corresponding (to)
86. **analogy**—comparison
87. **anarchy**—absence of government
88. **anathema**—curse
89. **anchorite**—hermit

90. **aneroid**—using no fluid
91. **aneurism**—swelling of artery
92. **animadversion**—criticism
93. **animalcule**—microscopic animal
94. **antediluvian**—old
95. **anterior**—front; earlier
96. **anthology**—literary selections
97. **anthropoid**—resembling man
98. **anthropology**—the science of man
99. **antipathy**—dislike
100. **apartheid**—South African racial segregation
101. **apathetic**—indifferent
102. **aperture**—opening
103. **apex**—peak
104. **aphorism**—proverb
105. **apiary**—place where bees are kept
106. **aplomb**—poise
107. **apocalypse**—revelation
108. **apocryphal**—of doubtful authority
109. **apogee**—highest point
110. **apostasy**—forsaking one's religion
111. **apothegm**—aphorism
112. **apotheosis**—deification
113. **appellation**—name; title
114. **append**—attach
115. **apposite**—appropriate

116. **appraise**—set a value on
117. **apprehend**—to arrest; understand
118. **apprehensive**—fearing
119. **apprise**—to give notice
120. **approbation**—approval
121. **apropos**—pertinent
122. **aquiline**—hooked
123. **arbiter**—judge
124. **arbitration**—compromise
125. **arbitrary**—despotic
126. **arboreal**—living among trees
127. **archaic**—out of use
128. **archetype**—example
129. **archive**—record
130. **arduous**—laborious
131. **argot**—slang
132. **armada**—fleet of armed ships
133. **aroma**—fragrance
134. **arraign**—to bring before a court
135. **arrogate**—to claim without right
136. **arroyo**—dry river bed
137. **artifacts**—products of primitive art
138. **artifice**—deception
139. **ascetic**—practicing self-denial
140. **ascribe**—to attribute
141. **aseptic**—free from bacteria
142. **asperity**—harshness
143. **aspersion**—slanderous remark

144. **assay**—to evaluate
145. **assent**—to comply
146. **assert**—to state positively
147. **asseverate**—to assert
148. **assiduous**—constant; devoted
149. **assimilate**—to absorb
150. **assuage**—to ease
151. **astral**—relating to stars
152. **astute**—shrewd
153. **atone**—to make amends
154. **atrophy**—wasting away
155. **attenuate**—to make slender
156. **attest**—to bear witness to
157. **attrition**—repentance
158. **atypical**—not normal
159. **augment**—to increase
160. **augur**—to foretell
161. **aural**—pert. to hearing
162. **aureate**—gilded
163. **auspicious**—indicating success
164. **austral**—southern
165. **autocrat**—absolute monarch
166. **autopsy**—inspection of corpse
167. **auxiliary**—adjunct
168. **avarice**—greed
169. **averse**—reluctant
170. **avocation**—hobby
171. **avow**—declare openly
172. **avuncular**—like an uncle
173. **badger**—to tease or annoy
174. **badinage**—banter
175. **baffle**—to perplex
176. **baleful**—destructive
177. **banal**—commonplace
178. **baneful**—evil
179. **banter**—good-natured ridicule
180. **baroque**—highly ornate
181. **barrister**—counselor-at-law
182. **barter**—to trade
183. **bastion**—fortification
184. **bauble**—trinket
185. **bazaar**—market place
186. **beatify**—to make happy
187. **bedizen**—to adorn gaudily
188. **bedlam**—wild confusion
189. **beguile**—to cheat
190. **belabor**—to beat soundly
191. **bellicose**—warlike
192. **benediction**—blessing
193. **benign**—kindly
194. **berate**—to scold vehemently
195. **besom**—a broom
196. **bestow**—to grant
197. **bicameral**—consisting of two branches
198. **biennial**—every two years
199. **bigotry**—fanaticism
200. **biped**—two-footed animal
201. **blanch**—to bleach

202. **blasphemy**—irreverence
203. **blatant**—noisy
204. **blithe**—joyous
205. **bombastic**—pompous
206. **bourne**—boundary
207. **bourse**—a foreign exchange
208. **bovine**—cowlike
209. **boycott**—to withhold business
210. **brace**—to fasten
211. **brazen**—impudent
212. **brevity**—conciseness
213. **broach**—introduce
214. **brochure**—a pamphlet
215. **bromidic**—tiresome; dull
216. **bruit**—to rumor
217. **brunt**—shock
218. **brusque**—blunt in manner
219. **bucolic**—rustic
220. **buffoon**—a clown
221. **bull**—a papal letter
222. **bullion**—gold or silver in bars
223. **burgeon**—to sprout
224. **burnish**—to polish by rubbing
225. **butt**—object of a jest
226. **buxom**—plump
227. **cabal**—conspiracy
228. **cabala**—any occult science
229. **cache**—hiding place
230. **cadaver**—dead body
231. **cadence**—rhythm
232. **cadre**—framework
233. **caduceus**—symbol of the medical profession
234. **cairn**—heap of stones used as a tombstone
235. **cajole**—coax
236. **caliber (calibre)**—ability
237. **calk, caulk**—to fill a seam
238. **calligraphy**—penmanship
239. **callow**—immature; innocent
240. **calumniate**—to slander
241. **calumny**—slander
242. **canaille**—rabble; mob
243. **candid**—straightforward
244. **candor**—frankness
245. **cant**—slang; pretense
246. **cantilever**—type of bridge
247. **capacious**—spacious
248. **capitulate**—to surrender
249. **capricious**—whimsical; fickle
250. **captious**—faultfinding
251. **carafe**—coffee bottle
252. **carcinoma**—cancer
253. **careen**—to tip to one side
254. **caricature**—distorted sketch
255. **carnage**—destruction of life
256. **carnal**—of the body
257. **carnivorous**—flesh-eating
258. **carrion**—decaying flesh

259. **carte blanche**—unrestricted authority
260. **cartilage**—firm elastic tissue
261. **cassock**—long church garment
262. **castigate**—to criticize; punish
263. **casuistry**—false reasoning
264. **cataclysm**—sudden, violent change
265. **catalyst**—substance causing change
266. **catastrophe**—calamity
267. **catechism**—elementary religious book
268. **categorical**—certain
269. **catholic**—universal
270. **caudal**—near the tail
271. **causerie**—a chat
272. **cauterize**—to cut with a hot iron
273. **caveat**—warning
274. **cavil**—to find fault
275. **cede**—yield
276. **celerity**—swiftness
277. **celestial**—heavenly
278. **celibacy**—unmarried state
279. **cenotaph**—monument for the dead
280. **censure**—to blame
281. **cephalic**—pert. to the head
282. **ceramic**—pert. to clay
283. **cerebral**—pert. to the brain
284. **cerebration**—process of thought
285. **cervical**—pert. to the neck
286. **chagrin**—disappointment, vexation
287. **challis**—soft cotton fabric
288. **chameleon**—lizard
289. **champ**—to bite
290. **chandler**—dealer in candles
291. **chaotic**—completely confused
292. **charlatan**—imposter
293. **charnel**—burial place
294. **chary**—careful, stingy
295. **chassis**—frame
296. **chaste**—pure
297. **chastisement**—punishment
298. **chattel**—property
299. **chauvinism**—zealous patriotism
300. **chicanery**—fraud
301. **chide**—to rebuke
302. **chimerical**—imaginary
303. **chiropractic**—healing by manipulating
304. **chiropodist**—foot doctor
305. **chivalrous**—gallant
306. **choleric**—angry
307. **chrysalis**—the pre-butterfly stage
308. **chutney**—seasoning
309. **cicada**—locust
310. **circuitous**—roundabout
311. **circumlocution**—talking around a subject
312. **circumspect**—watchful

313. **circumvent**—to go around
314. **cirrus**—thin, fleecy cloud
315. **citadel**—fortress
316. **cite**—to quote
317. **clairvoyant**—foretelling the future
318. **clandestine**—secret
319. **claque**—hired applauders
320. **claustrophobia**—fear of enclosed places
321. **clavicle**—collarbone
322. **clavier**—musical keyboard
323. **cleave**—to adhere; to split
324. **clemency**—leniency
325. **cliché**—over-worked expression
326. **climacteric**—critical
327. **coadjutor**—helper
328. **coalesce**—to grow together
329. **codicil**—amendment to a will
330. **coerce**—to compel
331. **cogent**—convincing
332. **cogitate**—to think
333. **cognate**—related
334. **cognizant**—aware
335. **coherent**—connected
336. **cohesion**—sticking together
337. **cohort**—a company or band
338. **colander**—strainer
339. **collateral**—accompanying
340. **collate**—to collect in order
341. **collation**—a light meal
342. **colligate**—arrange in order
343. **colloquialism**—informal conversation
344. **colloquy**—conference
345. **collusion**—secret agreement
346. **colophon**—inscription in a book
347. **comatose**—lethargic
348. **comity**—friendly feeling
349. **commensurate**—equal; corresponding
350. **comminuted**—reduced to fine particles
351. **commiseration**—sympathy
352. **commodious**—roomy
353. **commutation**—substitution
354. **compact**—agreement
355. **compatible**—harmonious
356. **compensate**—to make up for
357. **complacent**—self-satisfied
358. **complaisant**—calm
359. **complement**—full quantity
360. **compliant**—yielding
361. **component**—ingredient
362. **comprise**—to include
363. **compunction**—remorse
364. **concatenate**—to connect

365. **concentric**—with the same center
366. **conception**—original idea
367. **concerted**—agreed upon
368. **conciliate**—to pacify
369. **concise**—brief
370. **conclave**—a private meeting
371. **concomitant**—accompanying
372. **concordat**—covenant
373. **concupiscent**—lustful
374. **concurrent**—running together
375. **condign**—well-deserved
376. **condiment**—spice
377. **condole**—to express sympathy
378. **condone**—to pardon
379. **conduce**—to lead to
380. **conduit**—pipe
381. **confidant**—one confided in
382. **confiscate**—to seize
383. **conflagration**—large fire
384. **conformity**—agreement
385. **confute**—to overwhelm by argument
386. **congeal**—to change from a fluid to a solid
387. **congenital**—dating from birth
388. **conglomerate**—mixture
389. **congruent**—in agreement

390. **congruous**—becoming
391. **conic**—cone-shaped
392. **conjecture**—guess
393. **conjoin**—to unite
394. **conjugal**—pert. to marriage
395. **conjure**—to produce by magic
396. **connive**—to assist in wrongdoing
397. **connubial**—pert. to marriage
398. **consanguinity**—blood relationship
399. **consecrate**—to dedicate
400. **consign**—to transfer merchandise
401. **consonance**—agreement
402. **consort**—wife or husband
403. **constituency**—body of voters
404. **constrain**—to compel
405. **construe**—to interpret
406. **consummate**—to complete
407. **contagious**—infectious; communicable
408. **contemn**—to despise
409. **contentious**—quarrelsome
410. **contiguous**—next to
411. **contingent**—conditional
412. **contravene**—to oppose
413. **contrition**—repentance
414. **contrive**—to plan

415. **controvert**—to dispute
416. **contumacious**—stubbornly disobedient
417. **contumely**—contempt
418. **contusion**—bruise
419. **convene**—to assemble
420. **converge**—to move nearer
421. **conversant**—having knowledge of
422. **conveyance**—vehicle
423. **convivial**—gay
424. **convoke**—to call together
425. **convulsion**—spasm
426. **copious**—plentiful
427. **cordillera**—chain of mountains
428. **cordovan**—type of leather
429. **cornucopia**—horn of plenty
430. **coronary**—pert. to the arteries
431. **corporeal**—bodily
432. **corpulent**—very fat
433. **correlate**—to have a relationship
434. **corroborate**—to confirm
435. **corrugate**—to bend into folds
436. **cortege**—procession
437. **cosmopolitan**—belonging to the world
438. **coterie**—small informal group
439. **cotillion**—a social dance
440. **cotter**—pin
441. **couchant**—lying down
442. **coulee**—gulch
443. **countermand**—to revoke an order
444. **coup d'état**—overthrow of government
445. **couturier**—dressmaker
446. **covenant**—agreement
447. **covert**—hidden
448. **covetous**—envious
449. **cower**—to shrink from fear
450. **cranium**—skull
451. **crass**—stupid
452. **craven**—cowardly
453. **credence**—belief
454. **credulous**—inclined to believe
455. **creed**—statement of faith
456. **cremate**—to burn a dead body
457. **cretinism**—dwarfism
458. **criterion**—standard of judging
459. **crouton**—piece of toasted bread
460. **cruciate**—cross-/shaped
461. **cryptic**—mysterious
462. **culinary**—relating to the kitchen
463. **culmination**—acme
464. **culpable**—guilty
465. **cuneate**—wedge-shaped
466. **cult**—sect
467. **cumulus**—rounded cloud
468. **cupidity**—greed

469. **curmudgeon**—churlish person
470. **cursory**—superficial
471. **curtail**—to reduce
472. **cygnet**—young swan
473. **dactyl**—a metrical foot
474. **daguerreotype**—type of early photograph
475. **dale**—valley
476. **dalliance**—dawdling
477. **damask**—a figured fabric
478. **dank**—damp
479. **dappled**—marked with small spots
480. **dastard**—coward
481. **davit**—crane for hoisting boats
482. **dawdle**—to waste time
483. **dearth**—scarcity
484. **debase**—to reduce in dignity
485. **debauch**—to corrupt
486. **debilitate**—to weaken
487. **debonair**—courteous
488. **decamp**—to depart; flee
489. **decant**—to pour off gently
490. **decanter**—ornamental wine bottle
491. **deciduous**—leaf-shedding
492. **declivity**—downward slope
493. **décolleté**—low-necked
494. **decorous**—proper
495. **decrepit**—old

496. **decry**—to clamor against
497. **deduce**—to derive by reasoning
498. **deem**—to have an opinion
499. **de facto**—actual
500. **defalcation**—embezzlement
501. **defamation**—slander
502. **default**—neglect
503. **deference**—act of respect
504. **defile**—to make filthy
505. **defunct**—dead
506. **deify**—to make as a god
507. **deign**—to condescend
508. **de jure**—according to law
509. **delectable**—delightful
510. **delete**—to erase; remove
511. **deleterious**—harmful
512. **delineate**—to mark off
513. **demagogue**—leader who incites
514. **demean**—to debase
515. **demesne**—possession of land
516. **demur**—to hesitate
517. **demure**—serious
518. **denizen**—inhabitant
519. **dénouement**—solution
520. **deposition**—testimony outside court
521. **depraved**—corrupt
522. **deprecate**—to belittle
523. **depreciate**—decrease in value

524. **depredation**—plundering
525. **deranged**—insane
526. **derelict**—something abandoned
527. **deride**—to laugh at
528. **derogatory**—disparaging
529. **descry**—to spy out
530. **desecrate**—to profane
531. **despicable**—contemptible
532. **despoil**—to plunder
533. **despot**—absolute ruler
534. **destitute**—in extreme want
535. **desultory**—aimless
536. **deterrent**—thing which discourages
537. **detonate**—to explode
538. **detract**—to take away
539. **detriment**—harm
540. **deviate**—to stray
541. **devise**—to plan
542. **devolve**—to hand down
543. **dexterity**—skill
544. **diabolic**—devilish
545. **diadem**—a crown
546. **diaphanous**—translucent; filmy
547. **dichotomy**—division
548. **dictum**—authoritative statement
549. **didactic**—instructive
550. **diffidence**—timidity
551. **diffuse**—to spread out
552. **digress**—to wander
553. **dilapidated**—in disrepair
554. **dilate**—to expand
555. **dilatory**—dawdling
556. **dilemma**—difficult choice
557. **dilettante**—a dabbler
558. **diluvial**—pert. to the flood
559. **diminution**—reduction in size
560. **dipsomaniac**—an alcoholic (person)
561. **dirk**—a kind of dagger
562. **discernible**—identifiable
563. **disciple**—student
564. **disclaim**—to renounce
565. **discomfit**—to defeat
566. **disconcert**—to throw into confusion
567. **discordant**—not harmonious
568. **discretion**—judgment
569. **discursive**—rambling
570. **disdain**—to reject
571. **disingenuous**—not innocent
572. **disinterested**—unprejudiced
573. **disjoin**—to separate
574. **disparage**—to belittle
575. **disparity**—inequality
576. **disputation**—controversy
577. **dissemble**—to disguise
578. **disseminate**—to spread
579. **dissertation**—formal essay

580. **dissimulation**—disguise
581. **dissipate**—to squander
582. **dissolute**—immoral
583. **dissonant**—inharmonious
584. **dissuade**—to advise against
585. **distaff**—woman's work
586. **distend**—to stretch
587. **distortion**—twisting out of shape
588. **distraught**—bewildered
589. **dithyramb**—choral song
590. **diurnal**—daily
591. **diva**—prima donna
592. **diverge**—to extend in different directions
593. **diversity**—variety
594. **divest**—to deprive
595. **divination**—foreseeing the future
596. **divot**—turf cut out by a stroke
597. **divulge**—to reveal
598. **docile**—easily led
599. **doctrinaire**—impractical theorist
600. **dogma**—system of beliefs
601. **dogmatic**—arbitrary
602. **doldrums**—boredom
603. **dole**—free food or money
604. **doleful**—sorrowful
605. **dolorous**—grievous
606. **dolphin**—porpoise
607. **domicile**—residence
608. **doomsday**—day of judgment
609. **dormant**—sleeping
610. **dorsal**—referring to the back
611. **dossier**—file on a person
612. **dotage**—senility
613. **dotard**—senile person
614. **doublet**—man's coat
615. **doughty**—valiant
616. **dour**—sullen
617. **dowry**—money given at time of marriage
618. **doxology**—hymn praising God
619. **dray**—open cart
620. **driblet**—small part
621. **drivel**—foolish talk
622. **droll**—amusing
623. **dross**—waste matter
624. **dryad**—wood nymph
625. **dubious**—doubtful
626. **ductile**—able to be molded
627. **dudgeon**—resentment
628. **duenna**—Spanish chaperone
629. **duplicity**—hypocrisy
630. **durance**—imprisonment
631. **ebullience**—boiling up
632. **éclat**—brilliancy of achievement
633. **ecology**—science of environment
634. **eclogue**—pastoral poem
635. **eclectic**—selective

636. ecstasy—extreme happiness
637. ecumenical—general
638. edict—public notice
639. edify—to instruct
640. educe—to bring out
641. efface—to wipe out
642. effete—worn-out
643. effigy—image
644. effrontery—boldness
645. effulgent—illuminated
646. effusive—gushing
647. egocentric—self-centered
648. egotism—conceit
649. egress—exit
650. elated—elevated in spirit
651. electorate—voting body
652. eleemosynary—devoted to charity
653. elegy—mournful poem
654. elicit—to draw out
655. elision—omission
656. elucidate—to make clear
657. emanate—to issue forth
658. embellish—to adorn
659. embody—to render concrete
660. embolism—blood clot
661. embrocate—to rub with a lotion
662. emetic—inducing vomiting
663. emissary—messenger
664. emollient—soothing
665. emolument—reward
666. empirical—pert. to experience
667. emporium—trade center
668. empyreal—celestial
669. empyrean—heavenly
670. emulate—to try to equal
671. enclave—area within foreign territory
672. encomium—praise
673. encroach—to infringe
674. encyclopedic—covering a wide range
675. endemic—peculiar to an area
676. endive—lettuce-like plant
677. endogenous—originating from within
678. enervate—to weaken
679. engender—to produce
680. engrossed—fully absorbed
681. engulf—to swallow up
682. enhance—to improve; add to
683. enigma—a riddle
684. ennui—weariness
685. enormity—outrageous offense
686. ensnare—to trap
687. enteric—intestinal
688. enthrall—to charm; subjugate
689. entrepreneur—employer
690. enunciate—to pronounce clearly

691. **envenom**—to embitter
692. **environs**—surroundings
693. **eolithic**—stone age
694. **ephemeral**—temporary
695. **epicure**—lover of good food
696. **epigram**—witty thought
697. **epilogue**—concluding literary portion
698. **epistle**—a letter
699. **epithet**—descriptive adjective
700. **epitome**—condensation
701. **epoch**—period of time
702. **equanimity**—calm temper
703. **equestrian**—pert. to horses
704. **equipoise**—equilibrium
705. **equivocal**—uncertain
706. **equivocate**—to deceive
707. **eradicate**—to wipe out
708. **erode**—to wear away
709. **erotic**—amatory
710. **eruct**—to belch
711. **erudite**—scholarly
712. **erupt**—to break out
713. **escadrille**—airplane squadron
714. **eschew**—to avoid
715. **escritoire**—writing desk
716. **esculent**—edible

717. **escutcheon**—shield
718. **esoteric**—secret
719. **esthetic**—beautiful; artistic
720. **estranged**—separated
721. **estuary**—river mouth
722. **ethereal**—spirit-like
723. **ethical**—highly moral
724. **ethnic**—referring to a race
725. **etiolate**—to whiten
726. **etiology**—study of causes of disease
727. **etymology**—derivation of words
728. **eugenics**—improvement in offspring
729. **eulogy**—praise
730. **euphemism**—mild expression
731. **euphonious**—pleasant-sounding
732. **euphoria**—sense of well-being
733. **euphuism**—affected way of writing
734. **euthanasia**—painless death
735. **evacuate**—to empty
736. **evanescent**—transitory
737. **evasion**—a subterfuge
738. **evince**—to make evident
739. **eviscerate**—to disembowel
740. **exacting**—severe
741. **exchequer**—treasury
742. **excoriate**—to skin; denounce
743. **execrable**—extremely bad

744. **execrate**—to abhor
745. **exemplary**—deserving imitation
746. **exhort**—to incite
747. **exhortation**—recommendation
748. **exhume**—to dig out
749. **exigency**—necessity
750. **existentialism**—philosophy of a purposeless world
751. **exogenous**—derived externally
752. **exonerate**—to free from guilt
753. **exorbitant**—unreasonable
754. **exorcise**—to expel evil spirits
755. **exordium**—beginning part of an oration
756. **expedient**—advantageous
757. **expedite**—to speed up
758. **expiate**—to atone
759. **expeditious**—prompt
760. **explicate**—to explain
761. **expostulate**—to protest
762. **expressly**—especially
763. **expulsion**—driving out
764. **expurgate**—to remove objectionable matter
765. **exquisitely**—accurately
766. **extemporaneous**—impromptu; offhand
767. **extirpate**—to destroy entirely
768. **extrinsic**—foreign; external

769. **extrude**—to expel
770. **façade**—front of a building
771. **facetious**—humorous
772. **facilitate**—to make easy
773. **facile**—expert
774. **factious**—contrary; petulant
775. **factotum**—employee with many duties
776. **faint**—feeble
777. **fallacious**—misleading
778. **fallible**—capable of erring
779. **falter**—to hesitate
780. **fanatic**—ardent
781. **farraginous**—mixed; jumbled
782. **farrier**—blacksmith
783. **fasces**—emblem of power
784. **fastidious**—very critical
785. **fathom**—six feet
786. **fatuous**—foolish
787. **feasible**—suitable
788. **feckless**—ineffectiv
789. **feculent**—foul; impure
790. **felicitate**—to congra ulate
791. **ferret**—to search
792. **ferrous**—containing iron
793. **fetish**—superstition
794. **fetus**—unborn babe
795. **fiasco**—ridiculous failure
796. **fickle**—changeable

797. **finesse**—subtlety; craftiness
798. **finite**—having a limit
799. **firth**—narrow inlet
800. **fissure**—a crack
801. **flagitious**—wicked
802. **flammable**—same as **inflammable** (see)
803. **flatulent**—causing gas
804. **flex**—to bend
805. **florescence**—flowering
806. **flotsam**—ship wreckage
807. **fluctuate**—to rise and fall
808. **flume**—valley
809. **foliaceous**—leaflike
810. **foray**—plundering raid
811. **formidable**—frightening; impressive
812. **foulard**—a tie silk
813. **fractious**—unruly
814. **frenetic**—frantic
815. **frivolous**—not serious
816. **frond**—divided leaf
817. **fugue**—musical composition
818. **furbelow**—trimming
819. **fustian**—worthless
820. **futile**—useless
821. **gabardine**—woven fabric
822. **gabble**—to talk without meaning
823. **gall**—to wear away
824. **gallinaceous**—pert. to fowl
825. **gainsay**—to deny
826. **gamut**—the complete range
827. **garish**—flashy
828. **garrulity**—talkativeness
829. **generate**—to beget
830. **generic**—pert. to a race or kind
831. **genus**— a kind or class
832. **geriatrics**—care for the aged
833. **germane**—pertinent
834. **gerund**—a verbal noun
835. **gestation**—pregnancy
836. **gibber**—to talk foolishly
837. **gist**—essence
838. **glaucous**—sea-green
839. **glucose**—sugar
840. **gluttonous**—greedy for food
841. **gnostic**—wise
842. **goad**—to urge on
843. **golgotha**—a place of sacrifice; cemetery
844. **gonad**—sex gland
845. **gossamer**—sheer
846. **gourmet**—a judge of food
847. **grail**—a shallow vessel
848. **grandeur**—splendor
849. **granular**—grain-like
850. **graphology**—study of handwriting
851. **grapple**—to seize
852. **gratuitous**—free
853. **gratuity**—tip
854. **grimace**—to distort the features
855. **grimalkin**—old cat
856. **grimly**—fiercely

857. **grommet**—a metal ring
858. **grouse**—to complain
859. **grueling**—exhausting
860. **gruff**—rough
861. **gudgeon**—simpleton
862. **guile**—deceit
863. **gullible**—easily deceived
864. **gusty**—windy
865. **guzzle**—to drink much
866. **gynecology**—science of women's diseases
867. **gyrate**—to spin
868. **gyroscope**—rotating wheel
869. **gyve**—shackle
870. **habiliment**—clothes
871. **habitable**—livable
872. **haft**—handle
873. **haggard**—gaunt; careworn
874. **halberd**—axlike weapon
875. **halcyon**—peaceful
876. **hallucination**—delusion
877. **haphazard**—random
878. **harass**—to annoy
879. **harbinger**—forecast
880. **harridan**—vicious old woman
881. **hassock**—cushion used as stool
882. **hauteur**—pride
883. **haycock**—pile of hay
884. **hawser**—a large rope
885. **hegemony**—leadership

886. **heinous**—hateful; atrocious
887. **helix**—coil of wire
888. **heptagon**—seven-sided polygon
889. **herbivorous**—feeding on herbs
890. **heretical**—not agreeing
891. **hermitage**—monastery
892. **heterodox**—having unorthodox opinions
893. **heterogeneous**—different
894. **hexapod**—having six feet
895. **hidalgo**—Spanish nobleman
896. **hieratic**—priestly
897. **hinder**—to retard
898. **hirsute**—hairy
899. **histology**—science of organic tissue
900. **histrionic**—theatrical
901. **hoary**—white with age
902. **holocaust**—great destruction
903. **holograph**—personally handwritten document
904. **homage**—respect
905. **homeopathy**—method of treating disease
906. **homiletics**—art of preaching
907. **homily**—sermon
908. **homogeneous**—essentially alike
909. **homogenous**—derived from the same source

910. **homologous**—similar
911. **homunculus**—dwarf
912. **hone**—to sharpen
913. **hormone**—internal secretion
914. **hortatory**—encouraging
915. **hostile**—antagonistic
916. **hoyden**—tomboy
917. **huddle**—to crowd together
918. **humanist**—classical scholar
919. **humerus**—arm bone
920. **humility**—humbleness
921. **hummock**—small hill
922. **humus**—fertilizer
923. **hustings**—electioneering platform
924. **hydrous**—containing water
925. **hygroscope**—instrument indicating humidity
926. **hymeneal**—pert. to marriage
927. **hyperbole**—exaggeration
928. **hypertension**—high blood pressure
929. **hypochondria**—fancies of poor health
930. **hypothesis**—assumption
931. **ichthyology**—science of fish
932. **iconoclast**—image breaker
933. **ideology**—body of ideas
934. **idiosyncrasy**—peculiar tendency
935. **idyllic**—simple or poetic
936. **igneous**—of volcanic origin
937. **ignoble**—base, unworthy
938. **ignominious**—contemptible
939. **illicit**—unlawful
940. **illusion**—deception
941. **illusory**—unreal
942. **imbecility**—weakness of mind
943. **impale**—fix on a point
944. **impassioned**—animated; excited
945. **impeccable**—faultless
946. **impecunious**—poor
947. **impede**—to hinder
948. **impediment**—obstacle
949. **imperceptible**—not easily seen
950. **imperishable**—indestructible
951. **imperturbable**—tranquil
952. **impervious**—not to be penetrated
953. **impetuous**—impulsive
954. **importune**—to beg
955. **impotent**—incapable
956. **imprecation**—curse
957. **impresario**—manager
958. **imprimatur**—license to publish
959. **impudence**—shamelessness
960. **impugn**—to question
961. **impunity**—exemption from punishment

962. **impute**—to blame
963. **inadequate**—insufficient
964. **inadvertence**—carelessness
965. **inalienable**—not transferable
966. **inarticulate**—not distinct
967. **incarcerate**—to imprison
968. **incarnadine**—flesh-colored
969. **incessant**—uninterrupted
970. **incision**—cut
971. **incognito**—with identity concealed
972. **incommensurate**—not adequate
973. **incompatibility**—inconsistency
974. **incongruous**—not suitable
975. **inconsiderable**—trivial
976. **incorrigible**—beyond reform
977. **incubus**—burden
978. **inculpate**—to blame
979. **indenture**—contract
980. **indict**—to accuse
981. **indigenous**—native
982. **indigent**—poor
983. **indiscriminate**—not selective
984. **indolent**—lazy
985. **indubitable**—undeniably true
986. **induct**—to bring in
987. **indurate**—hardened
988. **inebriated**—drunk

989. **inexhaustible**—unfailing
990. **inexorable**—unyielding
991. **inference**—conclusion
992. **inflammable**—burnable
993. **ingenuous**—innocent
994. **ingratiate**—to establish in favor
995. **inhibition**—restraint
996. **iniquitous**—sinful
997. **initiation**—beginning
998. **innocuous**—harmless
999. **innuendo**—insinuation
1000. **inscrutable**—unfathomable
1001. **insensate**—withou sensation
1002. **insidious**—treache ous
1003. **insinuate**—to sugg subtly
1004. **insolvent**—bankru
1005. **insouciant**—carefr
1006. **instigate**—to incite
1007. **insufficient**—inadequate
1008. **insular**—pert. to an island
1009. **integral**—pert. to th whole
1010. **integrate**—to absorb into one group
1011. **intercede**—to interpose in behalf of
1012. **interdict**—official order

1013. **intermittent**—recurrent
1014. **interregnum**—interval between reigns
1015. **interpolate**—to insert new material
1016. **intractable**—stubborn
1017. **intransigent**—uncompromising
1018. **intravenous**—through a vein
1019. **intrepid**—brave
1020. **intrinsic**—essential
1021. **introvert**—to turn inward
1022. **inveigh**—to attack
1023. **inverse**—in reversed position
1024. **invidious**—odious
1025. **invocation**—calling on God
1026. **ionosphere**—outer layers
1027. **irony**—contradiction
1028. **irreconcilable**—incompatible
1029. **isobar**—weather map line
1030. **isotope**—chemical element
1031. **isthmus**—narrow land strip
1032. **iterate**—to repeat
1033. **itinerant**—traveling on a circuit
1034. **jaded**—worn out
1035. **jargon**—confused talk
1036. **jaundiced**—envious
1037. **jeremiad**—lamentation

1038. **jettison**—to cast overboard
1039. **jocose**—humorous
1040. **jodhpurs**—riding pants
1041. **jollity**—noisy mirth
1042. **judicious**—prudent
1043. **juridical**—legal
1044. **juxtaposed**—close together
1045. **kaleidoscope**—optical instrument
1046. **karat**—1/24th part gold
1047. **kinetics**—science of pure motion
1048. **kiosk**—stand open on one side
1049. **kith**—friends
1050. **knead**—to work dough
1051. **lacerate**—to tear
1052. **laconic**—brief
1053. **lachrymose**—tearful
1054. **lamented**—mourned
1055. **landed**—having an estate in land
1056. **languid**—listless
1057. **languish**—to become weak
1058. **lascivious**—lewd
1059. **lassitude**—weariness
1060. **latent**—concealed
1061. **latex**—milky fluid
1062. **legerdemain**—trickery
1063. **legitimate**—genuine
1064. **lethargic**—drowsy
1065. **liable**—exposed to
1066. **libel**—defamation
1067. **licentiate**—one who has a license

1068. limitation—restriction
1069. lithe—supple
1070. livid—black and blue
1071. longitudinal—pert. to length
1072. loquacious—talkative
1073. ludicrous—ridiculous
1074. lugubrious—sad
1075. macabre—gruesome
1076. macadamize—to cover with broken stones
1077. macerate—to soften by dipping
1078. madrigal—short musical poem
1079. maelstrom—whirlpool
1080. magisterial—authoritative
1081. magnanimous—generous
1082. magnate—tycoon
1083. mahatma—extraordinary person
1084. mahout—elephant driver
1085. maladroit—clumsy
1086. malaise—discomfort
1087. malapropism—word misused ridiculously
1088. malfeasance—wrongful act
1089. malignant—harmful
1090. malpractice—improper professional conduct
1091. mandate—a specific order
1092. mange—skin disease
1093. mantilla—head scarf
1094. marline—a nautical cord
1095. marquee—canopy
1096. marsupial—pert. to animals such as kangaroos
1097. martinet—disciplinarian
1098. matrix—a mold
1099. masticate—to chew
1100. mawkish—nauseating
1101. medicinal—healing
1102. mediocre—ordinary
1103. medley—mixture
1104. mega—million
1105. megrim—low spirits
1106. melange—m.. re
1107. mellifluent— .. ly flowing
1108. menace—to thr
1109. menage—househ
1110. mendacious—lyin
1111. mendicant—beggar
1112. meniscus—crescent-shaped
1113. meretricious—showily attractive
1114. metamorphose—to transform
1115. militate—to operate against
1116. minnow—small fish
1117. misanthropy—dislike of mankind
1118. misappropriate—to use for a wrong purpose

1119. **miscalculate**—to calculate erroneously
1120. **miscegenation**—interbreeding of races
1121. **mischievous**—annoying
1122. **misconceive**—to misunderstand
1123. **misconstruction**—wrong interpretation
1124. **miscreant**—villain
1125. **misdemeanor**—evil conduct
1126. **missal**—prayer book
1127. **mistral**—cold dry northerly wind
1128. **mitigate**—to lessen
1129. **mnemonics**—memory device
1130. **modicum**—small quantity
1131. **modulate**—to soften
1132. **molest**—to bother
1133. **monetary**—pert. to money
1134. **monolith**—large piece of stone
1135. **montage**—blending of pictures
1136. **mordant**—biting; sarcastic
1137. **moribund**—dying
1138. **motley**—miscellaneous
1139. **muddle**—to confuse
1140. **mufti**—civilian dress
1141. **murrain**—cattle disease
1142. **mutation**—change
1143. **muzhik**—Russian peasant
1144. **myopia**—near-sightedness
1145. **nacre**—mother-of-pearl
1146. **naïve**—innocent
1147. **nape**—back of neck
1148. **narcissism**—love of oneself
1149. **natatorial**—pert. to swimming
1150. **nauseate**—to sicken
1151. **nebulous**—hazy
1152. **necessitate**—to compel
1153. **nefarious**—wicked
1154. **negative**—expressing refusal
1155. **negotiable**—transferable
1156. **neophyte**—new convert
1157. **neolithic**—pert. to later Stone Age
1158. **neuralgia**—nerve pain
1159. **neurasthenia**—nervous exhaustion
1160. **neutralize**—to counteract
1161. **niggardly**—stingy
1162. **nihilism**—disbelief in religion
1163. **nimbus**—halo
1164. **nirvana**—freedom from pain
1165. **noctambulist**—sleepwalker
1166. **nocturne**—a piece of dreamy music
1167. **node**—knob
1168. **nomenclature**—names of things

1169. **nonagenarian**—person in the 90's
1170. **nonchalant**—indifferent
1171. **noncompliance**—failure to comply
1172. **nonpareil**—without equal
1173. **nonsensical**—absurd
1174. **non sequitur**—illogical argument
1175. **noxious**—harmful
1176. **nuncio**—representative of Pope
1177. **nuzzle**—to nestle
1178. **obdurate**—callous; hardened
1179. **obeisance**—bowing
1180. **obelisk**—four-sided pillar
1181. **obesity**—excessive fatness
1182. **obfuscate**—to confuse
1183. **obituary**—death notice
1184. **obliterate**—to demolish
1185. **oblivious**—absorbed; absent-minded
1186. **obloquy**—disgrace
1187. **obnoxious**—hateful
1188. **obsequious**—servile
1189. **obscene**—indecent
1190. **obscure**—not easily understood
1191. **obsess**—to trouble
1192. **obsolescent**—becoming out-of-date
1193. **obstreperous**—noisy
1194. **obtrude**—to thrust forth

1195. **obturate**—to stop or close
1196. **obtuse**—dull
1197. **obviate**—to prevent
1198. **obvious**—self-evident
1199. **occidental**—Western
1200. **occipital**—pert. to back of head
1201. **occlude**—to close
1202. **ocellated**—having eyelike spots
1203. **octamerous**—having eight parts
1204. **odoriferous**—fragrant
1205. **oleaginous**—oily
1206. **omega**—last letter
1207. **omit**—to leave out
1208. **omnipotent**—all-powerful
1209. **onerous**—difficult
1210. **opprobrious**—shameful
1211. **optimum**—the best
1212. **orbicular**—circular
1213. **ordnance**—military weapons
1214. **ordinance**—law
1215. **ordure**—filth
1216. **oriel**—a bay window
1217. **orifice**—opening
1218. **oscillate**—to vibrate
1219. **ostensible**—apparent
1220. **ostentatious**—pretentious
1221. **pachyderm**—elephant
1222. **pacific**—calm
1223. **paisley**—colorful fabric

1224. **paean**—song of praise
1225. **palanquin**—bed carried on poles
1226. **palaver**—smooth talk
1227. **palliate**—to mitigate
1228. **palpitate**—to beat rapidly
1229. **pamper**—to indulge
1230. **panacea**—remedy for all ills
1231. **panegyric**—eulogy
1232. **panic**—terror
1233. **panoply**—set of armor
1234. **pantheism**—belief of God-nature unity
1235. **paradigm**—model
1236. **paradox**—contra-d:tion
1237. **uralyze**—to render ineffective
123&. **parapet**—barricade
12?. **paregoric**—pain-reliever
**pariah**—outcast
**parietal**—pert. to side of skull
2. **parity**—equality
3. **parochial**—provin-cial
244. **paroxysm**—a fit
245. **parsimonious**—stingy
1246. **peccadillo**—a small fault
1247. **pectoral**—pert. to chest
1248. **peculate**—to em-bezzle
1249. **pecuniary**—financial

1250. **pedantic**—bookish
1251. **pediculous**—infested with lice
1252. **peduncle**—flower stalk
1253. **peevish**—fretful
1254. **peignoir**—dressing gown
1255. **pejorative**—dispar-aging
1256. **pelagic**—pert. to ocean
1257. **penchant**—strong inclination
1258. **pending**—awaiting decision
1259. **pensile**—hanging
1260. **pennate**—winged
1261. **penurious**—stingy
1262. **perambulate**—to walk about
1263. **perceive**—to feel; comprehend
1264. **perception**—aware-ness
1265. **percussion**—impact
1266. **peregrination**—traveling
1267. **peremptory**—posi-tive
1268. **perigee**—point near-est earth
1269. **periphery**—external surface
1270. **peristaltic**—pert. to alternate waves
1271. **permeable**—pene-trable
1272. **permutation**—changing
1273. **pernicious**—injuri-ous

1274. **perquisite**—incidental compensation
1275. **peroration**—last part of a speech
1276. **perspicuity**—clearness in expression
1277. **petulance**—peevishness
1278. **phylum**—grouping in biology
1279. **picaresque**—pert. to rogues
1280. **pilaster**—part of column
1281. **pileous**—pert. to hair
1282. **piquant**—pungent
1283. **pique**—to wound
1284. **piscatorial**—pert. to fishing
1285. **pixilated**—amusingly eccentric
1286. **platitude**—trite remark
1287. **plectrum**—small piece used to pluck
1288. **plethora**—over-supply
1289. **plinth**—lower part of column
1290. **pogrom**—organized massacre
1291. **poignant**—keenly affecting
1292. **polemics**—art of disputing
1293. **polity**—method of government
1294. **polonaise**—slow Polish dance
1295. **polymer**—chemical compound
1296. **pontificate**—to speak pompously
1297. **porringer**—soup plate
1298. **posterity**—succeeding generations
1299. **poultice**—soft, moist mass
1300. **pragmatic**—practical
1301. **precarious**—uncertain
1302. **precipitous**—steep
1303. **preclude**—to prevent
1304. **precocious**—advanced in development
1305. **precursor**—predecessor
1306. **predatory**—plundering
1307. **predilection**—preference
1308. **preëminent**—superior
1309. **premeditation**—forethought
1310. **preposterous**—very absurd
1311. **prerogative**—privilege
1312. **preternatural**—supernatural
1313. **prevaricate**—to lie
1314. **primordial**—first in order
1315. **probity**—integrity
1316. **proclivity**—tendency
1317. **procrastinate**—to put off
1318. **prodigious**—large

1319. **profligate**—utterly immoral
1320. **prolix**—long-winded
1321. **promiscuous**—without discrimination
1322. **propinquity**—nearness
1323. **proscenium**—front of stage
1324. **proselyte**—convert
1325. **protagonist**—leading character
1326. **prototype**—example
1327. **protuberance**—projection
1328. **provender**—food for animals
1329. **providential**—fortunate
1330. **psychic**—mental; supernatural
1331. **psychoneurosis**—emotional disorder
1332. **puissant**—powerful
1333. **punctilious**—exact
1334. **purloin**—to embezzle
1335. **purulent**—discharging pus
1336. **pusillanimous**—afraid
1337. **putative**—supposed
1338. **putrefy**—to decay
1339. **Pyrrhic victory**—victory at great cost
1340. **pythonic**—prophetic
1341. **quadrennial**—comprising four years
1342. **quandary**—doubt
1343. **quench**—to extinguish
1344. **query**—question

1345. **quidnunc**—curious person
1346. **quiescent**—inactive
1347. **quintessence**—concentrated essence
1348. **quirk**—a turn
1349. **quiver**—to shake
1350. **quixotic**—visionary
1351. **quote**—to cite
1352. **quotidian**—daily
1353. **rabbet**—groove
1354. **rabble**—vulgar, noisy people
1355. **rabid**—furious
1356. **raillery**—banter
1357. **ramification**—a division
1358. **rampant**—springing; climbing
1359. **ramshackle**—out of repair
1360. **ratiocination**—reasoning
1361. **recalcitrant**—stubborn
1362. **recapitulate**—to summarize
1363. **receptive**—receiving
1364. **reciprocal**—in return
1365. **recollect**—to recall
1366. **redundant**—excess wordage
1367. **regal**—royal
1368. **regimen**—manner of living
1369. **rehabilitate**—to restore
1370. **reimburse**—to refund
1371. **relegate**—to assign

1372. **reliquary**—receptacle
1373. **reminiscence**—memory of things past
1374. **renascent**—being reborn
1375. **repine**—to complain
1376. **reprehension**—rebuke
1377. **reprisal**—injury in return
1378. **repudiate**—to refuse
1379. **requital**—repayment
1380. **resilient**—rebounding
1381. **resplendent**—shining
1382. **restitution**—compensation
1383. **resurgent**—rising again
1384. **resuscitate**—to revive
1385. **retaliate**—give evil for evil
1386. **reticent**—silent
1387. **reticulate**—net-like
1388. **retroactive**—applying to the past
1389. **retrogression**—going back
1390. **retroussé**—turned up
1391. **rhesus**—type of monkey
1392. **rhinitis**—inflammation of nose
1393. **risibility**—disposition to laugh
1394. **rubicund**—red
1395. **rue**—to regret
1396. **rubric**—direction
1397. **ruminate**—to ponder
1398. **rusticate**—to live in the country
1399. **sabot**—wooden shoe
1400. **saccharine**—pert. to sugar
1401. **sagacious**—wise
1402. **salacious**—obscene
1403. **salient**—prominent
1404. **salubrious**—healthful
1405. **salutary**—wholesome
1406. **salvation**—the act of preserving
1407. **sanctimonious**—affectedly holy
1408. **sanctity**—holiness
1409. **sanguine**—confident
1410. **saponify**—to make fat into soap
1411. **sardonic**—ironic
1412. **satiate**—to supply excess
1413. **satrap**—governor province
1414. **saturate**—to fill
1415. **scapular**—pert. to shoulder
1416. **scarab**—ornament
1417. **scarify**—to make scratches
1418. **schism**—division
1419. **schist**—a type of rock
1420. **sciatic**—pert. to the hip
1421. **scintilla**—bit
1422. **scruple**—reluctance
1423. **secular**—not religious
1424. **sedition**—rebellion

1425. sedulous—painstaking
1426. seismic—caused by an earthquake
1427. semantic—pert. to meaning
1428. senescent—growing old
1429. sententious—magisterial
1430. sentient—feeling
1431. sequester—to seclude
1432. seraglio—harem
1433. shibboleth—a pet phrase
1434. silicosis—lung disease
1435. simony—profit from sacred things
1436. simian—pert. to a monkey
1437. sinecure—job requiring little work
1438. sinuous—with many curves
1439. skepticism—disbelief
1440. slatternly—slovenly
1441. slough—soft, muddy ground
1442. solicitude—concern
1443. somatic—bodily
1444. sonorous—resonant
1445. sophism—fallacy
1446. spatula—flat, broad instrument
1447. specious—deceptive
1448. speculum—mirror
1449. splenetic—peevish
1450. spontaneous—unconstrained
1451. sporadic—occasional
1452. stalactite—hanging calcium deposit
1453. stalagmite—calcium deposit on cave floor
1454. stentorian—loud
1455. stigma—blemish
1456. stipulate—to make a demand
1457. stoical—impassive
1458. stratagem—scheme
1459. strident—grating
1460. suave—smoothly polite
1461. subcutaneous—beneath the skin
1462. subdue—to overcome
1463. subjoin—to add
1464. subpoena—summons for witness
1465. subsidy—financial aid
1466. sufficiency—ampleness
1467. suffuse—to overspread
1468. supersede—to take the place of
1469. supercilious—proud and haughty
1470. supplicate—to beg
1471. surfeit—excess
1472. surreptitious—secret
1473. surrogate—deputy
1474. surveillance—watching
1475. susceptible—sensitive
1476. suture—stitch of a wound

1477. **sybarite**—person devoted to luxury
1478. **sycophant**—flatterer
1479. **syllogism**—deductive reasoning
1480. **sylvan**—pert. to woods
1481. **symposium**—meeting for discussion
1482. **syncope**—contradiction of a word
1483. **synthesis**—combination
1484. **taboret**—small stool
1485. **tachometer**—instrument for measuring speed
1486. **tacitly**—silently
1487. **taint**—to infect
1488. **talus**—slope
1489. **tautology**—useless repetition
1490. **tendon**—connective tissue
1491. **thesis**—essay
1492. **thoracic**—between neck and abdomen
1493. **thrombosis**—blood clot
1494. **tirade**—vehement speech
1495. **tithe**—tax of one tenth
1496. **tocsin**—alarm
1497. **tolerate**—to permit
1498. **toque**—hat without a brim
1499. **torpor**—dullness
1500. **tortilla**—large, round, thin cake
1501. **trachea**—windpipe
1502. **tractable**—easily led
1503. **traduce**—to slander
1504. **tranquillity**—calmness
1505. **transcendent**—surpassing others
1506. **transfuse**—to pour from one to another
1507. **transgression**—sin
1508. **transition**—change
1509. **transmute**—to change
1510. **transverse**—lying across
1511. **trauma**—wound
1512. **travail**—labor
1513. **travesty**—burlesque
1514. **treacle**—molasses
1515. **trenchant**—sharp
1516. **trepidation**—trembling from fear
1517. **tribulation**—trouble
1518. **tumbrel**—farmer's cart
1519. **tumid**—swollen
1520. **turbulent**—violent
1521. **turgid**—swollen
1522. **turpitude**—shameful depravity
1523. **tutelage**—instruction
1524. **tyke**—mischievous child
1525. **tyro**—novice
1526. **ubiquity**—omnipresence
1527. **ukase**—Russian government order
1528. **ultimately**—as a final result
1529. **ululation**—a wailing
1530. **umbilicus**—navel

**1531.** umbrage—offense

**1532.** unaccountable—not responsible

**1533.** uncouth—unrefined

**1534.** undulating—waving

**1535.** ungainly—clumsy

**1536.** unravel—to explain

**1537.** unwieldly—ponderous

**1538.** upbraid—to reproach

**1539.** uproarious—noisy

**1540.** urbane—refined

**1541.** urchin—mischievous boy

**1542.** urn—vase

**1543.** ursine—pert. to bears

**1544.** usurpation—wrongful seizure

**1545.** uxorious—fond of a wife

**1546.** vacuous—empty

**1547.** vain—unsuccessful

**1548.** vapid—dull

**1549.** varicosity—swollen veins

**1550.** vacillation—unsteadiness

**1551.** vacuity—stupidity

**1552.** validity—strength

**1553.** valor—courage

**1554.** vandalism—destruction

**1555.** vanguard—leaders

**1556.** vanquish—to conquer

**1557.** vaquero—cowboy

**1558.** variable—changing

**1559.** variegate—to diversify

**1560.** vendetta—feud

**1561.** venerate—to revere

**1562.** venous—pert. to veins

**1563.** ventricle—cavity

**1564.** verbatim—word for word

**1565.** verbose—wordy

**1566.** verdant—green; fresh

**1567.** verge—edge

**1568.** verify—to prove to be true

**1569.** verisimilitude—appearance of truth

**1570.** verity—honesty

**1571.** vernacular—native language

**1572.** vernal—pert. to spring

**1573.** vertex—top

**1574.** vertigo—dizziness

**1575.** vicissitude—change

**1576.** vilify—to defame

**1577.** vindicate—to uphold

**1578.** viridity—greenness

**1579.** vituperate—to defame

**1580.** vociferate—to shout

**1581.** volatility—frivolity

**1582.** volition—will

**1583.** voracious—ravenous

**1584.** waft—current of wind

**1585.** waggery—mischievous merriment

**1586.** wainscot—wood paneling

**1587.** warp—to bend slightly

**1588.** wassail—a toast

1589. **wastrel**—spend-thrift
1590. **waterlogged**—soaked with water
1591. **wayward**—irregular
1592. **wean**—to detach
1593. **weld**—to unite
1594. **welter**—to roll like a wave
1595. **wheedle**—to coax
1596. **whimsical**—fantastic; quaint
1597. **whimsy**—odd notion
1598. **whey**—milk water
1599. **wizened**—withered
1600. **wont**—custom
1601. **woof**—fabric

1602. **writ**—formal legal order
1603. **wry**—twisted
1604. **xylem**—woody tissue of plants
1605. **yak**—species of ox
1606. **yearn**—to long for
1607. **yen**—monetary unit of Japan
1608. **yodel**—a vocalization
1609. **yogi**—an ascetic
1610. **yowl**—wailing cry
1611. **zany**—clown
1612. **zeal**—enthusiasm
1613. **zenith**—highest point

# PART THREE

# SCHOLASTIC APTITUDE TEST

## (SAMPLE)

*This test closely resembles the actual test. Take this Sample Test now for guidance to determine how best to pinpoint your practice and study effort.*

*The actual test which you are going to take m̲a̲y̲, ̲i̲n̲ some areas, have more difficult questions than you will encounter in this Sample Test. On the other hand, the questions may be less difficult, but don't bank on this. We trust that in your use of this book, you will gain confidence not overconfidence.*

# PART ONE
## MATHEMATICS

### 28 QUESTIONS—30 MINUTES

*Directions:* For each of the following questions, select the choice which best answers the question or completes the statement.

1. Under certain conditions, sound travels at about 1100 ft. per second. If 88 ft. per second is approximately equivalent to 60 miles per hour, the speed of sound, under the above conditions, is, of the following, closest to:
   (A) 730 miles per hour
   (B) 740 miles per hour
   (C) 750 miles per hour
   (D) 760 miles per hour.

2. Of the following, the most nearly accurate set of equivalence is:
   (A) 1 foot equals 30.48 centimeters
   (B) 1 centimeter equals 2.54 inches
   (C) 1 rod equals 3.28 meters
   (D) 1 meter equals 1.09 feet.

3. The sum of an odd number and an even number is:
   (A) sometimes an even number
   (B) always divisible by 3 or 5 or 7
   (C) always an odd number
   (D) always a prime number (not divisible).

4. If one angle of a triangle is three times a second angle and the third angle is 20 degrees more than the second angle, the second angle is (in degrees):
   (A) 32                    (B) 34
   (C) 40                    (D) 50.

5. Assuming that on a blueprint ¼ inch equals 12 inches, the actual length in feet of a steel bar represented on the blueprint by a line 3⅜ inches long is:
   (A) 3⅜                    (B) 6¾
   (C) 2½                    (D) 13½.

6. A plane leaves Denver, Colo., (Mountain Standard Time Zone) on June 1 at 2 p.m. and arrives at New York City (Eastern Standard Time Zone) June 2 at 2 a.m. Eastern Standard is two hours later than Mountain Standard. The actual time of flight was:
   (A) 10 hours              (B) 11 hours
   (C) 12 hours             (D) 13 hours.

7. Of the following, the value closest to that of
   $$\frac{41.10 \times .0003}{.002}$$ is:
   (A) .063                  (B) .63
   (C) 6.3                   (D) 63.

8. If Mrs. Jones bought 3¾ yards of dacron at $1.1 per yard and 4⅔ yards of velvet at $3.87 per yard, the amount of change she receives from $25 is:
   (A) $2.12                 (B) $2.28
   (C) $2.59                 (D) $2.63.

9. The water level of a swiming pool, 75 feet by 42 feet, is to be raised four inches. The number of gallons of water needed for this is:
   (A) 140                   (B) 7,875
   (C) 31,500               (D) 94,500.

10. The part of the total quantity represented by a 24 degree sector of a circle graph is:
    (A) 6⅔%                (B) 12%
    (C) 13⅓%               (D) 24%.

11. If shipping charges to a certain point are 62 cents for the first five ounces and 8 cents for each additional ounce, the weight of a package for which the charges are $1.66 is:
    (A) 13 ounces          (B) 1⅛ pounds
    (C) 1¼ pounds          (D) 1½ pounds.

12. If 15 cans of food are needed for seven men for two days, the number of cans needed for four men for seven days is:
    (A) 15                 (B) 20
    (C) 25                 (D) 30.

13. The total saving in purchasing 30 13-cent ice cream pops for a class party at a reduced rate of $1.38 per dozen is:
    (A) $.35               (B) $.40
    (C) $.45               (D) $.50.

14. Find the value of x in the equation $2x - .2x = 9$
    (A) $x = 0$            (B) $x = 4.5$
    (C) $x = 5$            (D) $x = 18$.

15. An automobile traveled 6 hours at an average speed of 40 miles per hour. It averaged only 30 miles per hour on the return trip. What was the average speed per hour, to the nearest mile, for the round trip?
    (A) 34 mph             (B) 35 mph
    (C) 36 mph             (D) 37 mph.

16. What is the value of the following fraction?
$$\frac{3.2 \times .5 \times .25}{.08}$$

(A)  .05                    (B)  .50
(C)  5.0                    (D)  50.

17. A gallon of water is equal to 231 cubic inches. How many gallons of water are needed to fill a fish tank that measures 11″ high, 14″ long, and 9″ wide?
(A)  6 gal.                 (B)  8 gal.
(C)  9 gal.                 (D)  14 gal.

18. A savings and loan association pays 4% interest which is compounded quarterly. At this rate, what is the interest on $600 for one quarter?
(A)  $4                     (B)  $6
(C)  $24                    (D)  $60.

19. At an end-of-season sale, an air conditioner was sold at a 40% discount. If the sale price was $135.00, what was the list price?
(A)  $54                    (B)  $81
(C)  $189                   (D)  $225.

20.   26   Which of the following statements is the most
    —19   meaningful explanation of this subtraction ex-
      ―     ample?
      7

(A)  Take one from the 2 and place it in front of the 6 to make 16.
(B)  Exchange 1 ten for 10 ones, giving 16 ones.
(C)  Borrow 1 from the 2 and pay it back.
(D)  We cannot subtract 9 from 6.

**Common Information:** In each question, information concerning one or both of the quantities to be compared is given in the Item column. A symbol that appears in any column represents the same thing in Column A as it does in Column B.

**Numbers:** All numbers used are real numbers.

**Figures:** Assume that the position of points, angles, regions, and so forth, are in the order shown.

Assume that the lines shown as straight are indeed straight.

Figures are assumed to lie in a plane unless otherwise indicated.

Figures accompanying questions are intended to provide information you can use in answering the questions. However, unless a note states that a figure is drawn to scale, you should solve the problems by using your knowledge of mathematics, and NOT by estimating sizes by sight or by measurement.

*Directions:* For each of the following questions two quantities are given . . . one in Column A; and one in Column B. Compare the two quantities and mark your answer sheet with the correct, lettered conclusion. These are your options:

A: if the quantity in Column A is the greater;

B: if the quantity in Column B is the greater;

C: if the two quantities are equal;

D: if the relationship cannot be determined from the information given.

| Item | Column A | Column B |
|------|----------|----------|
| 21. | $(\frac{1}{3})^{-1}$ | $\frac{1}{3}$ |
| 22. | 50% of $\frac{4}{5}$ | $\frac{4}{5}$ of $\frac{1}{2}$ |

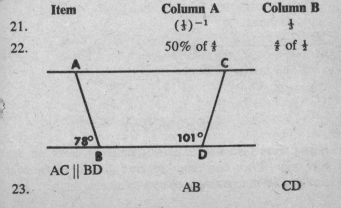

AC ‖ BD

| | | |
|---|---|---|
| 23. | AB | CD |

| Item | Column A | Column B |
|------|----------|----------|
| 24. | .01 ÷ .1 | .01 × .1 |

25.

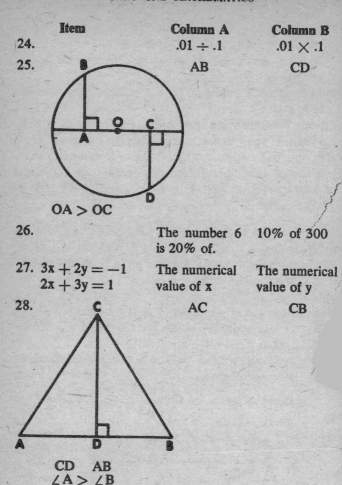

| | Column A | Column B |
|---|---|---|
| | AB | CD |

OA > OC

| | Column A | Column B |
|---|---|---|
| 26. | The number 6 is 20% of. | 10% of 300 |

| 27. $3x + 2y = -1$ $2x + 3y = 1$ | The numerical value of x | The numerical value of y |
|---|---|---|

28.

| | Column A | Column B |
|---|---|---|
| | AC | CB |

CD    AB
∠A > ∠B

## END OF PART

*If you finish before the allotted time is up, work on this part only. When time is up, proceed directly to the next part and do not return to this part.*

# PART TWO
## VERBAL ABILITY

### 44 QUESTIONS—30 MINUTES

**Vocabulary**

### TIME: 10 MINUTES

*Directions:* For each question in this test, select the appropriate letter preceding the word that is opposite in meaning to the capitalized word.

1. FETID
    - (A) in an embryonic state
    - (B) easily enraged
    - (C) acclaimed by peers
    - (D) reduced to skin and bones
    - (E) having a pleasant odor

2. CHIMERICAL
    - (A) nimble
    - (B) realistic
    - (C) powerful
    - (D) underrated
    - (E) remarkable

3. APOCALYPTIC
    - (A) concealed
    - (B) pure
    - (C) steep
    - (D) paralyzed
    - (E) authentic

4. ABERRANCE
    - (A) refusal
    - (B) criticism
    - (C) adherence
    - (D) exhuming
    - (E) easing

5. DISCRETE
   - (A) orderly
   - (B) antisocial
   - (C) crude
   - (D) joking
   - (E) grouped

6. CONTUMACIOUS
   - (A) swollen
   - (B) scandalous
   - (C) sanguine
   - (D) concise
   - (E) obedient

7. CAMARADERIE
   - (A) deviation
   - (B) glee
   - (C) aristocracy
   - (D) noise
   - (E) plunder

8. DOUR
   - (A) gay
   - (B) sweet
   - (C) wealthy
   - (D) responsive
   - (E) noiseless

9. MENDACIOUS
   - (A) charitable
   - (B) efficacious
   - (C) truthful
   - (D) destructive
   - (E) brilliant

10. ENERVATE
    - (A) debilitate
    - (B) fortify
    - (C) introduce
    - (D) conclude
    - (E) escalate

11. POLTROON
    - (A) plutocrat
    - (B) hero
    - (C) amateur
    - (D) partisan
    - (E) sage

12. PUNCTILIOUS
    - (A) late
    - (B) scrupulous
    - (C) disorganized
    - (D) apathetic
    - (E) repulsive

*Directions:* In these test questions the first two words are related to each other in some way. From the choices offered you are to select the one which completes the relationship with the three given items.

13. DISCIPLE is to MENTOR as PROSELYTE is to
    (A) opinion       (B) expedition
    (C) leader       (D) football

14. ARTIFICE is to FINESSE as INEPT is to
    (A) inefficient       (B) artistic
    (C) tricky       (D) insatiable

15. CAPTAIN is to STEAMSHIP as PRINCIPAL is to
    (A) interest       (B) school
    (C) agent       (D) concern

16. DIME is to SILVER as PENNY is to
    (A) mint       (B) copper
    (C) currency       (D) value

17. REVERT is to REVERSION as SYMPATHIZE is to
    (A) sympathic       (B) symposium
    (C) sympathy       (D) sympathizer

18. REGRESSIVE is to REGRESS as STERILE is to
    (A) sterilization       (B) sterilize
    (C) sterility       (D) sterilizer

19. DOWN is to DOWNY as AGE is to
    (A) aging       (B) old
    (C) ancient       (D) historic

20. I is to MINE as MAN is to
    (A) men       (B) his
    (C) man's       (D) mine

21. DISLOYAL is to FAITHLESS as IMPERFECTION
   is to
   (A) contamination       (B) depression
   (C) foible              (D) decrepitude
   (E) praise

22. NECKLACE is to PEARLS as CHAIN is to
   (A) metal               (B) prisoner
   (C) locket              (D) silver
   (E) links

23. DRIFT is to SNOW as DUNE is to
   (A) hill                (B) rain
   (C) sand                (D) hail
   (E) desert

24. DILIGENT is to UNREMITTING as DIAMETRIC
   is to
   (A) pretentious         (B) geographical
   (C) adamant             (D) contrary
   (E) opposite

## Reading Comprehension

### TIME: 20 MINUTES

*Directions:* The reading passage given below is followed
by questions based on its content. After reading the passage, choose the best answer to each question and blacken
the space beneath the appropriate letter on the answer
sheet. The questions are to be answered on the basis of
what is stated or implied in the passage.

Educators are seriously concerned about the high rate
of dropouts among the doctor of philosophy candidates
and the consequent loss of talent to a nation in need of
Ph.D.'s. Some have placed the dropout loss as high as

50 per cent. The extent of the loss was, however, largely a matter of expert guessing.

Last week a well-rounded study was pub'' ''ed. It was based on 22,000 questionnaires sent to former graduate students who were enrolled in 24 universities between 1950 and 1954 and seemed to show many past fears to be groundless.

The dropout rate was found to be 31 per cent, and in most cases the dropouts, while not completing the Ph.D. requirements, went on to productive work.

They are not only doing well financially, but, according to the report, are not far below the income levels of those who went on to complete their doctorates.

The study, called "Attrition of Graduate Students at the Ph.D. Level in the Traditional Arts and Sciences," was made at Michigan State University under a $60,000 grant from the United States Office of Education. It was conducted by Dr. Allan Tucker, former assistant dean of the university and now chief academic officer of the Board of Regents of the State University System of Florida.

Discussing the study last week, Dr. Tucker said the project was initiated "because of the concerns frequently expressed by graduate faculties and administrators that some of the individuals who dropped out of Ph.D. programs were capable of completing the requirements for the degree.

"Attrition at the Ph.D. level is also thought to be a waste of precious faculty time and a drain on university resources already being used to capacity. Some people expressed the opinion that the shortage of highly trained specialists and college teachers could be reduced by persuading the dropouts to return to graduate school to complete the Ph.D. program."

"The results of our research," Dr. Tucker concluded, "did not support these opinions."

The study found that:

(1) Lack of motivation was the principal reason for dropping out.

(2) Most dropouts went as far in their doctoral programs as was consistent with their levels of ability or their specialties.

(3) Most dropouts are now engaged in work consistent with their education and motivation.

(4) The dropout rate was highest in the humanities (50%) and lowest in the natural sciences (29%)—and is higher in lower-quality graduate schools.

Nearly 75 per cent of the dropouts said there was no academic reason for their decision, but those who mentioned academic reasons cited failure to pass qualifying examinations, uncompleted research and failure to pass language exams.

"Among the single most important personal reasons identified by dropouts for noncompletion of their Ph.D. program," the study found, "lack of finances was marked by 19 per cent."

As an indication of how well the dropouts were doing, a chart showed that 2 per cent whose studies were in the humanities were receiving $20,000 and more annually while none of the Ph.D.'s with that background reached this figure. The Ph.D.'s shone in the $7,500 to $15,000 bracket with 78 per cent at that level against 50 per cent for the dropouts. This may also be an indication of the fact that top salaries in the academic fields, where Ph.D.'s tend to rise to the highest salaries, are still lagging behind other fields.

In the social sciences 5 per cent of the Ph.D.'s reached the $20,000 plus figure as against 3 per cent of the dropouts but in the physical sciences they were neck-and-neck with 5 per cent each.

Academic institutions employed 90 per cent of the hu-

manities Ph.D.'s as against 57 per cent of the humanities
dropouts. Business and industry employed 47 per cent of
the physical science Ph.D.'s and 38 per cent of the physical
science dropouts. Government agencies took 16 per cent
of the social science Ph.D.'s and 32 per cent of the social
science dropouts.

As to the possibility of getting dropouts back on cam-
pus, the outlook was glum.

"The main conditions which would have to prevail for at
least 25 per cent of the dropouts who might consider re-
turning to graduate school would be to guarantee that they
would retain their present level of income and in some
cases their present job."

1. The author states that many educators feel that
   (A) steps should be taken to get the dropouts back
       to school particularly in certain disciplines
   (B) since the dropout does just about as well finan-
       cially as the Ph.D. degree-getter, there is no
       justifiable reason for the former to return to his
       studies
   (C) the high dropout rate is largely attributable to
       the lack of stimulation on the part of faculty
       members
   (D) the dropout should return to a lower quality
       school to continue his studies
   (E) the Ph.D. holder is generally a better adjusted
       person than the dropout

2. The article states that
   (A) not having sufficient funds to continue their edu-
       cation accounts for more Ph.D. dropouts than
       all the other reasons combined
   (B) in fields as English, philosophy, and the arts,
       the dropouts are doing better in the higher sal-
       ary brackets than the Ph.D.'s

- (C) at the $10,000 earning level, there is a higher percentage of dropouts than the percentage of Ph.D.'s
- (D) in physics, geology, and chemistry, the Ph.D.'s are twice as numerous in the higher salary brackets than the dropouts
- (E) the government agencies employ twice as many dropouts as they do Ph.D.'s

3. Research has shown that
- (A) dropouts are substantially below Ph.D.'s in financial attainment
- (B) the incentive factor is a minor one in regard to pursuing Ph.D. studies
- (C) the Ph.D. candidate is likely to change his field of specialization if he drops out
- (D) about one-third of those who start Ph.D. work do not complete the work to earn the degree
- (E) there are comparatively few dropouts in the Ph.D. humanities disciplines

4. Meeting foreign language requirements for the Ph.D.
- (A) is the most frequent reason for dropping out
- (B) is more difficult for the science candidate than for the humanities candidate
- (C) is considered part of the so-called "qualification" examination
- (D) is an essential part of many Ph.D. programs
- (E) does not vary in difficulty among universities

5. Dr. Tucker felt that
- (A) a primary purpose of his research project was to arrive at a more efficient method for dropping incapable Ph.D. applicants
- (B) a serious aspect of the dropout situation was the deplorable waste of productive talent
- (C) one happy feature about the dropout situation

was that the dropouts went into college teaching rather than into research

(D) his project should be free of outside interference and so he rejected outside financial assistance for the project

(E) it was important to determine how well Ph.D. dropouts did in comparison to those who completed their program

6. After reading the article, one would refrain from concluding that

(A) colleges and universities employ a substantial number of Ph.D. dropouts

(B) Ph.D.'s are not earning what they deserve in nonacademic positions

(C) the study, *Attrition of Graduate Students at the Ph.D. Level in the Traditional Arts and Sciences*, was conducted with efficiency and validity

(D) a Ph.D. dropout, by and large, does not have what it takes to earn the degree

(E) optimism reigns in regard to getting Ph.D. dropouts to return to their pursuit of the degree

*Directions:* Each of the completion questions in this test consists of an incomplete sentence. Each sentence is followed by a series of lettered words, one of which best completes the sentence. Select the word that best completes the meaning of each sentence, and mark the letter of that word opposite that sentence.

7. He _____ his speech heavily with jargon of the trade.

(A) retards               (B) brakes
(C) disburses             (D) inflates
              (E) lards

8. It really looked as if the outclassed Portuguese were about to make as _____ an exit from the _____ as had the Italians.
   (A) ignominious . . . competition
   (B) differential . . . forum
   (C) emphatic . . . cavern
   (D) surreptitious . . . vista
   (E) opportune . . . palladium

9. The growing of cereals on a large scale was the first stage in a revolution that was to replace a food-gathering _____ -existence by an urban civilization based on agriculture.
   (A) paternal        (B) herbivorous
   (C) sedulous        (D) nomadic
             (E) urbane

10. But a _____ wind built up during the race, and shortly most of the summertime boats turned to and went home.
    (A) infamous       (B) helpless
    (C) snarling       (D) ravishing
              (E) vacillating

11. To be director of the most important, largest, and surely richest art museum in the country demands _____ concentration and strong personal _____.
    (A) continued . . . antipathy
    (B) invaluable . . . attachment
    (C) hectic . . . interposition
    (D) unseemly . . . charm
    (E) unflagging . . . involvement

12. The novel, describing the experience of a man who is brought back from the dead by a new scientific tech-

nique, is a _____ on doctors, research foundations, and many _____ of contemporary society.

(A) treatise . . . remorses
(B) satire . . . foibles
(C) dossier . . . infallibilities
(D) criticism . . . nostalgias
(E) capsule . . . validities

13. The sales of Jules Verne's books continue to _____ like a runaway balloon.
(A) flit
(B) advance
(C) revive
(D) soar
(E) leap

14. Everything about her is borrowed, temporary, _____ as a soap bubble—even her name.
(A) unstable
(B) harebrained
(C) obstinate
(D) pliable
(E) obscure

15. Beginning with the brief period of open _____ in the early spring, there is ample opportunity for insects to make crossings between very _____ plants.
(A) insemination . . . recalcitrant
(B) pollination . . . diverse
(C) stigmatization . . . similar
(D) exposure . . . amorphous
(E) pollution . . . responsive

16. We should _____ if we said that all writers today felt that their independence as creative artists was threatened—yet, all writers, creative and other, participate in the _____ that reigns throughout the world.
    (A) apologize . . . naturalism
    (B) rescind . . . euphoria
    (C) reflect . . . enormity
    (D) recant . . . absolution
    (E) exaggerate . . . malaise

7. The human intelligence that created industrial civilization now has the assignment of making that civilization _____ man's basic needs.
    (A) compatible with      (B) reducible to
    (C) assignable to        (D) warrantable for
                (E) characteristic of

8. He was foredoomed by his _____ with the inventions and mechanisms that were transforming agrarian post-bellum America.
    (A) roustabout           (B) infatuation
    (C) superciliousness     (D) saturation
                (F) justification

9. One felt a little shiver of _____ at the thought of venturing out into that world where our footsteps _____ as we walked.
    (A) condescension . . . talked
    (B) indecision . . . squeaked
    (C) compunction . . . disappeared
    (D) apprehension . . . echoed
    (E) remorse . . . retraced

0. Students in small colleges often reveal their own status-seeking _____ by asking their favorite teachers why they stay in such a college.

(A) selfishness        (B) ambiguities
(C) reliance           (D) dubiety
            (E) propensities


## END OF PART


*If you finish before the allotted time is up, work on this part only. When time is up, proceed directly to the next part and do not return to this part.*

# PART THREE
## MATHEMATICS

### 24 QUESTIONS—30 MINUTES

**Common information:** In each question, information concerning one or both of the quantities to be compared is given in the Item column. A symbol that appears in any column represents the same thing in Column A as it does in Column B.

**Numbers:** All numbers used are real numbers.

**Figures:** Assume that the position of points, angles, regions, and so forth, are in the order shown.

Assume that the lines shown as straight are indeed straight.

Figures are assumed to lie in a plane unless otherwise indicated.

Figures accompanying questions are intended to provide information you can use in answering the questions. However, unless a note states that a figure is drawn to scale, you should solve the problems by using your knowledge of mathematics, and NOT by estimating sizes by sight or by measurement.

*Directions:* For each of the following questions two quantities are given . . . one in Column A; and one in Column B. Compare the two quantities and mark your answer sheet with the correct, lettered conclusion. These are your options:

    A: if the quantity in Column A is the greater;
    B: if the quantity in Column B is the greater;
    C: if the two quantities are equal;

D: if the relationship cannot be determined from the information given.

| Item | Column A | Column B |
|---|---|---|
| 1. $n < 0$<br>$a < 0$ | $n + a$ | $n - a$ |
| 2. | The average of: 22, 24, 26, 28, 30 | The average of: 17, 19, 21, 23, 25, 27, 29, 31, 33 |

3.

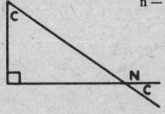

| | $n - c$ | $90°$ |
|---|---|---|

| 4. $0 < y < 5$<br>$0 < n < 7$ | y | n |
|---|---|---|
| 5. $5n - 5a = 25$ | n | a |
| 6. In isosceles $\triangle$<br>NCY | C | Y |

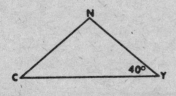

| 7. $\dfrac{m}{2} = c^2$ | m | c |
|---|---|---|

| Item | Column A | Column B |
|------|----------|----------|
| 8. | c | a |

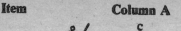

9.          arc RT       chord RT

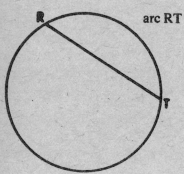

10.      $5 + 16(3 - 2)$    $21 + 5 - 3(4 - 3)(0)$

11.      $8[2x - 3(4x - 6) - 9]$    $6[3x - 2(6x - 3) + 2]$

12.      h           y

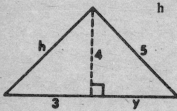

*Directions:* For each of the following questions, select the choice which best answers the question or completes the statement.

13. In the solution of a certain problem, three numbers of two digits each were added and their sum proved to be a number of two digits. It follows, therefore, that
    (A) at least two of the addends were less than 50
    (B) each addend was less than 50
    (C) the addends were not equal
    (D) none of the addends exceed 50

14. The number of grams in one ounce is 28.35. The number of grams in a kilogram is 1000. Therefore, the number of kilograms in one pound is approximately
    (A) 2.2          (B) 1.0
    (C) 0.45         (D) 4.5

15. If one-third of the liquid contents of a can evaporates on the first day and three-fourths of the remainder evaporates on the second day, the fractional part of the original contents remaining at the close of the second day is
    (A) 5/12         (B) 7/12
    (C) ⅙            (D) ½

16. The equation expressing the relationship between r and t in the table

    | r | 3 | 4 | 5 | 6 |
    |---|---|---|---|---|
    | t | 7 | 10 | 13 | 16 |

    is
    (A) $r = 3t - 2$        (B) $t = 2r + 1$
    (C) $t - 2 = 3r$        (D) none of the foregoing

17. The square of a proper fraction is
    (A) less than the original fraction
    (B) greater than the original fraction
    (C) greater than 1
    (D) not necessarily any of the preceding

18. Three of the following are mathematically correct expressions for the sum of 2½ and 3½. Which one is *not*?
    (A) 5%
    (B) $\dfrac{7}{2} + \dfrac{5}{2}$
    (C) $(2 \times \frac{1}{2}) + (2 + 3)$
    (D) $\dfrac{2 + 2}{5 + 7}$

19. If n and d represent positive whole numbers
    (n > d > 1), the fractions

    I. $\dfrac{d}{n}$      II. $\dfrac{d + 1}{n + 1}$      III. $\dfrac{d - 1}{n - 1}$      IV. $\dfrac{n}{d}$

    V. $\dfrac{n - 1}{d - 1}$

    arranged in ascending order of magnitude, are represented correctly by
    (A) III, II, I, V, IV
    (B) IV, V, III, I, II
    (C) III, I, II, IV, V
    (D) III, V, IV, I, II

20. The formula for the selling price S of an article sold at a loss of r% of its cost C is

    (A) $S = C(1 - r)$      (B) $S = \dfrac{C(100 - r)}{100}$

    (C) $S = \dfrac{C(1 - r)}{100}$      (D) none of these

21. The principle of inverse operation is indicated with symbols as
    (A) $a + b = c$,  $b + a = c$
    (B) $a + b = c$,  $c - b = a$
    (C) $a(b + c) = ab + ac$
    (D) $(a + b) + c = a + (b + c)$

22. 8 divided by zero is equivalent to
    (A) $8\overline{)0}$
    (B) 0
    (C) 8
    (D) none of these

23. Decimals are fractions with denominators of
    (A) multiples of 10
    (B) powers of 10
    (C) reciprocals of multiples of 10
    (D) reciprocals of powers of 10

24. Which one of the following numbers is *not* a perfect square?
    (A) .16
    (B) 1.6
    (C) 16
    (D) 1,600

**END OF PART**

*If you finish before the allotted time is up, work on this part only. When time is up, proceed directly to the next part and do not return to this part.*

### 42 QUESTIONS—30 MINUTES

**Reading Comprehension**

### TIME: 20 MINUTES

*Directions:* Each of the completion questions in this test consists of an incomplete sentence. Each sentence is followed by a series of lettered words, one of which best completes the sentence. Select the word that best completes the meaning of each sentence, and mark the letter of that word opposite that sentence.

1. Art is long and time is _____.
   - (A) fervid
   - (B) fallow
   - (C) nebulous
   - (D) evanescent

2. The _____ flower was also _____.
   - (A) pretty – redolent
   - (B) drooping – potable
   - (C) pale – opulent
   - (D) blooming – amenable

3. The _____ effects of the drug made her very weary.
   - (A) succinct
   - (B) spurious
   - (C) soporific
   - (D) supine

4. Being _____, the child was not permitted to have his supper.
   (A) refractory          (B) reticent
   (C) vernal              (D) unctuous

5. The chairman's _____ speech swayed the audience to favor his proposal.
   (A) cursory             (B) blatant
   (C) ancillary           (D) cogent

6. He is quite _____ and, therefore, easily _____.
   (A) callow – deceived       (B) lethal – perceived
   (C) fetal – conceived       (D) limpid – received

*Directions:* Below each of the following passages, you will find questions or incomplete statements about the passage. Each statement or question is followed by lettered words or expressions. Select the word or expression that most satisfactorily completes each statement or answers each question in accordance with the meaning of the passage. Write the letter of that word or expression on your answer paper.

It is almost a definition of a gentleman to say he is one who never inflicts pain. This description is both refined and, as far as it goes, accurate. He is mainly occupied in merely removing the obstacles which hinder the free and unembarrassed action of those about him; and he concurs with their movements rather than takes the initiative himself. His benefits may be considered as parallel to what are called comforts or conveniences in arrangements of a personal nature: like an easy chair or a good fire, which do their part in dispelling cold and fatigue, though nature provides both means of rest and animal heat without them. The true gentleman, in like manner, carefully avoids whatever may cause a jar or a jolt in the minds of those with

whom he is cast;—all clashing of opinion, or collision of
feeling, all restraint, or suspicion, or gloom, or resentment;
his great concern being to make everyone at their ease and
at home. He has his eyes on all his company; he is tender
towards the bashful, gentle towards the distant, and merciful towards the absurd; he can recollect to whom he is
speaking; he guards against unseasonable allusions, or
topics which may irritate; he is seldom prominent in conversation, and never wearisome. He makes light of favors
while he does them, and seems to be receiving when he
is conferring. He never speaks of himself except when
compelled, never defends himself by a mere retort, he
has no ears for slander or gossip, is scrupulous in imputing
motives to those who interfere with him, and interprets
everything for the best. He is never mean or little in his
disputes, never takes unfair advantage, never mistakes
personalities or sharp sayings for arguments, or insinuates
evil which he dare not say out. From a longsighted pru-
dence, he observes the maxim of the ancient sage, that we
should ever conduct ourselves towards our enemy as if
he were one day to be our friend. He has too much good
sense to be affronted at insults, he is too well employed to
remember injuries, and too indolent to bear malice. He
is patient, forbearing, and resigned, on philosophical principles; he submits to pain, because it is inevitable, to be-
reavement, because it is irreparable, and to death, because
it is his destiny. If he engages in controversy of any kind,
his disciplined intellect preserves him from the blundering
discourtesy of better, perhaps, but less educated minds;
who, like blunt weapons, tear and hack instead of cutting
clean, who mistake the point in argument, waste their
strength on trifles, misconceive their adversary, to leave the
question more involved than they find it. He may be right
or wrong in his opinion, but he is too clear-headed to be

unjust; he is as simple as he is forcible, and as brief as he is decisive. Nowhere shall we find greater candor, consideration, indulgence: he throws himself into the minds of his opponents, he accounts for their mistakes. He knows the weakness of human reason as well as its strength, its province, and its limits. If he be an unbeliever, he will be too profound and large-minded to ridicule religion or to act against it; he is too wise to be a dogmatist or fanatic in his infidelity. He respects piety and devotion; he even supports institutions as venerable, beautiful, or useful, to which he does not assent; he honors the ministers of religion, and it contents him to decline its mysteries without assailing or denouncing them. He is a friend of religious toleration, and that, not only because his philosophy has taught him to look on all forms of faith with an impartial eye, but also from the gentleness and effeminacy of feeling, which is the attendant on civilization.

Not that he may not hold a religion too, even when he belongs to no formal congregation. In that case his religion is one of imagination and sentiment; it is the embodiment of those ideas of the sublime, majestic, and beautiful, without which there can be no large philosophy. Sometimes he acknowledges the being of God, sometimes he invests an unknown principle or quality with the attributes of perfection. And this deduction of his reason, or creation of his fancy, he makes the occasion of such excellent thoughts, and the starting-point of so varied and systematic a teaching, that he even seems like a disciple of Christianity itself. From the very accuracy and steadiness of his logical powers, he is able to see what sentiments are consistent in those who hold any religious doctrines at all, and he appears to others to feel and to hold a whole circle of theological truths, which exist, in his mind no otherwise than as a number of deductions.

7. According to the passage, the gentleman when engaged in debate is
   - (A) soothing and conciliatory
   - (B) brilliant and insightful
   - (C) opinionated and clever
   - (D) concise and forceful
   - (E) quiet and charming

8. A gentleman, here, is equated with
   - (A) a jar or jolt
   - (B) an easy chair or a good fire
   - (C) a blunt weapon
   - (D) a sharp saying
   - (E) collisions and restraints

9. A person who is "scrupulous in imputing motives" is
   - (A) careful about accusing others
   - (B) eager to prove another guilty
   - (C) willing to falsify
   - (D) unable to make decisions
   - (E) suspicious concerning the actions of others

10. This passage does not take into account a commonly held concept of a gentleman—namely,
    - (A) consideration for others
    - (B) refusal to slander
    - (C) leniency toward the stupid
    - (D) neatness in attire
    - (E) willingness to forgive

11. The most appropriate title for this passage would be
    - (A) A Gentleman Now and Before
    - (B) Definition of a Gentleman
    - (C) Intellectualism and the Gentleman
    - (D) Can a Gentleman Be Religious?
    - (E) Gentlemen Prefer Easy Chairs

12. The word "effeminacy" as used in this selection really
means
(A) femininity
(B) childishness          (D) indecision
(C) cowardice             (E) delicacy

Monseigneur, one of the great lords in power at the
Court, held his fortnightly reception in his grand hotel in
Paris. Monseigneur was in his inner room, his sanctuary
of sanctuaries, the Holiest of Holiests to the crowd of
worshippers in the suite of rooms without. Monseigneur
was about to take his chocolate. Monseigneur could swallow a great many things with ease, and was by some few
sullen minds supposed to be rather rapidly swallowing
France; but, his morning's chocolate could not so much
as get into the throat of Monseigneur, without the aid of
four strong men besides the Cook.
Yes. It took four men, all four a-blaze with gorgeous
decoration, and the Chief of them unable to exist with
fewer than two gold watches in his pocket, emulative of
the noble and chaste fashion set by Monseigneur, to conduct the happy chocolate to Monseigneur's lips. One lac-
quey carried the chocolate-pot into the sacred presence;
a second milled and frothed the chocolate with the little
instrument he bore for that function; a third presented
the favoured napkin; a fourth (he of the two gold watches)
poured the chocolate out. It was impossible for Monseigneur to dispense with one of these attendants on the
chocolate and hold his high place under the admiring
Heavens. Deep would have been the blot upon his escutcheon if his chocolate had been ignobly waited on by only
three men; he must have died of two.
Monseigneur had been out at a little supper last night,
where the Comedy and the Grand Opera were charmingly

represented. Monseigneur was out at a little supper most
nights, with fascinating company. So polite and so im-
pressible was Monseigneur, that the Comedy and the
Grand Opera had far more influence with him in the tiresome articles of state affairs and state secrets, than the
needs of all France. A happy circumstance for France, as
the like always is for all countries similarly favoured!—
always was for England (by way of example), in the re-
gretted days of the merry Stuart who sold it.

Monseigneur had one truly noble idea of general public
business, which was, to let everything go on in its own
way; of particular public business, Monseigneur had the
other truly noble idea that it must all go his way—tend to
his own power and pocket. Of his pleasures, general and
particular, Monseigneur had the other truly noble idea,
that the world was made for them. The text of his order
(altered from the original by only a pronoun, which is
not much) ran: "The earth and the fulness thereof are
mine, saith Monseigneur."

13. The locale of this passage is
    (A)  the opera
    (B)  a sweet shop          (D)  an apartment
    (C)  the field of battle    (E)  a church

14. The tone of the selection is
    (A)  serious
    (B)  sarcastic             (D)  objective
    (C)  inquiring             (E)  informative

15. The chronological placement is the
    (A)  twentieth century
    (B)  eighteenth century
    (C)  sixteenth century
    (D)  fourteenth century
    (E)  indefinite past or future

16. Monseigneur represents
    (A) a person who elicits sympathy
    (B) a simpleton who cannot provide for himself
    (C) a profligate who cares little about others
    (D) an intellectual who dabbles in business matters
    (E) a miser who has moments of extravagance

17. The style of the passage suggests that it is part of
    (A) an historical document
    (B) a textbook on sociology
    (C) an essay against political favoritism
    (D) a magazine article on good etiquette
    (E) a story about abuse of power

18. The author is, with his reference to Monseigneur, using a literary device called
    (A) onomatopoeia
    (B) denouement         (D) psychogenesis
    (C) symbolism          (E) euphemism

## Vocabulary

### TIME: 10 MINUTES

*Directions:* In these test questions each of the two CAPITALIZED words have a certain relationship to each other. Following the capitalized words are other pairs of words, each designated by a letter. Select the lettered pair wherein the words are related in the same way as the two CAPITALIZED words are related to each other.

1. ADVERSITY : HAPPINESS ::
    (A) fear : misfortune
    (B) solace : adversity
    (C) vehemence : serenity
    (D) troublesome : petulance
    (E) graduation : felicitation

2. MARACAS : RHYTHM ::
   (A) flute : base
   (B) xylophone : percussion
   (C) drum : harmony
   (D) violin : concert
   (E) piano : octave

3. FEATHERS : PLUCK ::
   (A) goose : duck
   (B) garment : weave
   (C) car : drive
   (D) wool : shear
   (E) duck : down

4. MODESTY : ARROGANCE ::
   (A) debility : strength
   (B) cause : purpose
   (C) passion : emotion
   (D) finance : Wall Street
   (E) practice : perfection

5. BLOW : HORN ::
   (A) switch : tracks
   (B) turn on : lights
   (C) go over : map
   (D) accelerate : engine
   (E) tune : radio

6. BAY : SEA ::
   (A) mountain : valley
   (B) plain : forest
   (C) peninsula : land
   (D) cape : reef
   (E) island : sound

7. DECEMBER : WINTER ::
   (A) April : showers
   (B) September : summer

(C) June : fall
(D) March : spring
(E) February : autumn

8. NECKLACE : ADORNMENT ::
   (A) medal : decoration ::
   (B) bronze : medal
   (C) scarf : dress
   (D) window : house
   (E) pearl : diamond

9. LIQUOR : ALCOHOLISM ::
   (A) pill : dope
   (B) tranquilizer : emotions
   (C) perfume : smell
   (D) candy : overweight
   (E) atomizer : sinusitis

10. INTERRUPT : SPEAK ::
    (A) shout : yell
    (B) intrude : enter
    (C) interfere : assist
    (D) telephone : telegraph
    (E) concede : defend

11. ENCOURAGE : RESTRICT ::
    (A) gain : succeed
    (B) deprive : supply
    (C) see : believe
    (D) detain : deny
    (E) finish : complete

12. SETTING : STONE ::
    (A) pen : paper
    (B) glass : window
    (C) socket : bulb
    (D) ring : finger
    (E) locket : chain

*Directions:* For each question in this test, select the appropriate letter preceding the word that is opposite in meaning to the capitalized word.

13. CAVIL
   - (A) dishonest behavior
   - (B) frequent occurrence
   - (C) serious complaint
   - (D) small price
   - (E) light burden

14. TYRO
   - (A) promulgate effectively
   - (B) possess rightfully
   - (C) eradicate completely
   - (D) protect skillfully
   - (E) play freely

15. ARROGATE
   - (A) promulgate
   - (B) possess
   - (C) eradicate
   - (D) protect
   - (E) play

16. RECONDITE
   - (A) obvious
   - (B) renewed
   - (C) blighted
   - (D) noisy
   - (E) bright

17. PROTEAN
   - (A) depriving
   - (B) flowering
   - (C) unchanging
   - (D) universal
   - (E) united

18. COGENT
   - (A) repetitive
   - (B) urgent
   - (C) complicated
   - (D) confined
   - (E) unconvincing

19. DENIGRATE
    - (A) approve
    - (B) exasperate
    - (C) defy
    - (D) integrate
    - (E) usurp

20. INCARCERATE
    - (A) remit
    - (B) offend
    - (C) decline
    - (D) feign
    - (E) release

21. SAVORY
    - (A) firm
    - (B) tasteless
    - (C) bitter
    - (D) watery
    - (E) worthy

22. EXTANT
    - (A) constant
    - (B) prolific
    - (C) giddy
    - (D) destroyed
    - (E) equivalent

23. HISTRIONIC
    - (A) current
    - (B) living
    - (C) laughing
    - (D) fictitious
    - (E) natural

24. TENUOUS
    - (A) irritable
    - (B) inevitable
    - (C) tough
    - (D) willful
    - (E) arduous

### END OF PART

*If you finish before the allotted time is up, work on this part only. When time is up, proceed directly to the next part and do not return to this part.*

# PART FIVE
# MATHEMATICS

## 20 QUESTIONS—30 MINUTES

*Directions:* Each question below is followed by two numbered facts. Decide whether the data given is sufficient for answering the question. Sometimes the two facts do not give enough information to answer the question. Sometimes the two facts give just enough data to answer the question. And sometimes one of the facts alone is sufficient to answer the question. Read each question and the two facts that follow it; then mark your answer on the answer sheet that follows.

Mark "A" if statement 1 alone is sufficient to answer the question, but statement 2 alone is not sufficient.

Mark "B" if statement 2 alone is sufficient to answer the question, but statement 1 alone is not sufficient.

Mark "C" if both statements together are needed to answer the question, but neither statement alone is sufficient.

Mark "D" if either statement by itself is sufficient to answer the question asked.

Mark "E" if not enough facts are given to answer the question.

1. Are the triangles congruent?
   (1) The triangles are isosceles.
   (2) The triangles have equal altitudes drawn to their bases.

2. How many dimes does Edna have in her hand?
   (1) She has 42¢ in coins in her hand.
   (2) Only four of her coins are nickels.

3. What are the dimensions of an isosceles triangle?
   (1) The altitude of the triangle is 8.
   (2) The perimeter of the triangle is 32.

4. In triangle ABC, find the measure of angle B.
   (1) AB:BC = 1:1
   (2) AB:AC = 1:1

5. The bases of an isosceles trapezoid are 14 inches and 18 inches. Find its area.
   (1) The nonparallel sides are each 12 inches.
   (2) The diagonals of the trapezoid are each 20 inches.

6. There are 50 students in a certain class who read book A, or book B, or both. How many students read each book?
   (1) 20 students read book A only.
   (2) 30 students read book B.

7. A table is 60″ long and 30″ wide. It is covered with three overlapping newspapers each 30″ wide. How long is each newspaper?
   (1) All the newspapers are of equal length.
   (2) If the table were $1\frac{1}{2}$ times longer, the newspapers would just cover the table without overlapping.

8. What is the value of x?
   (1) $x + y = 4$
   (2) $x - y = 6$

9. Find the area of parallelogram ABCD.
   (1) AB = 10
   (2) AD = 6

10. Find the fifth consecutive number.
    (1) The sum of the first three is 75.
    (2) The sum of the last two is 60.

*Directions:* For each of the following questions, select the choice which best answers the question or completes the statement.

Imagine that we are required to use a new number system. This new system consists of 5 digits, 0, 7 , ⌐ , ∠ , and ⌐/ corresponding respectively to the numbers 0, 1, 2, 3, and 4. The digit 0 is used in this new system in the same way as in our old system, so that 5 is written 70.

11. What is the equivalent of 7?
    (A) 7
    (B) 7 7
    (C) 7⌐
    (D) ⌐7

12. What is the sum of 7 + ⌐ + ⌐/ + ∠ ?
    (A) 70
    (B) ⌐0
    (C) ⌐/0
    (D) ∠0

13. A radio has a list price of $∠0 and is sold at $\frac{7}{\angle}$ off of list. What is the selling price?
    (A) $∠
    (B) $⌐0
    (C) $70
    (D) $∠∠

14. Which of the following means 13 feet?
    (A) ∠7
    (B) 7∠
    (C) ⌐∠
    (D) ⌐/7

15. What is the value of 7 × ⌐ ?
    (A) 7
    (B) ⌐
    (C) 7⌐
    (D) ∠

16. What is the quotient of ⌋ 7 divided by 7⌐ ?
    (A) ∠
    (B) ⌡
    (C) ⌐
    (D) 7

Let us take a four dimensional space with the coordinate axes r, s, t and u. Any point in this space may be identified by the coordinates of that point (r, s, t, u). It may be observed that the distance of any point from the origin (0, 0, 0, 0) is

$$\sqrt{r^2 + s^2 + t^2 + u^2}$$

It may also be assumed that for any choices of the number $r_0$, $s_0$, $t_0$, $u_0$, $r_1$, $s_1$, $t_1$, $u_1$, $r_2$, $s_2$, $t_2$, $u_2$, the distance between the points $(r_1\text{-}r_0, s_1\text{-}s_0, t_1\text{-}t_0, u_1\text{-}u_0)$ and $(r_2\text{-}r_0, s_2\text{-}s_0, t_2\text{-}t_0, u_2\text{-}u_0)$ is equal to the distance between the points $(r_1, s_1, t_1, u_1)$ and $(r_2, s_2, t_2, u_2)$.

In the following questions, we shall consider certain planes whose coordinates are some pair of the coordinates r, s, t, u. For example, the point (7, 8, 9, 10) of the four dimensional space has coordinates (7, 10) when viewed in (more precisely, "projected on") the (r, u) plane.

17. How far is point (0, 1, 2, 3) from point (0, 1, 2, 4)?
    (A)    1
    (B)    1.2
    (C)   $\sqrt{5}$
    (D)    5

18. Viewed only in terms of the (s, u) plane which diagram shows correctly the location of point A (4, 3, 1, 5)?

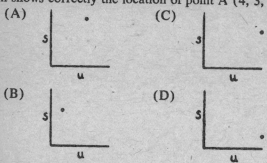

(A)

(C)

(B)

(D)

19. A box 1 yard long, 15 inches wide, and 6 inches deep will contain how many cubic feet of air?
    (A) 270
    (B) 1⅞
    (C) 22½
    (D) 90

20. When 5.1 is divided by 0.017 the quotient is
    (A) 30
    (B) 300
    (C) 3,000
    (D) 30,000

## END OF PART

*If you finish before the allotted time is up, work on this part only. When time is up, proceed directly to the next part and do not return to this part.*

# PART SIX
## USING WRITTEN ENGLISH

### 49 QUESTIONS—30 MINUTES

**English Usage**

### TIME: 15 MINUTES

*Directions:* This is a test of standard written English. The rules may differ from everyday spoken English. Many of the following sentences contain grammar, usage, word choice, and idiom that would be incorrect in written composition. Some sentences are correct. No sentence has more than one error. Any error in a sentence will be underlined and lettered; all other parts of the sentence are correct and cannot be changed. If the sentence has an error, choose the underlined part that is incorrect, and mark that letter on your answer sheet. If there is no error, mark E on your answer sheet.

1. He had a large amount of friends until he lost all his
   A              B                  C         D
   money. No error.
              E

2. John said, that he would transfer to another school
        A                    B
   at the end of the year. No error.
        C          D           E

3. Would you agree to Parsons having full control of the
      A           B           C
   operation? No error.
     D     E

4. "Your's is not to question why!" she declaimed
      A             B      C
   from the stage. No error.
      D     E

5. She was promoted because she had made less errors
          A                       B
   than the other secretary. No error.
    C          D     E

6. I would appreciate your treating me as if I was your
         A        B      C    D
   brother. No error.
       E

7. The teacher asked three of us, Dan Edward and I, to
              A                  B
   carry the plants down to the cafeteria. No error.
    C       D              E

8. Here, Jane, bring this note to the office. No error.
    A      B      C    D     E

9. Being that she was a newcomer to our organization,
     A             B         C
   Rose was shy. No error.
     D     E

10. My father, along with hundreds of other workers,
            A                  B
    have been on strike since New Year's Day. No error.
     C             D      E

11. The constant rise of prices and wages bring about
       A         B        C
    inflation. No error.
      D    E

12. That was the same identical damaged article that was
                    A              B                C
returned to the store last month. No error.
                        D              E

13. If I weren't dressed in this uniform, I wouldn't feel so
        A                      B            C
conspicuous. No error.
     D            E

14. It was not quite clear whether it was his friend or him
       A                   B                            C
who had requested the favor. No error.
     D                          E

15. After he had paid the fee and saw the pictures, he was
              A                B        C
quite satisfied. No error.
     D              E

16. Why should we give him our books, when he had
              A                B
extras why did he refuse to share them with us?
    C              D
No error.
    E

17. Jack likes all sports: tennis, basketball, football,
          A        B                          C
and etc. No error.
     D        E

18. That Bill's reasoning was fallacious was soon apparent
     A    B                   C
to all. No error.
   D        E

19. Neither John nor his children is likely to attend the
       A          B              C
ceremonies. No error.
     D            E

20. He <u>will give</u> the <u>message</u> to <u>whoever</u> <u>opens</u> the door.
      A              B           C         D
No error.
E

21. The <u>boy</u>, <u>as well as</u> his mother, <u>desperately</u> <u>need</u> help.
       A        B                      C              D
No error.
E

22. Because he <u>has always been</u> popular and
                    A
<u>with abundant wealth</u>, he <u>thoroughly</u> enjoyed his
          B                        C
<u>college years</u>. <u>No error</u>.
       D              E

23. <u>Having studied</u> your report carefully, I <u>am convinced</u>
          A                                           B
that <u>neither</u> of your solutions <u>are</u> correct. <u>No error</u>.
          C                            D               E

24. If he is successful in his attempt <u>to cross</u> the lake, he
                                           A
<u>will have swum</u> a <u>distance</u> of <u>twelve miles</u>. <u>No error</u>.
          B              C              D               E

25. <u>In spite of</u> his youth, <u>no faster</u> runner than <u>him</u>
          A                       B                        C
<u>will be found</u> in our school. <u>No error</u>.
          D                          E

## Sentence Correction

### TIME: 15 MINUTES

*Directions:* A sentence is given in which one part is underlined. Following the sentence are five choices. The first (A) choice simply repeats the underlined part. The subsequent four choices suggest other ways to express the underlined part of the original sentence. If you think that the underlined part is correct as it stands, write the answer A. If you believe that the underlined part is incorrect, select from among the other choices (B or C or D or E) the one you think is correct. Grammar, sentence structure, word usage, and punctuation are to be considered in your decision and the original meaning of the sentence must be retained.

1. Crossing the bridge, a glimpse of the islands was caught.
   - (A) a glimpse of the islands was caught.
   - (B) a glimpse of the islands were caught.
   - (C) we caught a glimpse of the islands.
   - (D) the islands were caught a glimpse of.
   - (E) we caught a glimpse of the islands' view.

2. This book has been laying here for weeks.
   - (A) laying here for weeks.
   - (B) laying here weeks.
   - (C) laying down here for weeks.
   - (D) lieing here for weeks.
   - (E) lying here for weeks.

3. When my brother will come home, I'll tell him you called.
   - (A) will come home,
   - (B) will come home
   - (C) will have come home,
   - (D) comes home,
   - (E) has come home,

4. After he graduated school, he entered the Army.
   - (A) After he graduated school,
   - (B) After he was graduated from school,
   - (C) When he graduated school,
   - (D) After he graduated school
   - (E) As he was graduated from school,

5. I think they, as a rule, are much more conniving than us.
   (A) as a rule, are much more conniving than us.
   (B) as a rule are much more conniving than us.
   (C) as a rule, are much more conniving than we.
   (D) as a rule; are much more conniving than us.
   (E) are, as a rule, much more conniving than us.

6. Sitting around the fire, mystery stories were told by each of us.
   (A) mystery stories were told by each of us.
   (B) mystery stories were told by all of us.
   (C) each of us told mystery stories.
   (D) stories of mystery were told by each of us.
   (E) there were told mystery stories by each of us.

7. The loud noise of the subway trains and the trolley cars frighten people from the country.
   (A) frighten people from the country.
   (B) frighten country people.
   (C) frighten persons from the country.
   (D) frightens country people.
   (E) frighten people who come from the country.

8. Inspecting Robert's report card, his mother noted that he had received high ratings in Latin and history.
   (A) his mother noted
   (B) it was noted by his mother
   (C) his mother had noted
   (D) a notation was made by his mother
   (E) Robert's mother noted

9. The old man told Mary and I many stories about Europe.
   (A) Mary and I
   (B) Mary and me
   (C) me and Mary

(D)  I and Mary

(E)  Mary together with me

10. The wild game hunter stalked the tiger slowly, cautiously, and in a silent manner.

(A)  and in a silent manner.

(B)  and silently.

(C)  and by acting silent.

(D)  and also used silence.

(E)  and in silence.

11. European film distributors originated the art of "dubbing"—the substitution of lip-synchronized translations in foreign languages for the original soundtrack voices.

(A)  —the substitution of lip-synchronized translations

(B)  ; the substitution of lip-synchronized translations

(C)  —the substitutions of translations synchronized by the lips

(D)  , the lip-synchronized substitution of translations

(E)  . The substitution of lip-synchronized translations

12. Every pupil understood the assignment except I.

(A)  except I.

(B)  excepting I.

(C)  outside of me.

(D)  excepting me.

(E)  except me.

13. Of the two candidates, I think he is the best suited.

(A)  he is the best suited.

(B)  that he is the best suited.

(C)  he is suited best.

(D)  he is the better suited.

(E)  he's the best suited.

14. You need not go unless you want to.
    (A) You need not go unless you want to.
    (B) You don't need to go not unless you want to.
    (C) You need go not unless you want to.
    (D) You need not go in case unless you want to.
    (E) You can go not unless you want to.

15. There is no man but would give ten years of his life to accomplish that deed.
    (A) no man but would give
    (B) no man but who would give
    (C) not no man who would not give
    (D) no man who would but give
    (E) not any man would give

16. I feel as though I was being borne bodily through the air.
    (A) as though I was being borne
    (B) as though I was being born
    (C) like I was being borne
    (D) like as though I was being borne
    (E) as though I were being borne

17. Honor as well as profit are to be gained by this work.
    (A) Honor as well as profit are to be gained by this work.
    (B) Honor as well as profit is to be gained by this work.
    (C) Honor in addition to profit are to be gained by this work.
    (D) Honor, as well as profit, are to be gained by this work.
    (E) Honor also profit is to be gained by this work.

18. He was neither in favor of or opposed to the plan.
    (A) He was neither in favor of or opposed to the plan.

    (B) He was not in favor of or opposed to the plan.

    (C) He was neither in favor of the plan or opposed
        to it.

    (D) He was neither in favor of the plan or opposed
        to the plan.

    (E) He was neither in favor of nor opposed to the
        plan.

19. I don't do well in those kinds of tests.

    (A) I don't do well in those kinds of tests.

    (B) I don't do well in those kind of tests.

    (C) I don't do good in those kinds of tests.

    (D) I don't do good in those kind of tests.

    (E) I don't do good in tests like those.

20. We were amazed to see the amount of people waiting
in line at Macy's.

    (A) amount of people waiting in line at Macy's.

    (B) number of people waiting in line at Macy's.

    (C) amount of persons waiting in line at Macy's.

    (D) amount of people waiting in line at Macys.

    (E) amount of people waiting at Macy's in line.

21. Whoever the gods wish to destroy, they first make
mad.

    (A) Whoever         (C) Whomever

    (B) Whoever,        (D) Whomever,

            (E) Whosoever

22. She is one of those girls who are always complaining.

    (A) who are

    (B) who is

    (C) whom are

    (D) whom is

    (E) whose

23. We buy only cherry plums since we like those kind best.

    (A)  those kind          (C)  that kind
    (B)  these kind          (D)  that kinds
              (E)  them kind

24. Making friends is more rewarding than to be antisocial.

    (A)  to be antisocial
    (B)  us being anti-social
    (C)  being anti social
    (D)  to be anti-social
    (E)  being antisocial


### END OF EXAM


*If you finish before the allotted time is up, work on this part only.*

# CORRECT ANSWERS FOR SAMPLE EXAMINATION

*(Please try to answer the questions on your own before looking at our answers. You'll do much better on your test if you follow this rule.)*

**Part One**
**Mathematics**

| | | | | |
|---|---|---|---|---|
| 1. C | 7. C | 13. C | 19. D | 25. B |
| 2. A | 8. C | 14. C | 20. B | 26. C |
| 3. C | 9. B | 15. A | 21. A | 27. B |
| 4. A | 10. A | 16. C | 22. C | 28. B |
| 5. D | 11. B | 17. A | 23. A | |
| 6. A | 12. D | 18. B | 24. A | |

**Part Two**
**Vocabulary**

| | | | | |
|---|---|---|---|---|
| 1. E | 6. E | 11. B | 16. B | 21. C |
| 2. B | 7. D | 12. C | 17. C | 22. E |
| 3. A | 8. A | 13. C | 18. B | 23. C |
| 4. C | 9. C | 14. A | 19. B | 24. E |
| 5. E | 10. B | 15. B | 20. C | |

**Reading Comprehension**

| | | | | |
|---|---|---|---|---|
| 1. A | 5. E | 9. D | 13. D | 17. A |
| 2. B | 6. E | 10. C | 14. A | 18. B |
| 3. D | 7. E | 11. E | 15. B | 19. D |
| 4. D | 8. A | 12. B | 16. E | 20. E |

## Part Three
## Mathematics

| | | | | |
|---|---|---|---|---|
| 1. B | 6. D | 11. D | 16. D | 21. B |
| 2. A | 7. A | 12. A | 17. A | 22. D |
| 3. C | 8. A | 13. A | 18. D | 23. B |
| 4. D | 9. A | 14. C | 19. C | 24. B |
| 5. A | 10. B | 15. C | 20. B | |

## Part Four
## Reading Comprehension

| | | | | |
|---|---|---|---|---|
| 1. D | 5. D | 9. A | 13. D | 17. E |
| 2. A | 6. A | 10. D | 14. B | 18. C |
| 3. C | 7. D | 11. B | 15. B | |
| 4. A | 8. B | 12. E | 16. C | |

## Vocabulary

| | | | | |
|---|---|---|---|---|
| 1. C | 6. C | 11. B | 16. A | 21. B |
| 2. B | 7. D | 12. C | 17. C | 22. D |
| 3. D | 8. A | 13. C | 18. E | 23. E |
| 4. A | 9. D | 14. A | 19. A | 24. C |
| 5. B | 10. B | 15. D | 20. E | |

## Part Five
## Mathematics

| | | | | |
|---|---|---|---|---|
| 1. E | 5. D | 9. E | 13. B | 17. A |
| 2. E | 6. E | 10. A | 14. C | 18. C |
| 3. C | 7. C | 11. C | 15. B | 19. B |
| 4. C | 8. D | 12. B | 16. A | 20. B |

## Part Six
## English Usage

| | | | | |
|---|---|---|---|---|
| 1. B | 6. D | 11. C | 16. B | 21. D |
| 2. A | 7. B | 12. A | 17. D | 22. B |
| 3. B | 8. B | 13. E | 18. E | 23. D |
| 4. A | 9. A | 14. C | 19. C | 24. E |
| 5. B | 10. C | 15. B | 20. E | 25. C |

## Sentence Correction

| | | | | |
|---|---|---|---|---|
| 1. C | 6. C | 11. A | 16. E | 21. C |
| 2. E | 7. D | 12. E | 17. B | 22. A |
| 3. D | 8. A | 13. D | 18. E | 23. C |
| 4. B | 9. B | 14. A | 19. A | 24. E |
| 5. C | 10. B | 15. A | 20. B | |

# Part Four

# PINPOINT PRACTICE TO RAISE

# YOUR MARK

VERBAL PRACTICE
MATHEMATICS PRACTICE
MATHEMATICS STUDY SECTION

# Pinpoint Practice to Raise Your Mark

## VERBAL PRACTICE

As you are well aware, after taking the sample test, the Verbal Section of the Scholastic Aptitude Test consists of the following areas:

1. OPPOSITES (also called ANTONYMS)*
2. COMPLETIONS
3. ANALOGIES
4. READING COMPREHENSION

In this Pinpoint Practice Section, we shall treat each of the foregoing areas and we shall, in treating them, analyze where necessary so that you will better attack the various types of verbal questions.

## SEVEN SIMPLE STEPS TO INCREASE YOUR VOCABULARY

1. LEARN LATIN . . . don't get scared. We are referring to Latin roots, prefixes, and suffixes. Remember

* To test your knowledge of words, the SAT gives you "opposites" questions rather than synonyms. There is a good reason for this—a synonym question merely tests your background in the meaning of words. On the other hand, an "opposites" question tests not only your knowledge of definitions but also your flexibility in handling words. However, since you must know the definition of a word before you can give its antonym, we are devoting considerable space in this Pinpoint Practice Section to synonym tests on various levels of difficulty.

that approximately 70 per cent of our English words are derived from Latin and Greek.

2. TAKE WORD TESTS . . . We have several Word Tests in this book.

3. STUDY WORD LISTS . . .

4. READ . . . not only novels. Non-fiction is good, too . . . and don't forget to read worthwhile newspapers and magazines.

5. LISTEN . . . to people who speak well. Tune in to worthwhile TV programs, also.

6. PLAY WORD GAMES . . . like Anagrams, Scrabble and Crossword Puzzles.

7. USE THE DICTIONARY . . . frequently and extensively.

This book will give you ample study and practice material in the first three steps listed:

LEARNING LATIN (AND GREEK)—The next few pages contain many useful Latin and Greek stems, prefixes, and suffixes. Learn them. By so doing, you will build up your vocabulary effectively and speedily.

TAKING WORD TESTS—This Practice Section has many word tests of different types.

USING WORD LISTS—We have one beginning on page 35.

In addition, may we suggest the following books which will help you considerably in your Verbal Practice preparation:

*2300 Steps to Word Power*—$1.45 (programmed)
Miller Analogies Test—*1400 Analogy Questions*—$4.00 (programmed)
　　　(Arco Publishing Co., 219 Park Avenue South, New York, N.Y. 10003)

## LATIN AND GREEK STEMS, PREFIXES, AND SUFFIXES

| LATIN STEM | MEANING | EXAMPLE |
|---|---|---|
| ag, ac | do | agenda, action |
| agr | farm | agriculture |
| aqua | water | aqueous |
| cad, cas | fall | cadence, casual |
| cant | sing | chant |
| cap, cep | take | captive, accept |
| capit | head | capital |
| cede | go | precede |
| celer | speed | celerity |
| cide, cis | kill, cut | suicide, incision |
| clud, clus | close | include, inclusion |
| cur, curs | run | incur, incursion |
| dict | say | diction |
| duct | lead | induce |
| fact, fect | make | factory, perfect |
| fer, lat | carry | refer, dilate |
| fring, fract | break | infringe, fracture |
| frater | brother | fraternal |
| fund, fus | pour | refund, confuse |
| greg | group | gregarious |
| gress, grad | move forward | progress, degrade |
| hom | man | homicide |
| ject | throw | reject |
| jud | right | judicial |
| junct | join | conjunction |
| lect, leg | read, choose | collect, legend |
| loq, loc | speak | loquacious, interlocutory |
| manu | hand | manuscript |
| mand | order | remand |
| mar | sea | maritime |
| mater | mother | maternal |
| med | middle | intermediary |
| min | lessen | diminution |
| mis, mit | send | remit, dismiss |
| mort | death | mortician |
| mote, mov | move | remote, remove |

| LATIN STEM | MEANING | EXAMPLE |
| --- | --- | --- |
| naut | sailor | astronaut |
| nom | name | nomenclature |
| pater | father | paternity |
| ped, pod | foot | pedal, podiatrist |
| pend | hang | depend |
| plic | fold | implicate |
| port | carry | portable |
| pos, pon | put | depose, component |
| reg, rect | rule | regicide, direct |
| rupt | break | eruption |
| scrib, scrip | write | inscribe, conscription |
| sec | cut | dissect |
| sed | remain | sedentary |
| sequ | follow | sequential |
| spect | look | inspect |
| spir | breathe | conspire |
| stat | stand | status |
| tact, tang | touch | tactile, tangible |
| ten | hold | retentive |
| term | end | terminal |
| vent | come | prevent |
| vict | conquer | evict |
| vid, vis | see | video, revise |
| voc | call | convocation |
| volv | roll | devolve |

| GREEK STEM | MEANING | EXAMPLE |
|---|---|---|
| anthrop | man | anthropology |
| arch | chief, rule | archbishop |
| astron | star | astronomy |
| auto | self | automatic |
| biblio | book | bibliophile |
| bio | life | biology |
| chrome | color | chromosome |
| chron | time | chronology |
| cosmo | world | cosmic |
| crat | rule | autocrat |
| dent, dont | tooth | dental, indent |
| eu | well, happy | eugenics |
| gamos | marriage | monogamous |
| ge | earth | geology |
| gen | origin, people | progenitor |
| graph | write | graphic |
| gyn | women | gynecologist |
| homo | same | homogeneous |
| hydr | water | dehydrate |
| logy | study of | psychology |
| meter | measure | thermometer |
| micro | small | microscope |
| mono | one | monotony |
| onomy | science | astronomy |
| onym | name | synonym |
| pathos | feeling | pathology |
| philo | love | philosophy |
| phobia | fear | hydrophobia |
| phone | sound | telephone |
| pseudo | false | pseudonym |
| psych | mind | psychic |
| scope | see | telescope |
| soph | wisdom | sophomore |
| tele | far off | telepathic |
| theo | god | theology |
| thermo | heat | thermostat |

| PREFIX * | MEANING | EXAMPLE |
| --- | --- | --- |
| ab, a | away from | absent, amoral |
| ad, ac, ag, at | to | advent, accrue, aggressive, attract |
| an | without | anarchy |
| ante | before | antedate |
| anti | against | antipathy |
| bene | well | beneficient |
| bi | two | bicameral |
| circum | around | circumspect |
| com, con, col | together | commit, confound, collate |
| contra | against | contraband |
| de | from, down | descend |
| dis, di | apart | distract, divert |
| ex, e | out | exit, emit |
| extra | beyond | extracurricular |
| in, im, il, ir, un | not | inept, impossible, illicit |
| inter | between | interpose |
| intra, intro, in | within | intramural, introspective |
| mal | bad | malcontent |
| mis | wrong | misnomer |
| non | not | nonentity |
| ob | against | obstacle |
| per | through | permeate |
| peri | around | periscope |
| poly | many | polytheism |
| post | after | post-mortem |
| pre | before | premonition |
| pro | forward | propose |
| re | again | review |
| se | apart | seduce |
| semi | half | semicircle |
| sub | under | subvert |
| super | above | superimpose |
| sui | self | suicide |
| trans | across | transpose |
| vice | instead of | vice-president |

* Latin and Greek.

| SUFFIX * | MEANING | EXAMPLE |
|---|---|---|
| able, ible | capable of being | capable, reversible |
| age | state of | storage |
| ance | relating to | reliance |
| ary | relating to | dictionary |
| ate | act | confiscate |
| ation | action | radiation |
| cy | quality | democracy |
| ence | relating to | confidence |
| er | one who | adviser |
| ic | pertaining to | democratic |
| ious | full of | rebellious |
| ize | to make like | harmonize |
| ment | result | filament |
| ty | condition | sanity |

\* Latin and Greek.

# Verbal Practice Tests

We are now ready to eliminate our weaknesses in preparation for the Verbal Part of the examination. The verbal questions which you encountered on the sample SAT (page 69 et seq.) should have spotlighted your verbal strong and weak points.

At this stage it is important for you to concentrate on the "soft spots" (your weaknesses). This Pinpoint Practice Section is so-called because you will, in the following pages, be able to locate accurately and quickly the areas in which you need the most work. You are strongly advised to deal first with the phases of the examination in which you need the most practice. You will find in the pages to come plenty of test material on three levels . . . EASY, DIFFICULT, and VERY DIFFICULT. The following areas of the verbal phase of the SAT are treated here:

SYNONYMS
OPPOSITES
COMPLETIONS
ANALOGIES
READING COMPREHENSION

Don't be alarmed if you do poorly in the DIFFICULT test. The actual Scholastic Aptitude Test "mixes them up"—EASY plus DIFFICULT questions in each grouping.

# SYNONYMS

You may wonder why the SAT does not include synonym questions—why are there "opposites" instead? There is a good reason for this—a synonym question merely tests your background in the meaning of words. On the other hand, an "opposites" question tests not only your knowledge of definitions but also your flexibility in handling words.

However, since you must know the definition of a word before you can give its antonym, we are devoting considerable space in the Pinpoint Section of this book to synonym tests on various levels of difficulty.

## SYNONYM TESTS BY LEVELS

### Level One—Easy Synonyms

*Directions:* In each question below, you will find one word followed by lettered words or phrases. In each case, choose the word or phrase that is closest in meaning to the first word.

### TEST 1—EASY SYNONYMS

1. controversial
   (A) faultfinding (B) pleasant (C) debatable (D) ugly (E) talkative

2. ghastly
   (A) hasty (B) furious (C) breathless (D) deathlike
   (E) spiritual

3. belligerent
   (A) worldly (B) warlike (C) loudmouthed (D) furious (E) artistic

4. proficiency
   (A) wisdom (B) oversupply (C) expertness (D) advancement (E) sincerity

5. compassion
   (A) rage (B) strength of character (C) forcefulness
   (D) sympathy (E) uniformity

6. dissension
   (A) treatise (B) pretense (C) fear (D) lineage (E) discord

7. intimate
   (A) charm (B) hint (C) disguise (D) frighten (E) hum

8. berate
   (A) classify (B) scold (C) underestimate (D) take one's time (E) evaluate

9. dearth
   (A) scarcity (B) width (C) affection (D) wealth (E) warmth

10. meditate
    (A) rest (B) stare (C) doze (D) make peace (E) reflect

11. neutralize
    (A) entangle (B) strengthen (C) counteract (D) combat (E) converse

12. insinuate
    (A) destroy (B) hint (C) do wrong (D) accuse (E) release

13. diminutive
    (A) proud (B) slow (C) small (D) watery (E) puzzling

14. plight
    (A) departure (B) weight (C) conspiracy (D) predicament (E) stamp

15. illicit
    (A) unlawful (B) overpowering (C) ill-advised (D) small-scale (E) unreadable

16. benign
    (A) contagious (B) fatal (C) ignorant (D) kindly (E) decorative

17. reverie
    (A) abusive language (B) love song (C) backward step (D) daydream (E) holy man

18. apprehensive
    (A) quiet (B) firm (C) curious (D) sincere (E) fearful

19. recoil
    (A) shrink (B) attract (C) electrify (D) adjust (E) enroll

20. guise
    (A) trickery (B) request (C) innocence (D) misdeed (E) appearance

### Answers Test 1

| | | | | |
|---|---|---|---|---|
| 1. C | 5. D | 9. A | 13. C | 17. D |
| 2. D | 6. E | 10. E | 14. D | 18. E |
| 3. B | 7. B | 11. C | 15. A | 19. A |
| 4. C | 8. B | 12. B | 16. D | 20. E |

## TEST 2—EASY SYNONYMS

1. stagnant
   (A) inactive (B) alert (C) selfish (D) difficult (E) scornful

2. mandatory
   (A) insane (B) obligatory (C) evident (D) strategic (E) unequaled

3. infernal
   (A) immodest (B) incomplete (C) domestic (D) second-rate (E) fiendish

4. exonerate
   (A) free from blame (B) warn (C) drive out (D) overcharge (E) plead

5. arbiter
   (A) friend (B) judge (C) drug (D) tree surgeon (E) truant

6. enmity
   (A) boredom (B) puzzle (C) offensive language (D) ill will (E) entanglement

7. discriminate
   (A) fail (B) delay (C) accuse (D) distinguish (E) reject

8. derision
   (A) disgust (B) ridicule (C) fear (D) anger (E) heredity

9. exultant
   (A) essential (B) elated (C) praiseworthy (D) plentiful (E) high-priced

10. ostensible
    (A) vibrating (B) odd (C) apparent (D) standard (E) ornate

11. acquit
    (A) increase (B) harden (C) clear (D) sharpen (E) sentence

12. dexterity
    (A) conceit (B) skill (C) insistence (D) embarrassment (E) guidance

13. assimilate
    (A) absorb (B) imitate (C) maintain (D) outrun (E) curb

14. despondency
    (A) relief (B) gratitude (C) dejection (D) hatred (E) poverty

15. buoyant
    (A) conceited (B) cautioning (C) youthful (D) musical (E) cheerful

16. culinary
    (A) having to do with cooking (B) pertaining to dressmaking (C) fond of eating (D) loving money (E) tending to be secretive

17. caprice
    (A) wisdom (B) ornament (C) pillar (D) whim (E) energy

18. deterrent
 (A) restraining (B) cleansing (C) deciding (D) concluding (E) crumbling

19. pugnacious
 (A) sticky (B) cowardly (C) precise (D) vigorous (E) quarrelsome

20. abscond
 (A) detest (B) reduce (C) swallow up (D) dismiss (E) flee

### Answers Test 2

| | | | | |
|---|---|---|---|---|
| 1. A | 5. B | 9. B | 13. A | 17. D |
| 2. B | 6. D | 10. C | 14. C | 18. A |
| 3. E | 7. D | 11. C | 15. E | 19. E |
| 4. A | 8. B | 12. B | 16. A | 20. E |

## Level Two—Difficult Synonyms

### TEST 3—DIFFICULT SYNONYMS

1. adumbrate
 (A) thunder (B) confuse (C) outline (D) deploy carefully

2. adventitious
 (A) risky (B) counterfeit (C) inventive (D) accidental

3. amulet
 (A) small vase (B) tribute (C) talisman (D) estuary

4. anhydrous
 (A) many-sided (B) carefully divided (C) many-headed (D) destitute of water

5. apiary
   (A) cage for primates (B) collection of beehives (C) bird cage (D) eagle's nest

6. arcane
   (A) obsolete (B) secret (C) exalted (D) curved

7. attainder
   (A) transfer of a faulty title (B) defendant's reply (C) extinction of civil rights (D) repossession of property

8. aureole
   (A) nesting place for birds (B) rising light of morning (C) distinctive atmosphere (D) ring of encircling light

9. bucolic
   (A) hymn-like (B) unripened (C) pastoral (D) doltish

10. burgee
    (A) nautical flag (B) colorful antipodean bird (C) hot parching wind (D) coarse sacking cloth

11. cachet
    (A) hidden compartment (B) intrigue (C) distinctive quality (D) esteem

12. caesura
    (A) imperial lineage (B) type of operation (C) division of time (D) break in rhythm of verse

13. caveat
    (A) codicil (B) unfortunate purchase (C) warning (D) agreement in principle

14. cloture
    (A) caucus (B) filibuster (C) closing (D) roll-call

15. comity
    (A) solace (B) beauty (C) union (D) courtesy

16. curvilinear
    (A) surrounded by glass (B) banked dangerously
    (C) bounded by curved lines (D) decorated exces-
    sively

17. debouch
    (A) pour gently (B) divert (C) seduce (D) emerge

18. dichotomy
    (A) cutting in two (B) ambiguous expression (C)
    tendency to digress (D) double entendre

19. discrete
    (A) not orderly (B) subtle (C) circumspect (D) dis-
    tinct

20. doctrinaire
    (A) pragmatic (B) abstruse (C) dogmatic (D) or-
    thodox

### Answers Test 3

| | | | | |
|---|---|---|---|---|
| 1. C | 5. B | 9. C | 13. C | 17. D |
| 2. D | 6. B | 10. A | 14. C | 18. A |
| 3. C | 7. C | 11. C | 15. D | 19. D |
| 4. D | 8. D | 12. D | 16. C | 20. C |

## TEST 4—DIFFICULT SYNONYMS

1. draw the longbow
   (A) prepare to fight (B) make a supreme effort (C)
   use a roundabout approach (D) indulge in exaggeration

2. duodecimal
   (A) expressed in the scale of twelve (B) type of ulcer
   (C) a twentieth portion (D) a musical dialogue

3. ecology
   (A) environmental study of organisms (B) study of
   business (C) doctrine of final causes (D) science of
   family life

4. ecumenical
   (A) metaphysical (B) universal (C) heretical (D)
   non-clerical

5. effulgent
   (A) radiant (B) dissembling (C) animated (D)
   abundant

6. embrasure
   (A) recess of a door (B) affectionate gesture (C)
   portable stove (D) gully

7. ewer
   (A) pitcher (B) metal pin (C) tender of sheep (D)
   wood craftsman

8. expatiate
   (A) clear of guilt (B) atone for (C) emit the last
   breath (D) enlarge on

9. exponential
   (A) discursive (B) involving exponents (C) neglect-
   ing explanations (D) advocating

10. fatuous
    (A) pompous (B) inane (C) fleshy (D) inexact

11. flaunt
    (A) disobey insolently (B) mock (C) escape (D)
    display brazenly

12. flummery
    (A) finery (B) treachery (C) scoffing remark (D) humbug

13. fuliginous
    (A) overflowing (B) luminous (C) smoky (D) angry

14. gazebo
    (A) gazelle-like animal (B) outdoor illumination (C) turret on a roof (D) basin for ablutions

15. gouache
    (A) awkward representation (B) method of painting (C) cowboy lore (D) lengendary material

16. gravamen
    (A) grievance (B) solemnity (C) carved idol (D) serving vessel

17. groat
    (A) silver coin (B) small animal (C) edible fish (D) worthless trifle

18. grommet
    (A) weight for sounding (B) metal eyelet (C) mischievous elf (D) crystalline gem

19. incommensurable
    (A) requiring limitless care (B) unbounded (C) not condensabic (D) having no common measure

20. incursion
    (A) invective (B) infusion (C) invasion (D) incision

### Answers Test 4

| | | | | |
|---|---|---|---|---|
| 1. D | 5. A | 9. B | 13. C | 17. A |
| 2. A | 6. A | 10. B | 14. C | 18. B |
| 3. A | 7. A | 11. D | 15. B | 19. D |
| 4. B | 8. D | 12. D | 16. A | 20. C |

## TEST 5—DIFFICULT SYNONYMS

1. interstice
   (A) crevice (B) reciprocal action (C) crossing (D) insertion

2. meed
   (A) exigency (B) reward (C) fermented drink (D) noble thought

3. meretricious
   (A) deserving (B) fawning (C) imitative (D) gaudy

4. minatory
   (A) advising (B) threatening (C) turret-like (D) monstrous

5. moiety
   (A) large majority (B) aggregate (C) tenderness (D) about half

6. moraine
   (A) glacial deposit (B) hilly country (C) small island (D) swamp

7. nadir
   (A) highest point (B) opposite of zenith (C) complete negation (D) apex of a right triangle

8. nebulous
   (A) false (B) basic (C) cloudy (D) starry

9. noisome
   (A) ear-splitting (B) uproarious (C) noxious (D) teasing

10. obi
    (A) movement expressing deferential courtesy (B) broad sash worn around the waist (C) mark used in ancient manuscripts (D) mammal closely related to the giraffe

11. outré
    (A) bizarre (B) chic (C) subtle (D) boycotted

12. palindrome
    (A) original pattern or model of a work (B) word,
    verse, or sentence that is the same when read back-
    ward or forward (C) in feudal times, a mounted man-
    at-arms serving a king (D) parchment which has
    been used twice or three times, the earlier writing
    having been erased

13. panegyric
    (A) frenzied petition (B) abusive oration (C) enco-
    mium (D) demagogic utterance

14. pellucid
    (A) radiant (B) limpid (C) discerning (D) trimmed
    with fur

15. pizzicato
    (A) rapid succession of notes (B) with a delicate
    stroke (C) in a humorous vein (D) plucking of musi-
    cal strings

16. prognathous
    (A) degenerate (B) diagnostic (C) having projecting
    jaws (D) prehuman

17. prosody
    (A) science of verse forms (B) dull style (C) prin-
    ciples of prose style (D) hymn of praise

18. protean
    (A) nutritious (B) mighty (C) variable (D) exem-
    plary

19. puncheon
    (A) pot-bellied person (B) puppet show (C) wooden
    mallet (D) large cask

20. putative
   (A) powerful (B) rotting (C) supposed (D) scolding

**Answers Test 5**

| | | | | |
|---|---|---|---|---|
| 1. A | 5. D | 9. C | 13. C | 17. A |
| 2. B | 6. A | 10. B | 14. B | 18. C |
| 3. D | 7. B | 11. A | 15. D | 19. D |
| 4. B | 8. C | 12. B | 16. C | 20. C |

## TEST 6—DIFFICULT SYNONYMS

1. Pyrrhic victory
   (A) victory gained at too great a cost (B) victory as a result of encirclement (C) total destruction of the enemy (D) victory as a result of a complete surprise

2. quirt
   (A) riding-whip (B) witty remark (C) idiosyncrasy (D) bludgeon

3. rara avis
   (A) cynosure (B) nonentity (C) gourmet (D) unusual person

4. sacerdotal
   (A) pertaining to the priesthood (B) pertaining to religious sacrifice (C) pertaining to contributions for religious purposes (D) pertaining to the lower back

5. saraband
   (A) stately dance (B) tiara-like ornament (C) small lute (D) insignia worn on left arm

6. saurian
   (A) ape-like (B) wicked (C) winged (D) lizard-like

7. sloe-eyed
   (A) of gentle look (B) almond-eyed (C) heavy-eyed
   (D) black-eyed

8. splayed
   (A) hunched (B) spread out (C) splashed (D)
   knobby

9. Star Chamber
   (A) secret tribunal (B) royal manifesto (C) illegal
   seizure (D) special jury

10. surrogate
    (A) will (B) substitute (C) court clerk (D) criminal
    court

11. tertian
    (A) recurring (B) subordinate (C) intermediate
    (D) remote in time

12. tessellate
    (A) quiver uncontrollably (B) arrange in a checkered
    pattern (C) adorn with random scraps of material
    (D) dry up rapidly

13. trammel
    (A) bore holes in (B) stamp on (C) impede (D)
    blend into one mass

14. truncated
    (A) abused (B) looped off (C) sharpened to a fine
    point (D) columnar

15. turbid
(A) insubordinate (B) distended (C) hooded (D) muddy

16. vitiate
(A) enliven (B) create (C) impair (D) defame

17. watershed
(A) artificial passage for water (B) sudden copious rainfall (C) drainage area (D) line marking ebb or flow of tide

18. welkin
(A) sky (B) countryside (C) fire gong (D) church bells

19. welter
(A) ridge (B) turmoil (C) vault of heaven (D) conglomeration

20. wherefore
(A) whilom (B) why (C) whence (D) whither

### Answers Test 6

| | | | | |
|---|---|---|---|---|
| 1. A | 5. A | 9. A | 13. C | 17. C |
| 2. A | 6. D | 10. B | 14. B | 18. A |
| 3. D | 7. D | 11. A | 15. D | 19. B |
| 4. A | 8. B | 12. B | 16. C | 20. B |

### TEST 7—DIFFICULT SYNONYMS

1. acanthus
(A) leaf-like architectural ornamentation (B) gummy substance used in stiffening fabrics (C) ethereal spirit (D) ornamental vessel

2. alfresco
   (A) fresh food (B) spring flood (C) watercolor (D) in the open air

3. animadversion
   (A) vitality (B) ire (C) taboo (D) stricture

4. aplomb
   (A) self-assurance (B) stodginess (C) foppishness (D) sturdiness

5. apocryphal
   (A) awesome (B) disease-bearing (C) of doubtful authority (D) threatening

6. artifact
   (A) product of human workmanship (B) stratagem (C) duplication (D) artful or skillful contrivance

7. atavistic
   (A) overeager (B) narrow-minded (C) reverting to a primitive type (D) pertaining to an uncle

8. baize
   (A) cereal plant (B) medicinal plant (C) tree marking (D) soft fabric

9. bowdlerize
   (A) ratiocinate (B) interpolate (C) asseverate (D) expurgate

10. carafe
    (A) glass water bottle (B) means of transportation (C) wineskin (D) bony case covering back of animal

11. carte blanche
    (A) demerit (B) symbol of cowardice (C) unconditional authority (D) press card

12. chapbook
    (A) style book used by publishers and printers (B) small book of popular literature (C) missal (D) compendium of usage

13. cicerone
    (A) orator (B) guide (C) buffoon (D) cavalier

14. colander
    (A) species of lizard (B) upright of a sluice (C) baking dish (D) vessel perforated for use as a sieve or strainer

15. complaisant
    (A) discontented (B) smug (C) obliging (D) satisfied

16. congeries
    (A) intricate plots (B) aggregation (C) clique (D) leave-takings

17. contumacious
    (A) stubbornly disobedient (B) deservedly disgraced (C) unduly pompous (D) gravely libelous

18. coryphee
    (A) shepherdess (B) priestess (C) ballet dancer (D) small fishing boat

19. covert
    (A) envious (B) secret (C) timid (D) protected

20. crepitate
    (A) enfeeble (B) worsen (C) depreciate (D) crackle

### Answers Test 7

| | | | | |
|---|---|---|---|---|
| 1. A | 5. C | 9. D | 13. B | 17. A |
| 2. D | 6. A | 10. A | 14. D | 18. C |
| 3. D | 7. C | 11. C | 15. C | 19. B |
| 4. A | 8. D | 12. B | 16. B | 20. D |

### TEST 8—DIFFCULT SYNONYMS

1. crepuscular
   (A) like crinkled fabric (B) resembling twilight (C) diminutive (D) transitory

2. denigrate
   (A) defame (B) contradict (C) digress (D) repudiate

3. doughty
   (A) flabby and pale (B) strong and valiant (C) weak and craven (D) crude and boorish

4. durance
   (A) penance (B) imprisonment (C) strength (D) toughness

5. entomology
   (A) study of plant fossils (B) study of relics of man (C) study of insects (D) study of derivatives

6. euphemistic
   (A) having good digestion (B) less offensive in phrasing (C) exhibiting great enjoyment (D) excessively elegant in style

7. euphoria
   (A) sense of well-being (B) assumption of friendliness (C) ability to speak well (D) eagerness to agree

8. exceptionable
   (A) not better than average (B) objectionable (C) out of the ordinary (D) captious

9. excoriate
   (A) rack (B) expel (C) disembarrass (D) flay

10. farrier
    (A) ship's carpenter (B) litter of pigs (C) blacksmith (D) trainman

11. fecund
(A) fruitful (B) decaying (C) offensive (D) feverish

12. fettle
(A) gala occasion (B) shackle (C) thriving condition (D) part of a horse's leg

13. fey
(A) appearing to be under a spell (B) happy-go-lucky (C) not clairvoyant (D) lacking vision

14. fiduciary
(A) faithful (B) speculative (C) yielding interest (D) holding in trust

15. forensic
(A) agreeable (B) exotic (C) logical (D) argumentative

16. fulminating
(A) hurling denunciation (B) reaching the highest point (C) fulfilling acceptably (D) remonstrating gently

17. halcyon days
(A) period of sowing wild oats (B) period of storms and turbulence (C) period of ominous portents (D) period of tranquility and peace

18. hyperbole
(A) exaggeration (B) plane curve (C) onomatopoeia (D) assumption

19. immure
(A) ossify (B) enclose (C) fertilize (D) inhere

20. indefeasible
(A) not probable (B) not justifiable (C) not practicable (D) not annullable

**Answers Test 8**

| | | | | |
|---|---|---|---|---|
| 1. B | 5. C | 9. D | 13. A | 17. D |
| 2. A | 6. B | 10. C | 14. D | 18. A |
| 3. B | 7. A | 11. A | 15. D | 19. B |
| 4. B | 8. B | 12. C | 16. A | 20. D |

## TEST 9—DIFFICULT SYNONYMS

1. indurate
   (A) harden (B) prolong (C) endow (D) suffer

2. internecine
   (A) pertaining to fraternal strife (B) mutually destructive (C) pertaining to sibling competition (D) excessively diffident

3. jeremiad
   (A) dolorous tirade (B) optimistic prophecy (C) prolonged journey (D) religious pilgrimage

4. kelp
   (A) military cap (B) sharp cry (C) disembodied spirit (D) seaweed ash

5. hegemony
   (A) body of officials disposed according to rank (B) preponderant influence (C) tendency to evade (D) protection against fluctuation in stock prices

6. lissome
   (A) supple (B) beautiful (C) strong (D) rippling

7. lodestar
   (A) guiding star (B) vein of ore (C) central star of constellation (D) celestial body exercising magnetic force

8. lucubrate
   (A) illuminate brilliantly (B) lament unduly (C) work or study laboriously (D) deprecate unceasingly

9. maunder
   (A) weep sentimentally (B) talk incoherently (C) flow swiftly (D) act insincerely

10. mead
    (A) upland (B) fermented drink (C) reward (D) fallow soil

11. nexus
    (A) gist (B) central portion of atom (C) opposing argument (D) connection

12. nubile
    (A) obscure (B) voluptuous (C) marriageable (D) oriental

13. obloquy
    (A) sacrifice (B) forgetfulness (C) calumny (D) indirectness

14. orthography
    (A) beautiful handwriting (B) correct spelling (C) autobiography (D) illegibility

15. otiose
    (A) long-winded (B) thick-skinned (C) inactive (D) hateful

16. panoply
    (A) comprehensive survey (B) full suit of armor (C) overhanging projection (D) elaborate display

17. patois
    (A) inner court (B) perfume (C) sympathetic sorrow (D) provincial speech

18. pertinacious
    (A) persistent (B) relevant (C) saucy (D) cohesive

19. potsherd
    (A) primitive agricultural implement (B) herdsman
    (C) fragment of earthern pot (D) caretaker

20. pragmatic
    (A) smoothly rehearsed (B) practical (C) absolute
    (D) bookish

### Answers Test 9

| | | | | |
|---|---|---|---|---|
| 1. A | 5. B | 9. B | 13. C | 17. D |
| 2. B | 6. A | 10. B | 14. B | 18. A |
| 3. A | 7. A | 11. D | 15. C | 19. C |
| 4. D | 8. C | 12. C | 16. B | 20. B |

## TEST 10—DIFFICULT SYNONYMS

1. proclivity
   (A) propensity (B) rapid descent (C) devoted adherence (D) buoyancy

2. prosthesis
   (A) attempt to convert (B) addition of an artificial part to the human body (C) complete exhaustion (D) figure of speech

3. pundit
   (A) prosy speaker (B) witty saying (C) learned man (D) harsh judge

4. quondam
   (A) which was to be done (B) having been formerly (C) to this extent (D) cited as an authority

5. recidivist
   (A) one who receives (B) one who relapses into criminality (C) one who remains behind (D) one who reciprocates

6. rubric
   (A) footnote (B) enigmatic representation of a word (C) manuscript title or heading (D) medicinal application

7. satrap
   (A) subordinate ruler (B) male woodland deity (C) form of basalt rock (D) device for entangling small game

8. sawbuck
   (A) antler (B) bucksaw (C) male deer (D) rack

9. sobriquet
   (A) musical comedy actress (B) nickname (C) puppet (D) habitual temperance

10. spoliate
    (A) decay (B) besmirch (C) wind on a bobbin (D) plunder

11. spoor
    (A) mutation (B) trail of wild animal (C) unicellular reproductive body (D) fetid odor

12. tamp
    (A) pound down (B) tread clumsily (C) curl (D) bind firmly

13. "cross the Rubicon"
    (A) pass into oblivion (B) overcome almost insurmountable difficulties (C) take an irrevocable step (D) change one's identity

14. "send to Coventry"
(A) doom to destruction (B) reduce in rank (C) send on a fool's errand (D) ostracize

15. touchstone
(A) instrument for sharpening tools (B) material for cleaning decks of ships (C) test for worth (D) fundamental cause

16. truckle
(A) transport (B) submit obsequiously (C) tighten securely (D) barter

17. turgid
(A) distended (B) muddy (C) agitated (D) sluggish

18. viable
(A) not excusable (B) open to corrupt influence (C) easily pulverized (D) capable of living

19. vouchsafe
(A) escort (B) acknowledge openly (C) grant (D) attest the truth of

20. wraith
(A) anger (B) perversity (C) calamity (D) apparition

**Answers Test 10**

| | | | | |
|---|---|---|---|---|
| 1. A | 5. B | 9. B | 13. C | 17. A |
| 2. B | 6. C | 10. D | 14. D | 18. D |
| 3. C | 7. A | 11. B | 15. C | 19. C |
| 4. B | 8. D | 12. A | 16. B | 20. D |

## Level Three—Very Difficult Synonyms

### TEST 11—VERY DIFFICULT SYNONYMS

1. alabaster
   (A) translucent calcite (B) detritus (C) ruff (D) antique ivory

2. althea
   (A) mockingbird (B) flowering shrub (C) balm (D) luscious fruit

3. ana
   (A) recipes (B) information (C) parables (D) nurses

4. aplomb
   (A) avoirdupois (B) assurance (C) neatness (D) headgear

5. apse
   (A) proclivity (B) recess (C) gibbon (D) legume

6. atelier
   (A) studio (B) winged messenger (C) prophet (D) unit of measure

7. cajolery
   (A) superstition (B) wheedling (C) obstreperousness (D) drollery

8. calender
   (A) to press between rollers (B) to tell time (C) to make a chronology (D) to standardize

9. caromed
   (A) rebounded (B) duly licensed (C) abutted (D) reversed

10. cavil
(A) fawn (B) petition (C) plot (D) quibble

11. cilia
(A) aquatic animals (B) eyelashes (C) heavenly bodies (D) swords

12. coryphee
(A) harbinger (B) caryatid (C) odalisk (D) ballet dancer

13. cosset
(A) drink mildly (B) deceive (C) pamper (D) fit closely

14. crepuscular
(A) crepe-like (B) glimmering (C) infirm (D) slow-moving

15. davit
(A) imprecation (B) sworn statement (C) crane (D) oarlock

16. denouement
(A) exordium (B) diabolism (C) solution (D) climax

17. descant
(A) comment freely (B) adjudicate fairly (C) authorize (D) disparage

18. descried
(A) discerned (B) belittled (C) barbarized (D) erred

19. didoes
(A) parts of wall surface (B) antics (C) heraldic devices (D) vampires

20. dystrophy
    (A) malnutrition (B) dysuria (C) atrophy (D) leukemia

**Answers Test 11**

| | | | | |
|---|---|---|---|---|
| 1. A | 5. B | 9. A | 13. C | 17. A |
| 2. B | 6. A | 10. D | 14. B | 18. A |
| 3. B | 7. B | 11. B | 15. C | 19. B |
| 4. B | 8. A | 12. D | 16. C | 20. A |

## TEST 12—VERY DIFFICULT SYNONYMS

1. echinated
   (A) fossil-like (B) isometric (C) interspersed (D) bristly

2. eclectic
   (A) comprehensive (B) omniscient (C) shocking (D) selecting

3. enfilade
   (A) a flaring up (B) raking fire (C) cataclysm (D) canard

4. escarpment
   (A) steep slope (B) trench (C) fishery (D) dashboard

5. etiology
   (A) epitome (B) inertia (C) cause (D) ecology

6. fatuous
   (A) pompous (B) stupid (C) swollen (D) sanguine

7. forensic
   (A) prohibiting (B) argumentative (C) oral (D) fluent

8. fortuitism
   (A) premeditation (B) gigantism (C) opportunism (D) philosophy of chance

9. franklin
   (A) merchant (B) freeholder (C) English archer (D) seller of pardons

10. frenum
    (A) membrane (B) state of anger (C) tributary (D) gratuity

11. gallimaufry
    (A) hodgepodge (B) omelet (C) harness (D) equipage

12. gimlet
    (A) adze (B) small boring tool (C) countersink (D) auger

13. godown
    (A) descent (B) warehouse (C) incline (D) sacrilege

14. higgle
    (A) beguile (B) bedim (C) chaffer (D) exorcise

15. hustings
    (A) coverings (B) plants (C) platform (D) sibilant sounds

16. hyperacusia
    (A) abnormal hearing (B) accusation (C) figure of speech (D) exaggeration

17. id
(A) alternate (B) psychic agent (C) calendar item
(D) essence

18. janissary
(A) Knight Templar (B) Turkish soldier (C) custodian (D) crusader

19. kestrel
(A) renegade (B) small falcon (C) sadiron (D) diffident

20. lissome
(A) agile (B) comely (C) fractious (D) diffident

**Answers Test 12**

| | | | | |
|---|---|---|---|---|
| 1. D | 5. C | 9. B | 13. B | 17. B |
| 2. D | 6. B | 10. A | 14. C | 18. B |
| 3. B | 7. B | 11. A | 15. C | 19. B |
| 4. A | 8. D | 12. B | 16. A | 20. A |

## TEST 13—VERY DIFFICULT SYNONYMS

1. litotes
(A) hyperbole (B) oxymoron (C) synecdoche (D) understatement

2. metathetic
(A) transposed (B) emetic (C) elastic (D) unsympathetic

3. misprision
(A) unlawful act (B) unjust incarceration (C) evil destiny (D) supplication

4. narial
   (A) negative (B) pertaining to the jaw (C) pelagic
   (D) pertaining to the nostrils

5. newel
   (A) prawn (B) threshold (C) acolyte (D) principal
   post

6. obturation
   (A) closing (B) irreconcilability (C) stubbornness
   (D) eulogy

7. ogive
   (A) leader (B) arch (C) prestidigitation (D) benediction

8. passim
   (A) inactive (B) secretive (C) everywhere (D) pe-
   rennial

9. pellucid
   (A) light producing (B) obscured (C) transparent
   (D) notorious

10. peregrine
    (A) ambulatory (B) deceptive (C) odious (D) alien

11. petroglyph
    (A) silicon (B) mermaid (C) rock carving (D) mys-
    terious manifestation

12. phaeton
    (A) nemesis (B) light carriage (C) prophet (D)
    sidecar

13. pismire
    (A) grass seed (B) demimonde (C) filth (D) ant

14. pizzicato
    (A) scanty (B) delicate (C) plucked (D) allegretto

15. poundal
   (A) unit of force (B) reverberation (C) iteration
   (D) monetary unit

16. prognathous
   (A) with jutting jaws (B) with martial stride (C)
   protean (D) herculean

17. psaltery
   (A) kneeling bench (B) sacred song (C) musical instrument (D) synagogue

18. pullulate
   (A) multiply (B) divide (C) supplicate (D) swell

19. rachitic
   (A) racy (B) regal (C) rosy (D) rickety

20. raddled
   (A) punctured (B) meretricious (C) zealous (D)
   rouged

**Answers Test 13**

| | | | | |
|---|---|---|---|---|
| 1. D | 5. D | 9. C | 13. D | 17. C |
| 2. A | 6. A | 10. D | 14. C | 18. A |
| 3. A | 7. B | 11. C | 15. A | 19. D |
| 4. D | 8. C | 12. B | 16. A | 20. D |

## TEST 14—VERY DIFFICULT SYNONYMS

1. ratiocination
   (A) ecstasy (B) zeal (C) reasoning (D) proportion

2. recidivism
   (A) relapse into criminal habits (B) addiction (C)
   rule by the proletariat (D) solvency

3. redaction
   (A) recoil (B) propaganda (C) movement of a rifle
   (D) new edition

4. replication
   (A) echo (B) repeat mechanism (C) analysis (D)
   erosion

5. reticulate
   (A) embellished (B) netlike (C) required (D) sub-
   servient

6. rote
   (A) indited (B) alternating (C) routine (D) spiral

7. rubric
   (A) rule of conduct (B) plain song (C) poem (D)
   vespers

8. rune
   (A) despoliation (B) contumely (C) alphabetical
   character (D) luminous meteor

9. rutabaga
   (A) alfalfa (B) kind of corn (C) turnip (D) relish

10. scutage
    (A) form of tax (B) armor plate (C) disposal plant
    (D) decapitation

11. sear
    (A) cut (B) striped (C) dried (D) aged

12. semasiology
    (A) logistics (B) semantics (C) sociology (D)
    petrology

13. sericeous
    (A) grain-like (B) silky (C) in order (D) antag-
    onistic

14. sib
   (A) error (B) blood relation (C) ingestion (D) weak cry

15. sobriquet
   (A) nickname (B) patronym (C) ottoman (D) waitress

16. sough
   (A) bow (B) shrink (C) sink (D) sigh

17. stertorousness
   (A) mercurial temper (B) heavy snoring (C) blowiness (D) reverberating tones

18. strobic
   (A) pausing (B) whirling (C) toothed (D) cosmic

19. susurrant
   (A) murmuring (B) crepitant (C) lambent (D) coruscating

20. svelte
   (A) wasteful (B) slender (C) suave (D) indecisive

### Answers Test 14

| | | | | |
|---|---|---|---|---|
| 1. C | 5. B | 9. C | 13. B | 17. B |
| 2. A | 6. C | 10. A | 14. B | 18. B |
| 3. D | 7. A | 11. C | 15. A | 19. A |
| 4. A | 8. C | 12. B | 16. D | 20. B |

## TEST 15—VERY DIFFICULT SYNONYMS

1. achromatic
   (A) spurious (B) colorless (C) brilliant (D) by small degree

2. acolyte
   (A) rite (B) attendant (C) mystery (D) celebrant

3. afflatus
   (A) conceit (B) expansion (C) inspiration (D) debris

4. agglutination
   (A) efflorescence (B) adhesion (C) acquisitiveness (D) softening

5. alembic
   (A) apparatus for distillation (B) term in prosody (C) plastic material (D) synthetic jewel

6. aliform
   (A) wing-like (B) symmetrical (C) foliated (D) many-sided

7. aliment
   (A) digestion (B) nutriment (C) discharge (D) waste

8. amaranthine
   (A) unfading (B) serpentine (C) pastoral (D) greenish

9. antiphony
   (A) fallacy (B) argument (C) discord (D) response

10. aphasia
    (A) loss of speech (B) deafness (C) loss of memory (D) tonguetiedness

11. apologue
    (A) fable (B) conclusion (C) preamble (D) apology

12. athanasia
    (A) mercy killing (B) sleeplessness (C) euphoria (D) immortality

13. austral
    (A) starry (B) southern (C) Australian (D) austere

14. autochthonous
    (A) independent (B) self-sufficient (C) indigenous
    (D) unattached

15. autoclave
    (A) air-tight vessel (B) cabal (C) gathering (D)
    self-governing country within the territory of another

16. avatar
    (A) throw-back (B) incantation (C) incarnation
    (D) immolation

17. baldric
    (A) coat (B) vest (C) belt (D) cape

18. batten
    (A) gather (B) seize (C) fatten (D) shatter

19. cachinnation
    (A) conspiracy to rob (B) immoderate laughter (C)
    noisy riot (D) subterranean vibration

20. cairn
    (A) small boy (B) base wretch (C) cave (D)
    memorial

### Answers Test 15

| | | | | |
|---|---|---|---|---|
| 1. B | 5. A | 9. D | 13. B | 17. C |
| 2. B | 6. A | 10. A | 14. C | 18. C |
| 3. C | 7. B | 11. A | 15. A | 19. B |
| 4. B | 8. A | 12. D | 16. C | 20. D |

## TEST 16—VERY DIFFICULT SYNONYMS

1. calumet
   (A) purge (B) false accusation (C) peace pipe (D) dagger

2. canard
   (A) hoax (B) ancient cannon (C) rabble (D) partisan

3. catachresis
   (A) exordium (B) question and answer method (C) misuse of words (D) atrophy

4. chrestomathy
   (A) anthology of plays (B) collection of passages (C) treasury of controversial essays (D) literary concordance

5. daedal
   (A) obdurate (B) ineffable (C) prostrate (D) intricate

6. debouch
   (A) indulge to excess (B) emerge (C) corrupt (D) remove an opening

7. deciduous
   (A) transitory (B) stubborn (C) paleolithic (D) staining

8. denigrate
   (A) contravene (B) sully (C) retract (D) render obscure

9. deracinated
   (A) unmanned (B) deprived of citizenship (C) uprooted (D) devalued

10. dipsomania
    (A) fear of water (B) irresistible craving for drink
    (C) urge for power (D) tendency to gamble

11. discrete
    (A) prudent (B) judicious (C) secretive (D) separate

12. divagation
    (A) primary formulation (B) digression (C) equitable apportionment (D) subterranean tunnel

13. doxology
    (A) right reasoning (B) canon law (C) papal bull
    (D) hymn of praise to God

14. dulcinea
    (A) organ stop (B) deceiver (C) sweetheart (D) elderly woman

15. ecological
    (A) tautological (B) bucolic (C) destructive (D) environmental

16. ecumenical
    (A) universal (B) ritualistic (C) excommunicatory
    (D) orthodox

17. endemic
    (A) local (B) sporadic (C) widespread (D) deadly

18. epicene
    (A) feminine (B) masculine (C) belonging to both sexes (D) unrelated to sex

19. epigraph
    (A) postscript (B) tombstone figurine (C) inscription (D) duplicating device

20. etiolation
    (A) ingestion (B) hardening (C) wasting away grad-
    ually (D) blanching

**Answers Test 16**

| | | | | |
|---|---|---|---|---|
| 1. C | 5. D | 9. C | 13. D | 17. A |
| 2. A | 6. B | 10. B | 14. C | 18. C |
| 3. C | 7. A | 11. D | 15. D | 19. C |
| 4. B | 8. B | 12. B | 16. A | 20. D |

## TEST 17—VERY DIFFICULT SYNONYMS

1. euthenics
   (A) dancing as an expression of emotion (B) painless death (C) race improvement (D) science of
   heredity

2. feral
   (A) fearful (B) wild (C) measured (D) veiled

3. fetid
   (A) hot (B) damp (C) noisome (D) decayed

4. fortuitous
   (A) lucky (B) hazardous (C) accidental (D) gratuitous

5. friable
   (A) susceptible to improvement (B) easily swayed
   (C) capable of maintaining life (D) easily crumbled

6. fustian
   (A) confusion (B) fine silk (C) bombast (D) un-
   necessary activity

7. gouache
   (A) watercolor (B) engraving (C) fresco (D) etching

8. halcyon
   (A) calm (B) warm (C) sunny (D) drowsy

9. halyard
   (A) sail (B) spar (C) flag (D) rope

10. illative
    (A) obscure (B) contradictory (C) illustrative (D) inferential

11. impudicity
    (A) insolence (B) contentiousness (C) immodesty (D) shiftlessness

12. incubus
    (A) nightmare (B) early printed book (C) fetus (D) sanctum

13. ineluctable
    (A) indefatigable (B) inescapable (C) incomprehensible (D) uncontrollable

14. insensate
    (A) undefiled (B) brutish (C) wrathful (D) taciturn

15. intercalation
    (A) calcification (B) altercation (C) intervention (D) insertion

16. jejune
    (A) puerile (B) trivial (C) ebullient (D) insipid

17. lacunae
    (A) gaps (B) mysteries (C) secrets (D) tear glands

18. lambent
   (A) bright (B) cool (C) flickering (D) diffused

19. lares
   (A) spining fates (B) household deities (C) animal dens (D) part of the windpipe

20. limn
   (A) trim (B) sprinkle (C) conjure (D) delineate

### Answers Test 17

| | | | | |
|---|---|---|---|---|
| 1. C | 5. D | 9. D | 13. B | 17. A |
| 2. B | 6. C | 10. D | 14. B | 18. C |
| 3. C | 7. A | 11. C | 15. D | 19. B |
| 4. C | 8. A | 12. A | 16. D | 20. D |

## TEST 18—VERY DIFFICULT SYNONYMS

1. littoral
   (A) shore (B) isthmus (C) peninsula (D) island

2. lustrum
   (A) bronze candelabrum (B) five-year period (C) detergent (D) glowing emanation

3. macerate
   (A) kill wantonly (B) soften by soaking (C) excise an internal organ (D) intertwine strands

4. maculated
   (A) purified (B) spotted (C) pulverized (D) serrated

5. marquetry
   (A) bas relief (B) inlay (C) carving (D) design

6. mendacity
(A) temerity (B) heedlessness (C) untruthfulness
(D) beggary

7. mimesis
(A) parody (B) imitation (C) cacophony (D) fate

8. minatory
(A) towering (B) minimizing (C) threatening (D)
mollifying

9. necropolis
(A) paradise (B) cemetery (C) mammoth industrial
center (D) small town

10. nescience
(A) occult knowledge (B) ignorance (C) stupor (D)
birth

11. nexus
(A) bond (B) crux (C) epitome (D) aggregation

12. nugatory
(A) inoperative (B) denying the truth (C) bearing
false witness (D) adversative

13. ochlocracy
(A) government by ukase (B) army rule (C) mob
rule (D) government by the select few

14. oriel
(A) sprite (B) kind of window (C) buttress (D)
song bird

15. otiose
(A) comatose (B) indolent (C) contemptible (D)
fat

16. palladium
(A) symbol of protection (B) source of atomic power (C) temple of the ancient gods (D) medieval knight

17. paradigm
(A) model (B) syllogism (C) perfection (D) similar case at law

18. parturition
(A) division of territory (B) discrepancy in allotment (C) childbirth (D) dietary regimen

19. peregrine
(A) immature (B) dilatory (C) spice for pickling (D) coming from abroad

20. petard
(A) hock (B) crane (C) ram (D) bomb

### Answers Test 18

| | | | | |
|---|---|---|---|---|
| 1. A | 5. B | 9. B | 13. C | 17. A |
| 2. B | 6. C | 10. B | 14. B | 18. C |
| 3. B | 7. B | 11. A | 15. B | 19. D |
| 4. B | 8. C | 12. A | 16. A | 20. D |

## TEST 19—VERY DIFFICULT SYNONYMS

1. pharisaical
(A) charitable (B) reconcilable (C) intransigent (D) hypocritical

2. pilaster
(A) column (B) lintel (C) capital (D) base

3. plangent
(A) resounding (B) heavy (C) complaining (D) translucent

4. plinth
(A) base of a statue (B) supporting column in a temple (C) full supply (D) rock formation

5. polity
(A) urbanity (B) form of government (C) crafty statesmanship (D) party platform

6. protocol
(A) Roman governor of a province (B) favorable legal opinion (C) military liaison officer (D) diplomatic etiquette

7. quiddity
(A) oddity (B) essence (C) quittance (D) quietus

8. recidivist
(A) incorrigible criminal (B) visionary theorist (C) fanatical reformer (D) unregenerate rebel

9. recusant
(A) recriminatory (B) accusative (C) non-conformist (D) recuperative

10. rutabaga
(A) tribal dance (B) turnip (C) Scandinavian poem (D) elf

11. scholiast
(A) commentator (B) pretender to learning (C) pedantic teacher (D) founder of a philosophical school

12. sebaceous
(A) subcutaneous (B) salacious (C) fatty (D) sweaty

13. sententious
    (A) pithy (B) testy (C) truculent (D) rhetorical

14. sirocco
    (A) hot, oppressive wind (B) equatorial tide (C) desert calm (D) residue of mist

15. tenebrous
    (A) stubborn (B) argumentative (C) gloomy (D) persuasive

16. thrasonical
    (A) brutal (B) boastful (C) idle (D) royal

17. transmogrified
    (A) transported in ecstasy (B) changed as by magic (C) disinterred (D) felled by terror

18. trope
    (A) direction of growth (B) microscopic particle (C) adverse criticism (D) figure of speech

19. truckle
    (A) yield (B) defy (C) saunter (D) load

20. votary
    (A) proxy (B) devotee (C) elective office (D) demagogue

### Answers Test 19

| | | | | |
|---|---|---|---|---|
| 1. D | 5. B | 9. C | 13. A | 17. B |
| 2. A | 6. D | 10. B | 14. A | 18. D |
| 3. A | 7. B | 11. A | 15. C | 19. A |
| 4. A | 8. A | 12. C | 16. B | 20. B |

# OPPOSITES

As we explained in the footnote at the beginning of the Verbal Practice section, the SAT tests your knowledge of words through "opposites" or antonyms. This requires you to think about and evaluate the meanings of words as well as to understand their meanings.

The following practice questions range in scale from the moderately difficult to the more difficult ones you will find on examinations of this type.

*Directions:* Select the lettered words below which are opposite in meaning or most nearly opposite in meaning to the capitalized word at the beginning of each question.

1. IMMUTABLE (A) erudite (B) abject (C) changeable (D) fantastic (E) aura
2. DUCTILE (A) fetid (B) alluvial (C) stubborn (D) abnormal (E) belabor
3. FASTIDIOUS (A) factitious (B) absurd (C) indifferent (D) sloppy (E) chary
4. TEMERITY (A) affinity (B) cherubim (C) humility (D) degenerate (E) celerity
5. ITINERANT (A) animosity (B) metaphor (C) perpetrator (D) resident (E) cerebrum
6. TACITURN (A) malevolent (B) loquacious (C) paltry (D) opaque (E) morbid
7. NEFARIOUS (A) grotesque (B) virtuous (C) jovial (D) pious (E) cerement
8. OBSEQUIOUS (A) harbinger (B) bold (C) heredity (D) quaff (E) falchion

9. OSTENTATION (A) emulsion (B) languid (C) modesty (D) kilogram (E) bey

10. CONTENTION (A) equation (B) oblivion (C) guild (D) pacification (E) bream

11. IMPUTATION (A) assiduous (B) radiant (C) challis (D) raiment (E) vindication

12. BENIGN (A) cavenne (B) relevant (C) robot (D) malevolent (E) precarious

13. COHERENT (A) perspicacious (B) zephyr (C) weal (D) chaotic (E) changeling

14. DEPREDATION (A) plethoric (B) gloss (C) restoration (D) usher

15. PROVOCATIVE (A) sedentary (B) capricious (C) vindictive (D) tawny (E) pacifying

16. SUBMISSION (A) authorized (B) defiance (C) assignment (D) defeat (E) belabor

17. AFFLUENT (A) immigrant (B) junction (C) insufficient (D) kin (E) clandestine

18. CHURLISH (A) exiguous (B) laudable (C) cheerful (D) maternal (E) civet

19. SYMMETRY (A) invocation (B) madrigal (C) distortion (D) satyr (E) cilia

20. DULCET (A) extrinsic (B) optimistic (C) unanimous (D) acerbate (E) chiffonette

21. PIQUANT (A) factitious (B) vain (C) insipid (D) vulture (E) chromatic

22. OPPORTUNE (A) dialectical (B) mutable (C) clinch (D) weird (E) inexpedient

23. PETULANT (A) irascible (B) cheerful (C) uncouth (D) abnormal (E) closure

24. SAVORY (A) apathy (B) clandestine (C) pliant (D) unpalatable (E) capillary

25. SATIATED (A) satirical (B) centaur (C) gorgeous (D) delectable (E) hungry

26. RECLUSIVE (A) empyreal (B) obscure (C) gregarious (D) rustication (E) chilblain

27. COURTEOUS (A) flaccid (B) emolient (C) insolent (D) scrupulous (E) chaffinch

28. USURP (A) succinct (B) predict (C) pacify (D) clematis (E) donate

29. ACRIMONIOUS (A) alluvial (B) apocalyptic (C) concourse (D) harmonious (E) carcanet

30. SKEPTIC (A) cryptic (B) bigot (C) discursive (D) eminent (E) caricature

31. RECONDITE (A) miniature (B) ceramic (C) arable (D) caraway (E) obvious

32. REDUNDANT (A) dilatory (B) apocryphal (C) astute (D) insufficient (E) calumny

33. INDUBITABLE (A) fetid (B) aesthetic (C) unmitigated (D) questionable (E) belabor

34. RESTITUTION (A) depredatory (B) cataclysm (C) acquisition (D) misogyny (E) changeling

35. ROTUNDITY (A) clemency (B) ebullient (C) angularity (D) contumely (E) chicory

36. SAGACIOUS (A) derelict (B) hazardous (C) article (D) verbose (E) ignorant

37. SANGUINARY (A) pacific (B) sanctuary (C) gastronomy (D) turgid (E) cambium

38. PARSIMONY (A) miasmic (B) endemic (C) clinch (D) fustian (E) prodigality

39. PERSPICUITY (A) cupidity (B) salubrious (C) ambiguity (D) discrimination (E) chrysolite

40. PREPOSTEROUS (A) complaisant (B) conceited (C) apologetic (D) rational (E) castellated

41. PROFUSION (A) travesty (B) valiant (C) scarcity (D) ordinance (E) laudanum

42. AGNOSTIC (A) aged (B) fanatic (C) truncheon (D) farmer (E) inebriate

43. MITIGATION (A) aggravation (B) verdant (C) obscene (D) restriction (E) interregnum

44. MISANTHROPE (A) angel (B) cauterize (C) supercilious (D) biologist (E) humanitarian

45. INIQUITY (A) equitable (B) rectitude (C) noxious (D) apostasy (E) taupie

46. PROTUBERANCE (A) cadence (B) habitation (C) indentation (D) appanage (E) timbrel

47. INGENUOUS (A) gimlet (B) hypothetical (C) spasmodic (D) sirocco (E) hypocritical

48. SANCTIMONIOUS (A) contumacious (B) flagitious (C) zany (D) ingenuous (E) impervious

49. EXTIRPATE (A) propogate (B) helot (C) ingratiate (D) emasculate (E) dauber

50. CAPRICIOUS (A) redoubtable (B) constant (C) bellicose (D) cretaceous (E) ignominious

51. CASUISTRY (A) wright (B) trilogy (C) sedentary (D) verity (E) salsify

52. CONTUMELY (A) pecuniary (B) imminence (C) eminence (D) augur (E) tractable

53. CREDULITY (A) litany (B) drollery (C) ablution (D) badinage (E) cynicism

54. PREDILECTION (A) sobriety (B) hostility (C) euphony (D) palliative (E) contentious

55. EFFULGENT (A) murky (B) petulant (C) mercenary (D) ludicrous (E) mundane

56. SEDULOUS (A) vociferous (B) indolent (C) concomitant (D) itinerant (E) onerous

57. IMPERTURBABLE (A) milieu (B) cynical (C) conical (D) agitated (E) Martian

58. CAPTIOUS (A) eulogistic (B) whimsical (C) jocose (D) lethargic (E) empyreal

59. DENOUEMENT (A) fusillade (B) redundance (C) modicum (D) limpet (E) introduction

60. TAUTOLOGY (A) oscillation (B) succinctness (C) investiture (D) interurban (E) curvet

61. CATEGORICAL (A) darnel (B) wherry (C) ambiguous (D) unregenerate (E) voluptuous

62. PREMEDITATED (A) superannuated (B) tractable (C) syncopated (D) impromptu (E) sebaceous

63. PROPINQUITY (A) remoteness (B) succulence (C) tantamount (D) tedium (E) glebe

64. SANGUINE (A) corporeal (B) tamarind (C) subaltern (D) ecliptic (E) apathetic

65. ALTERCATION (A) versus (B) consonance (C) provender (D) encomium (E) contrition

66. COLLIGATE (A) juxtaposition (B) coxswain (C) emendation (D) derange (E) integrate

67. ADJURE (A) shrive (B) derogate (C) extort (D) rehabilitate (E) viola

68. POSTULATE (A) undulate (B) prove (C) peculate (D) palpitate (E) disenchant

69. ARROGATE (A) earn (B) confabulate (C) imprecate (D) interstice (E) litigate

70. ALIENATE (A) hospice (B) profligate (C) conjoin (D) furbelow (E) desiccate

71. APOCRYPHAL (A) authentic (B) copse (C) eclat (D) nefarious (E) pipkin

72. IMPETUOUS (A) gyve (B) hypothetical (C) impediment (D) obstreperous (E) migratory

73. AMELIORATE (A) amorphous (B) vitiate (C) hempen (D) dissemble (E) curlew

74. BENIGN (A) dulcimer (B) dogmatic (C) dolorous (D) morose (E) coppice

75. ABRIDGE (A) epitomize (B) trivet (C) augment (D) cloy (E) zenith

76. AVERSION (A) amnesty (B) augury (C) affinity (D) wassail (E) valance

77. SOLICITUDE (A) nonchalance (B) truncheon
(C) ebullition (D) dereliction (E) diurnal
78. STOICISM (A) anemia (B) sensibility (C) detritus
(D) escutcheon (E) gossamer
79. EXCULPATIO` (A) hyperbolic (B) imputation
(C) monition (D) propinquity (E) xylem
80. SUBJOIN (A) delete (B) regress (C) wraith (D)
interpolate (E) deciduous
81. CONCOMITANT (A) hymeneal (B) synthesis (C)
pellucid (D) linnet (E) original
82. PROCLIVITY (A) furbelow (B) repugnance (C)
effrontery (D) doxology (E) contingency
83. ETHEREAL (A) synchronous (B) tamarind (C)
ponderous (D) plashy (E) egregious
84. EXTRANEOUS (A) doubloon (B) facetious (C)
germane (D) toxic (E) sequin
85. ANALOGOUS (A) expletive (B) septic (C) virulent (D) heterogeneous (E) defunct
86. ASSUAGE (A) corrugate (B) detestable (C) pro-
voke (D) traduce (E) reverberate
87. ASSEVERATE (A) striate (B) deny (C) wrapt
(D) misanthrope (E) integrate
88. PARABLE (A) annunciation (B) chronicle (C)
kaleidoscope (D) habergeon (E) eclogue
89. FUSION (A) schism (B) paradox (C) stratagem
(D) analogy (E) monastic
90. CAJOLE (A) enveigle (B) proselyte (C) repel
(D) zither (E) dissimulate
91. DILETTANTE (A) titmouse (B) pilaster (C)
strophe (D) professional (E) seraglio
92. AUGMENT (A) shirr (B) argot (C) conjunction
(D) badinage (E) dissever
93. AVERSE (A) sesame (B) habituated (C) tussah
(D) quiddity (E) porous

94. COMMENSURATE (A) inadequate (B) proem (C) sedimentary (D) amalgamate (E) phylactery

95. DISCIPLE (A) younker (B) pique (C) renegade (D) cortical (E) hidalgo

96. COTERMINOUS (A) sarcophagus (B) hyaline (C) spontaneous (D) remote (E) replica

97. MUCILAGINOUS (A) withe (B) sanctimonious (C) rotund (D) separable (E) prolix

98. PROCRASTINATE (A) elegiac (B) investiture (C) expedite (D) cordillera (E) mediate

99. VENERATE (A) abominate (B) suzerainty (C) wright (D) verile (E) purlieu

100. EMBELLISH (A) embolish (B) disfigure (C) wherry (D) demolish (E) derogate

101. DELETERIOUS (A) fractious (B) salubrious (C) pathetic (D) eulogy (E) antipathy

102. PUISSANCE (A) bicuspid (B) approbation (C) impotence (D) repudiation (E) erudition

103. SYCOPHANCY (A) colloquialism (B) innuendo (C) nihilism (D) frankness (E) apotheosis

104. ABERRATION (A) correctness (B) apathetic (C) attenuation (D) consanguinity (E) reticent

105. ANOMALOUS (A) capacious (B) vicious (C) explicated (D) covetous (E) systematic

106. COGNIZANCE (A) idiom (B) ignorance (C) abeyance (D) anecdote (E) fetish

107. QUIESCENT (A) restless (B) antipathy (C) malignant (D) mendicant (E) fiasco

108. ESCHEW (A) traduce (B) escheat (C) select (D) emanate (E) subvene

109. TACITURN (A) dubious (B) garrulous (C) eucharist (D) iniquitous (E) gullible

110. SENTENTIOUS (A) gullible (B) laconic (C) frustrated (D) prolix (E) sadistic

111. INAUGURATE (A) facilitate (B) ameliorate (C) inculcate (D) gesticulate (E) terminate

112. DUBIOUS (A) concomitant (B) cadaverous (C) immutable (D) hypochondriac (E) iconoclastic

113. CASTIGATION (A) cliche (B) panegyric (C) esthete (D) euphemism (E) gourmet

114. FORTUITY (A) transient (B) extenuation (C) corpuscle (D) foreordination (E) importune

115. PLEONASM (A) succinctness (B) ambiversion (C) braggadocio (D) connoisseur (E) demagogue

116. EMANCIPATION (A) scintillation (B) imprisonment (C) misadventure (D) pertinacity (E) ephod

117. INVIDIOUS (A) contingent (B) promiscuous (C) benignant (D) inadvertent

118. BUCOLIC (A) circumspect (B) urbane (C) abortive (D) laconic (E) punctilious

119. LUGUBRIOUS (A) jocose (B) volatile (C) agnostic (D) sagacious (E) puerile

120. INEXORABLE (A) erudite (B) impregnable (C) indulgent (D) perscipacious (E) quixotic

121. OSTENTATION (A) abasement (B) retrogression (C) extirpation (D) reprobation (E) procrastination

122. CONTUMACIOUS (A) puerile (B) compliant (C) primitive (D) pungent (E) profligate

123. ABJURE (A) expostulate (B) retaliate (C) vindicate (D) annotate (E) pompous

124. TENUOUS (A) unctuous (B) vacillate (C) sadistic (D) scurrilous (E) stout

125. OBSEQUIOUS (A) bicameral (B) esoteric (C) pompous (D) nebulous (E) omniscient

126. CONGRUOUS (A) monotonous (B) indecorous (C) vicarious (D) uxorious (E) moribund

127. INITIATION (A) martinet (B) virago (C) consummation (D) jingoism (E) polyglot

128. ALTRUISTIC (A) ostracized (B) polygamous (C) self-centered (D) penurious (E) schizophrenic

129. ACIDULOUS (A) chauvinistic (B) ambiguous (C) dulcet (D) bastinado (E) pernicious

130. PHILOSOPHY (A) saturnalia (B) cadaver (C) misanthrope (D) metamorphosis (E) persiflage

131. BOURNE (A) magnum (B) interior (C) cabal (D) sachem (E) minion

132. INTREPID (A) surreptitious (B) monotonous (C) paranoiac (D) pusillanimous (E) theocratic

133. DOGMATIC (A) stentorian (B) synchronous (C) compliant (D) clairvoyant (E) introvert

134. UNEQUIVOCAL (A) maudlin (B) gratulation (C) insatiable (D) ambiguous (E) lethargic

135. EXCULPATE (A) mulct (B) malinger (C) rusticate (D) penalize (E) impeach

136. ABSTEMIOUSNESS (A) sensuality (B) acrimonious (C) didactical (D) lethargic (E) machiavellian

137. CHIMERICAL (A) abortive (B) realistic (C) banal (D) diffident (E) loquacious

138. VITUPERATIVE (A) frustrate (B) emulate (C) liberate (D) vindicate (E) debate

139. PEDANTIC (A) ascetic (B) agnostic (C) untaught (D) indicted (E) pariah

140. CONTINGENCY (A) desuetude (B) euphony (C) exigency (D) demesne (E) foreordination

141. ACERBITY (A) cupidity (B) amiability (C) depredation (D) insomnia (E) facet

142. EXPEDITIOUS (A) lackadaisical (B) unique (C) ubiquitous (E) epicurean (E) portable

143. PERSPICACITY (A) obtuseness (B) argot (C) dipsomania (D) malediction (E) kleptomania

144. SPLENETIC (A) inane (B) complaisant (C) phlegmatic (D) querulous (E) sundered

145. JOYOUS (A) redundant (B) poignant (C) turbid (D) saturnine (E) sardonic
146. BLASPHEMY (A) gynecologist (B) benediction (C) podium (D) panacea (E) miscegenation
147. CONTUMACIOUS (A) punctillious (B) plenteous (C) obloquy (D) tractable (E) plebeian
148. ANTECEDENT (A) apothegm (B) quandary (C) auxiliary (D) posterior (E) orthodontist
149. TRANQUILITY (A) complacency (B) tumult (C) plagiary (D) prophecy (E) philately
150. APPOSITE (A) incongruous (B) diaphanous (C) vitriolic (D) truculent (E) unique
151. RETALIATION (A) distintegration (B) reconciliation (C) admonition (D) abjuration (E) ratiocination
152. HOMOGENEOUS (A) parsimonious (B) consciousness (C) heterogeneous (D) loquacious (E) unrequitted
153. AMALGAMATE (A) recriminate (B) procrastinate (C) scintillate (D) segregate (E) recuperate
154. DIFFIDENCE (A) imbroglio (B) temerity (C) cognomen (D) effervescence (E) monopoly
155. MUTATION (A) factotum (B) expiation (C) continuance (D) megalomania (E) numismatist

### Answer Key to Opposites Questions

| | | | | |
|---|---|---|---|---|
| 1. C | 9. C | 17. C | 25. E | 33. D |
| 2. C | 10. D | 18. C | 26. C | 34. C |
| 3. D | 11. E | 19. C | 27. C | 35. C |
| 4. C | 12. D | 20. D | 28. E | 36. E |
| 5. D | 13. D | 21. C | 29. D | 37. A |
| 6. B | 14. C | 22. E | 30. B | 38. E |
| 7. B | 15. E | 23. B | 31. E | 39. C |
| 8. B | 16. B | 24. D | 32. D | 40. D |

| | | | | |
|---|---|---|---|---|
| 41. C | 64. E | 87. B | 110. D | 133. C |
| 42. B | 65. B | 88. B | 111. E | 134. D |
| 43. A | 66. D | 89. A | 112. C | 135. E |
| 44. E | 67. C | 90. C | 113. B | 136. A |
| 45. A | 68. B | 91. D | 114. D | 137. B |
| 46. C | 69. A | 92. E | 115. A | 138. D |
| 47. E | 70. C | 93. B | 116. B | 139. C |
| 48. D | 71. A | 94. A | 117. C | 140. E |
| 49. A | 72. E | 95. C | 118. B | 141. B |
| 50. B | 73. B | 96. D | 119. A | 142. A |
| 51. D | 74. D | 97. D | 120. C | 143. A |
| 52. C | 75. C | 98. C | 121. A | 144. B |
| 53. E | 76. C | 99. A | 122. B | 145. C |
| 54. B | 77. A | 100. B | 123. C | 146. B |
| 55. A | 78. B | 101. B | 124. E | 147. D |
| 56. B | 79. B | 102. C | 125. C | 148. D |
| 57. D | 80. A | 103. D | 126. B | 149. B |
| 58. A | 81. E | 104. A | 127. C | 150. A |
| 59. E | 82. B | 105. E | 128. C | 151. B |
| 60. B | 83. C | 106. B | 129. C | 152. C |
| 61. C | 84. C | 107. A | 130. E | 153. D |
| 62. D | 85. D | 108. C | 131. B | 154. B |
| 63. A | 86. C | 109. B | 132. D | 155. C |

# OPPOSITES TESTS BY LEVELS

## Level One—Easy Opposites

*Directions:* In each question below, choose the word or expression that has most nearly the opposite meaning of the first word.

## TEST 1—EASY OPPOSITES

1. incredulous
   (A) argumentative (B) imaginative (C) indifferent (D) irreligious (E) believing

2. placate
   (A) amuse (B) antagonize (C) embroil (D) pity (E) reject

3. cognizant
   (A) afraid (B) ignorant (C) capable (D) aware (E) optimistic

4. dissonance
   (A) disapproval (B) disaster (C) harmony (D) disparity (E) dissimilarity

5. torsion
   (A) bending (B) compressing (C) sliding (D) stretching (E) straightening

6. accrued
   (A) subtracted (B) incidental (C) miscellaneous (D) special (E) unearned

7. effrontery
   (A) bad taste (B) conceit (C) dishonesty (D) shyness (E) snobbishness

8. acquiescence
   (A) advice (B) advocacy (C) opposition (D) friendliness (E) compliance

9. reticent
   (A) fidgety (B) repetitious (C) talkative (D) restful (E) truthful

10. pseudo
    (A) deep (B) obvious (C) honest (D) provoking (E) spiritual

11. awry
    (A) straight (B) deplorable (C) odd (D) simple (E) striking

12. nefarious
    (A) clever (B) necessary (C) negligent (D) shortsighted (E) kindly

13. glib
    (A) cheerful (B) de'ightful (C) dull (D) quiet (E) gloomy

14. paucity
    (A) lack (B) ease (C) hardship (D) abundance (E) stoppage

15. lucrative
    (A) debasing (B) fortunate (C) influential (D) monetary (E) unprofitable

16. indubitable
    (A) doubtful (B) fraudulent (C) honorable (D) safe (E) deniable

17. savant
    (A) diplomat (B) inventor (C) moron (D) thrifty
    person (E) wiseacre

18. incipient
    (A) concluding (B) dangerous (C) hasty (D) secret
    (E) widespread

19. virile
    (A) honest (B) loyal (C) effeminate (D) pugnacious
    (E) virtuous

20. assiduous
    (A) courteous (B) careless (C) discouraged (D)
    frank (E) slow

### Answers Test 1

| | | | | |
|---|---|---|---|---|
| 1. E | 5. E | 9. C | 13. D | 17. C |
| 2. B | 6. A | 10. C | 14. D | 18. A |
| 3. B | 7. D | 11. A | 15. E | 19. C |
| 4. C | 8. C | 12. E | 16. E | 20. B |

## TEST 2—EASY OPPOSITES

1. cataclysm
   (A) blunder (B) superstition (C) treachery (D)
   triumph (E) status quo

2. auspicious
   (A) condemnatory (B) conspicuous (C) unfavorable
   (D) questionable (E) spicy

3. banter
   (A) conversation (B) criticism (C) gossip (D) irony
   (E) serious talk

4. vernacular
   (A) literary speech (B) correct usage (C) long words
   (D) oratory (E) poetic style

5. emolument
   (A) capital (B) penalty (C) liabilities (D) loss (E)
   output

6. turgid
   (A) dusty (B) muddy (C) rolling (D) deflated (E)
   tense

7. expunge
   (A) clarify (B) cleanse (C) perpetuate (D) investi-
   gate (E) underline

8. panoramic
   (A) brilliant (B) pinpoint (C) pretty (D) fluores-
   cent (E) unique

9. ignominy
   (A) fame (B) isolation (C) misfortune (D) sorrow
   (E) stupidity

10. relevant
    (A) ingenious (B) inspiring (C) obvious (D) inap-
    propriate (E) tentative

11. apposite
    (A) irrelevant (B) contrary (C) different (D) spon-
    taneous (E) tricky

12. ambulatory
    (A) confined to bed (B) able to walk (C) injured
    (D) quarantined (E) suffering from disease

13. disparage
    (A) applaud (B) degrade (C) erase (D) reform (E)
    scatter

14. limpid
    (A) calm (B) turbid (C) crippled (D) delightful
    (E) sad

15. derisive
    (A) dividing (B) furnishing (C) reflecting (D) laud-
    atory (E) suggesting

16. debilitate
    (A) encourage (B) insinuate (C) prepare (D) turn
    away (E) strengthen

17. opulent
    (A) fearful (B) free (C) oversized (D) trustful (E)
    impoverished

18. blandishment
    (A) brunette (B) criticism (C) ostentation (D)
    praise (E) return

19. cryptic
    (A) appealing (B) arched (C) deathly (D) revealing
    (E) intricate

20. raucous
    (A) euphonious (B) loud (C) querulous (D) ra-
    tional (E) violent

**Answers Test 2**

| | | | | |
|---|---|---|---|---|
| 1. E | 5. B | 9. A | 13. A | 17. E |
| 2. C | 6. D | 10. D | 14. B | 18. B |
| 3. E | 7. C | 11. A | 15. D | 19. D |
| 4. A | 8. B | 12. A | 16. E | 20. A |

## TEST 3—EASY OPPOSITES

1. avidity
   (A) friendliness (B) generosity (C) resentment (D) speed (E) thirst

2. hiatus
   (A) branch (B) disease (C) gaiety (D) insect (E) closing

3. plenary
   (A) easy (B) stolid (C) empty (D) rewarding (E) untrustworthy

4. capricious
   (A) active (B) stable (C) opposed (D) sheeplike (E) slippery

5. specious
   (A) scanty (B) particular (C) genuine (D) suspicious (E) vigorous

6. extirpate
   (A) besmirch (B) clean (C) renew (D) favor (E) subdivide

7. equivocal
   (A) positive (B) medium (C) monotonous (D) musical (E) well-balanced

8. benison
   (A) approval (B) curse (C) gift (D) prayer (E) reward

9. sanguine
   (A) limp (B) mechanical (C) muddy (D) livid (E) stealthy

10. surcease
    (A) inception (B) hope (C) resignation (D) sleep
    (E) sweetness

11. sentient
    (A) emotional (B) callous (C) hostile (D) sympathetic (E) wise

12. obviate
    (A) grasp (B) reform (C) simplify (D) smooth (E) make necessary

13. rancor
    (A) dignity (B) affection (C) odor (D) spite (E) suspicion

14. dilatory
    (A) hairy (B) happy-go-lucky (C) ruined (D) punctual (E) well-to-do

15. ebullition
    (A) bathing (B) cooling (C) refilling (D) retiring (E) returning

16. relegate
    (A) welcome (B) deprive (C) designate (D) report (E) request

17. recondite
    (A) brittle (B) exposed (C) explored (D) concealed (E) uninformed

18. sublime
    (A) below par (B) highly praised (C) extreme (D) ignoble (E) settled

19. termagant
    (A) fever (B) quiet woman (C) sea bird (D) sedative (E) squirrel

20. sedulous
(A) deceptive (B) careless (C) grassy (D) hateful
(E) sweet

**Answers Test 3**

| | | | | |
|---|---|---|---|---|
| 1. B | 5. C | 9. D | 13. B | 17. B |
| 2. E | 6. C | 10. A | 14. D | 18. D |
| 3. C | 7. A | 11. B | 15. B | 19. B |
| 4. B | 8. B | 12. E | 16. A | 20. B |

## TEST 4—DIFFICULT OPPOSITES

1. alfresco
(A) indoors (B) art exhibit (C) sidewalk cafe (D) charcoal sketch

2. aliment
(A) illness (B) non-support (C) sidewise motion (D) wing-formation

3. animadversion
(A) favorable remark (B) soul sickness (C) whole-heartedness (D) opposing clique

4. antinomy
(A) name-calling (B) agreement of two laws (C) contrary viewpoint (D) metallic alloy

5. asyndeton
(A) periodic in structure (B) lacking parallelism (C) faulty in conclusion (D) inclusion of conjunctions

6. auscultation
(A) religious veneration (B) refusal to listen (C) political intrigue (D) indoor horticulture

7. basilic
   (A) fundamental (B) deadly (C) slaggy (D) lowly

8. bowdlerized
   (A) uncensored (B) chopped fine (C) swallowed whole (D) criticized severely

9. cabala
   (A) medieval tribunal (B) voodoo symbols (C) published doctrine (D) conspiratorial gathering

10. canorous
    (A) extremely hungry (B) euphoniously sonorous (C) cacophonous (D) hound-like

11. caveat
    (A) deception (B) roe (C) invitation (D) seizure

12. cerement
    (A) death mask (B) garment for the living (C) inscription on tomb (D) refrain in threnody

13. cicatrice
    (A) smooth surface (B) house pest (C) fabulous serpent (D) summer insect

14. congeneric
    (A) artificially reproduced (B) remotely related (C) carefree in nature (D) of a different kind

15. contumelious
    (A) compromising (B) mildly reproachful (C) laudatory (D) genuinely contrite

16. cupidity
    (A) passing fancy (B) restraint (C) foolish attraction (D) make-believe tenderness

17. demotic
    (A) tyrannical (B) mobile (C) selective (D) fiendish

18. dissidence
    (A) propinquity (B) efflorescence (C) dubiety (D) concurrence

19. divagation
    (A) operatic solo (B) adherence to topic (C) underwater study (D) summer travel

20. epideictic
    (A) modest (B) concise (C) intended to edify (D) concentrated upon

21. farinaceous
    (A) mealy (B) remote (C) rock-like (D) waxy

22. flacon
    (A) pennant (B) slender leaf (C) flaming torch (D) large bottle

23. froward
    (A) offensive (B) perverse (C) progressive (D) tractable

24. halidom
    (A) fief (B) martyrdom (C) ancestry (D) ungodliness

25. immured
    (A) guaranteed (B) free (C) iniquitous (D) suffered

**Answers Test 4**

| | | | | |
|---|---|---|---|---|
| 1. A | 6. B | 11. C | 16. B | 21. C |
| 2. B | 7. D | 12. B | 17. C | 22. D |
| 3. A | 8. A | 13. A | 18. D | 23. D |
| 4. B | 9. C | 14. D | 19. B | 24. D |
| 5. D | 10. C | 15. C | 20. A | 25. B |

## TEST 5—DIFFICULT OPPOSITES

1. inamorata
   (A) nameless person (B) enemy (C) assumed name
   (D) lovelorn person

2. inspissated
   (A) animated (B) thickened (C) attenuated (D)
   mixed thoroughly

3. interpellate
   (A) alter by inserting (B) clarify (C) admonish (D)
   answer informally

4. jardiniere
   (A) professional soldier (B) small flowerpot (C) fe-
   male gardener (D) beekeeper

5. lenitive
   (A) shortening (B) emollient (C) painful (D) elon-
   gating

6. litigious
   (A) ornate in literary style (B) illegally threatening
   (C) agreeable (D) close to the shoreline

7. lubricous
   (A) mercenary (B) rough (C) tubular (D) thrifty

8. lucubrate
   (A) write stupidly (B) whine incessantly (C) sail
   nearer the wind (D) remove friction

9. megacephaly
   (A) smallness of head (B) magnification of vision
   (C) malformation of feet (D) inordinate loss of hair

10. mendicity
    (A) lying (B) giving (C) venerating (D) repairing

11. nirvana
    (A) loss of auditory acuity (B) nervous tension (C) loss of courage (D) muscular atrophy

12. objurgate
    (A) appeal (B) forswear (C) praise (D) importune

13. oneiromancy
    (A) interpretation of actual occurrences (B) astrology (C) fortune-telling by cards (D) phrenology

14. outré
    (A) barren (B) out-of-bounds (C) usual (D) stylish

15. palinode
    (A) song of reassertion (B) fence post (C) wedding hymn (D) festival

16. pelagic
    (A) landlocked (B) horny (C) terrestrial (D) furry

17. pettifog
    (A) practice law in an honest way (B) spread smoke and haze (C) obstruct vision (D) shrink cloth

18. plashy
    (A) tawdry (B) rainy (C) pretentious (D) dry

19. repine
    (A) approve (B) retract (C) relax (D) confess

20. raffish
    (A) dour (B) carefree (C) sporty (D) reputable

21. provenance
    (A) last resting place (B) foresight (C) scion's inheritance (D) provisions

22. sacerdotal
    (A) priestly (B) baggy (C) sugary (D) profane

23. uxorious
(A) clamorous (B) lavish in display (C) loathing one's wife (D) hating one's spouse

24. velleity
(A) excusable error (B) sentimental weeping (C) strong wish (D) unfulfilled longing

25. whilom
(A) intermittent (B) old-fashioned (C) future (D) quaint

### Answers Test 5

| | | | | |
|---|---|---|---|---|
| 1. D | 6. C | 11. B | 16. C | 21. A |
| 2. C | 7. B | 12. C | 17. A | 22. D |
| 3. D | 8. A | 13. A | 18. D | 23. C |
| 4. B | 9. A | 14. C | 19. A | 24. C |
| 5. C | 10. B | 15. A | 20. D | 25. C |

# SENTENCE COMPLETIONS

The examination may include in its verbal part, questions which require you to complete a sentence in which one or two words are represented by blank spaces. Here it is necessary to look for the implication of a sentence, the underlying meaning. Usually this understanding does not require any special knowledge, but does require a solid vocabulary background. Here are practice questions.

*Directions:* Select from the lettered word or sets of words which follow, the word or words which best fit the meaning of the quotation as a whole.

1. In legislative investigations of _____ subjects, there will always be great risks that any standards set up will yield or be circumvented in one way or another. (A) delicate (B) innocuous (C) sublimal (D) controversial (E) parsimonious.

2. One of the objects of statutes relating to judicial procedures is the separating of the _____ from the deciding function, and the provision of a measure of independence for the person who is called on to decide. (A) jurisprudence (B) prosecuting (C) nonsensical (D) superficial (E) mitigating.

3. In many cases injured persons find it impossible, through their personal initiative and ambition, to _____ themselves to the extent that they are enabled to pursue some work which will bring them a good living. (A) consecrate (B) assimilate (C) rehabilitate (D) coordinate (E) educate.

4. The principal object of the _____ law is to define crime and prescribe punishments. (A) cure (B) parole (C) State (D) Federal (E) penal.

5. It is the source of our constitutional rule that serious criminal charges must be made by _____ of a grand jury. (A) indictment (B) conviction (C) consideration (D) interrogation (E) amelioration.

6. In the long run, ideas are more powerful than more _____ weapons. (A) lethal (B) military (C) atomic (D) legal (E) tangible.

7. The Constitution provides that no person shall be twice put in _____ for the same offense. (A) prison (B) jeopardy (C) the army (D) coventry (E) court.

8. Compulsory education was instituted for the purpose of preventing _____ of young children, and guaranteeing them a minimum of education. (A) malnutrition (B) ignorance (C) abuse (D) exploitation (E) delinquency.

9. Any person who is in _____ while awaiting trial is considered innocent until he has been declared guilty. (A) custody (B) prison (C) jeopardy (D) suspicion (E) probation.

10. Certain employers, among them those employing fewer than four persons as well as non-profit making institutions, are _____ under the law, but may elect to become subject to the law. (A) prohibited (B) eliminated (C) demoted (D) exempted (E) mortified.

11. The day will come when _____ will look back upon us and our time with a sense of superiority. (A)

teachers (B) posterity (C) scientists (D) ancestors
(E) sophisticates.

12. Now, many years later, with the benefit of much
_____, we see the activities in which these people
engaged in a very unfavorable light. (A) foresight
(B) education (C) hindsight (D) research (E)
Federal aid.

13. A majority of the membership constitutes a _____
_____ to do business in the Senate. (A) forum (B)
quorum (C) podium (D) minority (E) malfeasance.

14. The fact that the locations were a mile and a half
apart was welcomed by L'Enfant as conducing to
ceremonial intercourse, and by the practical Washington as _____ the importunities of the legislature,
a waste of time he suffered in New York and Phil-
adelphia. (A) creating (B) mitigating (C) multiplying (D) relegating (E) implementing.

15. Practically anything can be done in either House by
_____ consent except where the Constitution or
the rules specifically prohibit the presiding officer from
entertaining such a request. (A) presidential (B)
parliamentary (C) appropriate (D) congressional
(E) unanimous.

16. A "rider" is a (an) _____ provision incorporated
in an appropriation bill, with the idea of "riding"
through to enactment on the merits of the main
measure. (A) pusillanimous (B) mandatory (C)
influential (D) extraneous (E) macabre.

17. Monetary policy was _____ primarily through
the flexible use of both open market operations and ad-
justments in the discount rate. (A) implemented (B)
controlled (C) unified (D) deliberated (E) associated.

18. While lenses and frames form the focus of operations, the company also makes a host of other _____ products such as artificial eyes and instruments used to correct ocular defects as well as eyeglass cases. (A) panoramic (B) corporate (C) mutilated (D) optimistic (E) ocular.

19. A minor legal _____ developed early when the legislature passed a new law. (A) impediment (B) miscellany (C) diurnal (D) morais (E) syncopation.

20. Short of a further major _____ of business conditions, it is difficult to see how inventory liquidation could continue at current rates much beyond mid-year. (A) infiltration (B) delimitation (C) deterioration (D) machination (E) obliteration.

21. Dealers complying with our prices in fair trade states have been placed in a (an) _____ competitive position when located next to non-fair trade areas or in states where it has become increasingly difficult to secure injunctions promptly or adequate penalties to enforce them. (A) sensational (B) multilateral (C) unicameral (D) untenable (E) categorical.

22. Although there is reason to expect an improvement in business conditions, at least a seasonal rise would be necessary to show that the _____ of the slump has been passed. (A) nadir (B) minority (C) majority (D) economics (E) cycle.

23. The appearance of corruption in Washington clearly shows the need for closer scrutiny and stricter _____ for men chosen to direct our government. (A) discipline (B) grading (C) coercion (D) criteria (E) decisions.

24. It took great political courage for the President to face down the _____ farm lobby clamoring aggressively for greater handouts and to veto a bill to freeze farm price supports. (A) nefarious (B) militant (C) democratic (D) unconstitutional (E) communistic.

25. The strenuousness of the 102-hour week is further _____ when it is compared to the police forces in our American cities. (A) accentuated (B) demoralized (C) inculcated (D) cauterized (E) anaesthetized.

26. The meeting between this man of means and vision and the needy young architect came at an _____ moment when the needs of the country were greatest. (A) enlightened (B) usurious (C) ominous (D) auspicious (E) inspiring.

27. The gifted young man was soon _____ with local architects, helping with various minor civil commissions. (A) commiserating (B) scintillating (C) luxuriating (D) undulating (E) collaborating.

28. Objectives may be _____, the mistake may be nothing worse than excessive zeal, yet if all similar plans were adopted, the employees' predicament would be a sorry one. (A) subversive (B) laudable (C) nugatory (D) compensatory (E) precarious.

29. Specifically our proposal would be to establish sufficient journeyman level positions so that when capability and performance is achieved by individuals they would _____ achieve journeyman level positions. (A) derisively (B) never (C) automatically (D) consequently (E) eventually.

30. _____ of qualitative research on readers is costing newspapers considerable linage. (A) Accuracy (B) Delicacy (C) Monotony (D) Paucity (E) Simplicity.

31. As often with those who spend themselves in the agony of revolutionizing set patterns, many of the _____ for which he broke ground were left to be fully realized by others. (A) foundations (B) initiations (C) collaborations (D) provocations (E) innovations.

32. Attendance of museums and galleries increases by leaps and bounds, new exhibition facilities _____ and possession of works of art is becoming a badge of cultural honor. (A) proliferate (B) coagulate (C) asphyxiate (D) conglomerate (E) simulate.

33. A _____ statement shows the Toronto Star Ltd.'s net operating revenue for the year ending Sept. 30, 1957, as $1,596,403, as compared with $2,016,024 the previous year. (A) mercenary (B) notarized (C) economic (D) financial (E) judicial.

34. One of the clearest affirmations of the confidence which fifteenth-century intellectuals felt in the _____ of their art, their sense of belonging to a momentous epoch, their joy in conquest and spiritual discovery, is a letter written in May 1473. (A) consanguinity (B) rejuvenation (C) juxtaposition (D) rectitude (E) multiplicity.

35. While the government asks its employees to back a (an) _____ budget on the ground that the City must conserve every possible penny to make both ends meet, it does not say what the employees must do

to make both ends meet. (A) meticulous (B) inconspicuous (C) austerity (D) sententious (E) meritorious.

36. It has come to the attention of the court that a newspaper recently published a series of photographs
_____ taken during a session. (A) judiciously
(B) notoriously (C) economically (D) patiently (E)
surreptitiously.

37. Even as many of them _____ their pledges of
support, their actions belie their words. (A) conform
(B) renege (C) reiterate (D) decline (E) remand.

38. Jones has continued his _____ with athletics in
pictures of football, lacrosse, and boxing. (A) sensation (B) tension (C) schizophrenia (D) metamorphosis (E) preoccupation.

39. There has been an almost _____ fear of infla-
tion which has been especially terrifying to people
who live on unearned income exclusively. (A) neu-
rotic (B) salubrious (C) sadistic (D) concomitant
(E) puerile.

40. We would certainly be _____ if we did not report
the error. (A) malaise (B) derelict (C) consonant
(D) nominative (E) eleemosynary.

41. Publication of the article was timed to _____
with professor's fiftieth birthday. (A) coincide (B)
harmonize (C) amalgamate (D) terminate (E) elucidate.

42. Few institutions are more _____ than France's
provincial museums, but lately an effort has been
made to rouse them from their lethargy. (A) resistant
(B) conformist (C) conservative (D) mellifluous
(E) somnolent.

43. It could be that it will prove to be only the lively _____ to a more sumptuous drama or that the best has already passed. (A) dance (B) consummation (C) prelude (D) diversion (E) incarceration.

44. He owes most of his success to his calm, measured, analytical attack on the problems of advertising making order out of _____. (A) procedure (B) chaos (C) inquiry (D) letter (E) miscellany.

45. Genius, according to Schopenhauer, is _____ to the opinions of others—notably of authorities. (A) response (B) condolence (C) pertinence (D) malice (E) imperviousness.

46. His productions are not _____. The ideas usually are slow in building up. (A) comprehensible (B) conducive (C) matriarchal (D) spontaneous (E) mortified.

47. The fact is so _____ that no one ever succeeded even in defining it. (A) fragmentary (B) morbid (C) elusive (D) slanderous (E) mastoidal.

48. One of the few hard and fast "musts" around here is _____, which Webster defines as the ability to live, grow, and develop. (A) malleability (B) viability (C) flexibility (D) mortification (E) livid.

49. Honors go to Insley's drawings which have an unusual _____ quality, as if they had been traced by a misunderstanding hand, by a mind utterly unaccustomed to Western pictorial representation and haltingly trying to understand through copying. (A) dilettante (B) professional (C) primitive (D) snide (E) gauche.

50. Discretion and a gift for compensating a basic monotony of composition by subtle _____ also characterize his paintings. (A) modulations (B) aberrations (C) consolidations (D) analogies (E) complications.

51. If the dominant characteristic of a style is its _____—often confused with universality—then our time might appear to many as the last depositary of that secret force which periodically sweeps the world and showers it with monuments of collective fervor. (A) omniscience (B) category (C) ubiquity (D) materialism (E) putrescence.

### Answer Key to Sentence Completions

| | | | | |
|---|---|---|---|---|
| 1. D | 12. C | 23. D | 34. D | 45. E |
| 2. B | 13. B | 24. B | 35. C | 46. D |
| 3. C | 14. B | 25. A | 36. E | 47. C |
| 4. E | 15. E | 26. D | 37. C | 48. B |
| 5. A | 16. D | 27. E | 38. E | 49. E |
| 6. E | 17. A | 28. B | 39. A | 50. A |
| 7. B | 18. E | 29. C | 40. B | 51. C |
| 8. D | 19. A | 30. D | 41. A | |
| 9. A | 20. C | 31. E | 42. E | |
| 10. D | 21. D | 32. A | 43. C | |
| 11. B | 22. A | 33. D | 44. B | |

# SENTENCE COMPLETION TESTS BY LEVELS

## Level One—Easy Completions

*Directions:* Select from the words or sets of words, the word or words which best complete the meaning of the statement as a whole.

### TEST 1—EASY COMPLETIONS

1. Through his _____, he deceived us all.
   (A) whit (B) selvage (C) canard (D) petard

2. The lover of democracy has an _____ toward totalitarianism.
   (A) antipathy (B) empathy (C) antipode (D) idiopathy

3. An _____ may connect the names of members of a partnership.
   (A) addendum (B) ampersand (C) epigram (D) encomium

4. A _____ person cannot be expected to resist _____.
   (A) profligate - money (B) raucous - temptation (C) recreant - aggression (D) squalid - quarreling

5. He hated his father so intensely that he committed _____.
   (A) parricide (B) fratricide (C) genocide (D) matricide

6. Being very _____, he knew what was going on about him.
   (A) circumlocutory (B) choleric (C) caustic (D) circumspect

7. The convicted man resorted to _____ in attacking his accusers.
   (A) nepotism (B) anathema (C) panoply (D) bravura

8. The _____ woman was the _____ of all eyes.
   (A) titled - cupola (B) lonely - sinecure (C) ugly - doggerel (D) attractive - cynosure

9. A _____ is likely to give you the wrong advice.
   (A) nuance (B) panacea (C) charlatan (D) virago

10. The _____ professor put his wife out and went to sleep with the cat.
    (A) diurnal (B) distrait (C) dubious (D) dilatory

### Answers Test 1

| | | | | |
|---|---|---|---|---|
| 1. C | 3. B | 5. A | 7. B | 9. C |
| 2. A | 4. C | 6. D | 8. D | 10. B |

### TEST 2—EASY COMPLETIONS

1. Art is long and time is _____.
   (A) fervid (B) fallow (C) nebulous (D) evanescent

2. The _____ flower was also _____.
   (A) pretty - redolent (B) drooping - potable (C) pale - opulent (D) blooming - amenable

3. The _____ effects of the drug made her very weary.
   (A) succinct (B) spurious (C) soporific (D) supine

4. Being _____, the child was not permitted to have his supper.
   (A) refractory (B) reticent (C) vernal (D) unctuous

5. The chairman's _____ speech swayed the audience to favor his proposal.
   (A) cursory (B) blatant (C) ancillary (D) cogent

6. He is quite _____ and, therefore, easily _____.
   (A) callow - deceived (B) lethal - perceived (C) fetal - conceived (D) limpid - received

7. That _____ seems so out of place with those lovely little girls.
   (A) shard (B) hoyden (C) tyro (D) vanguard

8. The sculptor will convert this _____ piece of clay into a beautiful bust.
   (A) virulent (B) amorphous (C) taciturn (D) salient

9. His _____ had no place in our serious conversation.
   (A) badinage (B) viscosity (C) concatenation (D) valence

10. Her _____ manner embarrassed the others at the party.
    (A) affable (B) tractable (C) sapid (D) gauche

### Answers Test 2

| | | | | |
|---|---|---|---|---|
| 1. D | 3. C | 5. D | 7. B | 9. A |
| 2. A | 4. A | 6. A | 8. B | 10. D |

**Level Two—Difficult Completions**

## TEST 3—DIFFICULT COMPLETIONS

1. In a state of _____, we are likely to have _____.

   (A) ochlocracy - havoc  (B) bureaucracy - respect
   (C) theocracy - sin  (D) desuetude - activity

2. Knowledge cannot thrive where there is _____.
   (A) parturition  (B) nescience  (C) protocol  (D) neo-classicism

3. _____ is a phase of the study of penology.
   (A) Recidivism  (B) Eclecticism  (C) Hematosis  (D) Hydrometry

4. The _____ of war is death and cruelty.
   (A) sirocco  (B) rutabaga  (C) beldam  (D) quiddity

5. The conceited soldier was forward and _____ in his attitude.
   (A) mundane  (B) thrasonical  (C) gratuitous  (D) laconic

6. Being a man of maxims, he was _____ in what he said.
   (A) sententious  (B) transmogrified  (C) sebaceous
   (D) sentient

7. His _____ remarks are too stupid to be taken _____.

   (A) empyreal - lightly  (B) puerperal - slowly  (C) lacunal - violently  (D) vapid - seriously

8. The _____ was very informative during the trip.
   (A) censer  (B) centaur  (C) cicerone  (D) burgeon

9. A _____ and the principle of monogamy are poles apart.
(A) seraglio (B) purlieu (C) shallop (D) benison

10. The mourning throng was preparing for a _____.
(A) wimple (B) cirque (C) riposte (D) monody

**Answers Test 3**

| 1. A | 3. A | 5. B | 7. D | 9. A |
| 2. B | 4. D | 6. A | 8. C | 10. D |

# TEST 4—DIFFICULT COMPLETIONS

1. The will did not require _____ of witnesses since it was _____.
(A) subornation - genocidic (B) bribery - histrionic (C) attestation - holographic (D) consternation - ballistic

2. Man's fate is _____.
(A) ineluctable (B) cerulean (C) estivated (D) spatulated

3. How can you depend upon a person who is so _____?
(A) protean (B) somatic (C) pensile (D) empirical

4. A _____ would be interested in a _____ of that type.
(A) botanist - vignette (B) soldier - maverick (C) musician - caterwaul (D) butcher - brioche

5. In India, a wealthy person may travel in a _____ borne by means of poles resting on men's shoulders.
(A) palanquin (B) bibelot (C) gambrel (D) lampoon

6. Suffering from _____, he decided to stay indoors.
   (A) claustrophobia (B) agoraphobia (C) chicanery
   (D) patois

7. _____ that my uncle is, he can do just about everything.
   (A) Dipsomaniac (B) Factotum (C) Numismatist
   (D) Pachyderm

8. His _____ features reminded me of the missing link.
   (A) simian (B) euphemistic (C) vicarious (D) vertiginous

9. For insisting on "It is I" instead of "It is me," he was charged with _____.
   (A) calligraphy (B) anomaly (C) bellicosity (D) preciosity

10. In certain tropical areas, malaria is an _____ disease.
    (A) endocrine (B) introversive (C) endemic (D) interstitial

### Answers Test 4

| | | | | |
|---|---|---|---|---|
| 1. C | 3. A | 5. A | 7. B | 9. D |
| 2. A | 4. A | 6. B | 8. A | 10. C |

# ANALOGIES

## Two Forms of the Analogy Question

There are various forms of analogy questions. The type that appears most frequently on the SAT is that in which each question consists of two words which have some specific relationship to each other. From the four (or five) pairs of words which follow, you are to select the pair which is related in the same way as the words of the first pair.

*Type 1. Example:*
   SPELLING : PUNCTUATION :: (A) pajamas : fatigue (B) powder : shaving (C) bandage : cut (D) biology : physics
*SPELLING* and *PUNCTUATION* are elements of the mechanics of English; *BIOLOGY* and *PHYSICS* are two of the subjects that make up the field of science. The other choices do not possess this PART : PART relationship. Therefore, (D) is the correct choice.

   Another popular form of analogy (be prepared to meet it on the SAT) is the type in which two words are followed by a third word. The latter is related to one word in a group of choices in the same way that the first two words are related.

*Type 2. Example:*
   WINTER is to SUMMER as COLD to
      (A) wet (B) future (C) warm (D) freezing
*WINTER* and *SUMMER* bear an opposite relationship.

*COLD* and *WARM* have the same type of opposite relationship. Therefore, (C) is the correct answer.

## Two Important Steps to Analogy Success

**Step One**—Determine the relationship between the first two words.

**Step Two**—Find the same relationship among the choices which follow the first two words.

NOW LET US APPLY THESE TWO STEPS

*Directions:* Each question consists of two words which have some relationship to each other. From the five following pairs of words, select the one which is related in the same way as the words of the first pair:

ARC : CIRCLE :: (A) segment : cube (B) angle : triangle (C) tangent : circumference (D) circle : cube (E) cube : square

An arc is part of a circle, just as an angle is part of a triangle. The other choices do not bear this PART : WHOLE relationship. Therefore, (B) is correct.

With the foregoing line of reasoning, you probably eliminated choice (A) immediately. Choice (B) seemed correct. Did you give it FINAL acceptance without considering the remaining choices? In this analogy question, choice (B), as it turned out, was the correct choice. However, let us change the question slightly:

ARC : CIRCLE :: (A) segment : cube (B) angle : triangle (C) tangent : circumference (D) circle : cube (E) line : square

Note that the (E) choice has been changed. (E)—not (B)—is now the correct answer. REASON: An arc is *any* part of the drawn circle. Likewise, a line is *any* part of the drawn square. However, an angle is *not* any part of the drawn triangle. The correct answer is, therefore, (E) line : square.

This illustration should caution you not to "jump to conclusions." Consider *all* choices carefully before you reach your conclusion.

## Kinds of Relationship

In analogy questions, the relationship between the first two words may be one of several kinds. Following are relationship possibilities.

*1. Purpose Relationship*
   GLOVE : BALL :: (A) hook : fish (B) winter : weather (C) game : pennant (D) stadium : seats

*2. Cause and Effect Relationship*
   RACE : FATIGUE :: (A) track : athlete (B) ant : bug (C) fast : hunger (D) walking : running

*3. Part : Whole Relationship*
   SNAKE : REPTILE :: (A) patch : thread (B) removal : snow (C) struggle : wrestle (D) hand : clock

*4. Part : Part Relationship*
   GILL : FIN :: (A) tube : antenna (B) instrument : violin (C) sea : fish (D) salad : supper

*5. Action to Object Relationship*
   KICK : FOOTBALL :: (A) kill : bomb (B) break : pieces (C) question : team (D) smoke : pipe

*6. Object to Action Relationship*
   STEAK : BROIL :: (A) bread : bake (B) food : sell (C) wine : pour (D) sugar : spill

7. *Synonym Relationship*
ENORMOUS : HUGE :: (A) rogue : rock (B) muddy : unclear (C) purse : kitchen (D) black : white

8. *Antonym Relationship*
PURITY : EVIL :: (A) suavity : bluntness (B) north : climate (C) angel : horns (D) boldness : victory

9. *Place Relationship*
MIAMI : FLORIDA :: (A) Chicago : United States (B) New York : Albany (C) United States : Chicago (D) Albany : New York

10. *Degree Relationship*
WARM : HOT :: (A) glue : paste (B) climate : weather (C) fried egg : boiled egg (D) bright : genius

11. *Characteristic Relationship*
IGNORANCE : POVERTY :: (A) blood : wound (B) money : dollar (C) schools : elevators (D) education : stupidity

12. *Sequence Relationship*
SPRING : SUMMER :: (A) Thursday : Wednesday (B) Wednesday : Monday (C) Monday : Wednesday (D) Wednesday : Thursday

13. *Grammatical Relationship*
RESTORE : CLIMB :: (A) segregation : seem (B) into : nymph (C) tearoom : although (D) overpower : seethe

14. *Numerical Relationship*
4 : 12 :: (A) 10 : 16 (B) 9 : 27 (C) 3 : 4 (D) 12 : 6

15. *Association Relationship*
    DEVIL : WRONG :: (A) color : sidewalk (B) slipper : state (C) ink : writing (D) picture : bed

### Answers to Above Analogy Questions

| | | | | |
|---|---|---|---|---|
| 1. A | 4. A | 7. B | 10. D | 13. D |
| 2. C | 5. D | 8. A | 11. A | 14. B |
| 3. D | 6. A | 9. D | 12. D | 15. C |

# PRACTICE VERBAL ANALOGY QUESTIONS

*Directions:* Each of the two capitalized words below have a certain relationship to each other. Following are five other pairs of words, each designated by a letter. Select the lettered pair of words which are related in the same way as the words in the capitalized pair are related to each other.

1. ISLAND : OCEAN :: (A) pit : orange (B) filament : bulb (C) city : nation (D) water : oasis (E) pine : grove

2. FRUIT : ORCHARD :: (A) tree : forest (B) fish : sea (C) lumber : mill (D) seed : flower (E) money : cash

3. ALTITUDE : MOUNTAIN :: (A) height : weight (B) depth : ocean (C) mass : energy (D) latitude : country (E) incline : hill

4. SUN : DAY :: (A) moon : dusk (B) bulb : house (C) stars : night (D) heat : summer (E) earth : axis

5. FOREST : FLORA :: (A) zoo : animals (B) jungle : fauna (C) countryside : cows (D) orchard : trees (E) vase : flowers

6. IGNORANCE : BOOKS :: (A) study : learning (B) school : teacher (C) candy : store (D) darkness : lamps (E) publication : fame

7. AILMENT : DOCTOR :: (A) medicine : pharmacist (B) care : relief (C) victim : crime (D) fire : water (E) war : victory

8. RETREAT : DEFEAT :: (A) retrench : depression
(B) victory : charge (C) campaign : advance (D)
armistice : surrender (E) stand : death

9. OBLITERATE : PAINT :: (A) earthquake : city
(B) write : ink (C) destroy : house (D) drown :
water (E) artist : canvas

10. ADMIRATION : CHAMPION :: (A) hate : villain
(B) cry : misfortune (C) love : store (D) hero :
affection (E) sadness : pity

11. VICTORY : JUBILATION :: (A) defeat : consternation (B) graduation : congratulation (C) elec-
tion : celebration (D) wedding : felicitation (E)
slavery : emancipation

12. MONOTONY : BOREDOM :: (A) perseverence :
success (B) factory : salary (C) automation : saving
(D) interest : complication (E) repetition : in-
dolence

13. CONDONE : TREACHERY :: (A) punish :
criminal (B) mitigate : penitence (C) overlook :
aberrations (D) mistake : judgment (E) ignore :
loyalty

14. POWER : BATTERY :: (A) vitamins : metabolism
(B) exercise : strength (C) recuperation : con-
valescence (D) automobile : engine (E) light :
kerosene

15. DEPRESSION : UNEMPLOYMENT :: (A) capital : interest (B) legislation : lobbying (C) emacia-
tion : debilitation (D) deterioration : rust (E)
recession : inefficiency

16. DIETING : OVERWEIGHT :: (A) overeating : gluttony (B) poverty : sickness (C) gourmet : underweight (D) doctor : arthritis (E) exercise : weakness

17. STREPTOCOCCI : PNEUMONIA :: (A) boat : trip (B) quinine : malaria (C) cause : sickness (D) malnutrition : beriberi (E) medicine : sickness

18. NAIVE : CHEAT :: (A) sensible : succeed (B) hurt : retaliate (C) gullible : convince (D) contentious : scorn (E) simple : win

19. ERRORS : INEXPERIENCE :: (A) skill : mistakes (B) training : economy (C) news : publication (D) success : victory (E) thefts : carelessness

20. FORECAST : HAPPENING :: (A) prophesy : miracle (B) analyze : problem (C) exculpate : criminal (D) forestall : disaster (E) elucidate : explanation

21. CAT : FELINE :: (A) horse : equine (B) tiger : carnivorous (C) bird : vulpine (D) chair : furniture (E) sit : recline

22. ADVERSITY : HAPPINESS :: (A) fear : misfortune (B) troublesome : petulance (C) vehemence : serenity (D) solace : adversity (E) graduation : felicitation

23. NECKLACE : ADORNMENT :: (A) medal : decoration (B) bronze : medal (C) window : house (D) pearl : diamond (E) scarf : dress

24. GUN : HOLSTER :: (A) shoe : soldier (B) sword : warrior (C) ink : pen (D) books : school bag (E) cannon : plunder

25. ARCHAEOLOGIST : ANTIQUITY :: (A) theology : minister (B) flower : horticulture (C) ichthyologist : marine life (D) Bible : psalms (E) gold : silver

26. SHOE : LEATHER :: (A) passage : ship (B) trail : wagon (C) journey : boat (D) highway : asphalt (E) car : engine

27. LORD : FEUDALISM :: (A) laissez-faire : tariff (B) conservative : radical (C) entrepreneur : capitalism (D) child : parent (E) farm : castle

28. FIN : FISH :: (A) engine : auto (B) propeller : aeroplane (C) five : ten (D) teeth : stomach (E) leg : chair

29. PULP : PAPER :: (A) rope : hemp (B) box : package (C) paper : package (D) fabric : yarn (E) cellulose : rayon

30. SKIN : MAN :: (A) scales : fur (B) hide : hair (C) walls : room (D) roof : house (E) clothes : lady

31. RAIN : DROP :: (A) ice : winter (B) cloud : sky (C) flake : snow (D) ocean : stream (E) mankind : man

32. RAISIN : PRUNE :: (A) apricot : currant (B) grape : plum (C) orange : grapefruit (D) kumquat : orange (E) citron : marmalade

33. CONSTELLATION : STARS :: (A) continent : peninsula (B) state : country (C) archipelago : islands (D) dollar : penny (E) library : book

34. BOOKKEEPER : ACCOUNTANT :: (A) reporter : editor (B) typist : stenographer (C) lawyer : judge (D) boy : man (E) teacher : student

35. RUBBER : FLEXIBILITY :: (A) iron : pliability
(B) iron : elasticity (C) steel : rigidity (D) syn-
thetics : natural (E) wood : plastic

36. ABSENCE : PRESENCE :: (A) steady : secure
(B) safe : influential (C) poor : influential (D)
fresh : canned (E) stable : changeable

37. SAFETY VALVE : BOILER :: (A) fuse : motor
(B) house : wire (C) city : factory (D) brake :
automobile (E) extinguisher : fire

38. SCHOLARLY : UNSCHOLARLY :: (A) learned
: ignorant (B) wise : skilled (C) scholarly : literary
(D) knowledge : books (E) lies : knowledge

39. IMMIGRATION : ENTRANCE :: (A) file : knife
(B) travel : alien (C) native : foreigner (D)
emigration : departure (E) nest : bird

40. GOVERNOR : STATE :: (A) lieutenant : army
(B) ship : captain (C) admiral : navy (D) inmate
: institution (E) mother : home

41. LETTER CARRIER : MAIL :: (A) messenger :
value (B) delivery : easy (C) government : fast
(D) courier : dispatch (E) message : messenger

42. WOOL : COAT :: (A) doll : cover (B) gingham :
dress (C) tailor : suit (D) cover : box (E) yarn :
wool

43. BOAT : DOCK :: (A) wing : strut (B) engine
: chassis (C) contents : box (D) verb : sentence
(E) dirigible : hangar

44. OAT : BUSHEL :: (A) wheat : gram (B) hardness : usefulness (C) gold : karat (D) diamond :
carat (E) ornament : case

45. PHYSIOLOGY : SCIENCE :: (A) psychology : psychiatry (B) law : profession (C) contract : suit (D) painting : art (E) worker : work

46. INSTINCT : LEARNING :: (A) reflex : will (B) thought : idea (C) sight : image (D) development : project (E) research : development

47. CAPTAIN : VESSEL :: (A) guide : touring party (B) boat : travel (C) conductor : train (D) conductor : orchestra (E) musician : violin

48. FATHER : DAUGHTER :: (A) son : daughter (B) son-in-law : daughter (C) uncle : nephew (D) uncle : aunt (E) grandfather : mother

49. PISTOL : TRIGGER :: (A) sword : holster (B) dynamo : amperes (C) motor : switch (D) rifle : sight (E) gun : race

50. CUBE : PYRAMID :: (A) circle : triangle (B) France : Egypt (C) square : triangle (D) cylinder : trylon (E) hill : right angle

51. PROFIT : SELLING :: (A) cost : price (B) fame : bravery (C) praying : loving (D) medal : service (E) money : work

52. BINDING : BOOK :: (A) welding : tank (B) chair : table (C) wire : lamp (D) pencil : paper (E) glue : plate

53. GYMNASIUM : HEALTH :: (A) library : books (B) books : study (C) knowledge : school (D) library : knowledge (E) doctor : health

54. COKE : COAL :: (A) bread : eat (B) money : work (C) bread : dough (D) coal : rubber (E) dough : wheat

55. INDIAN : AMERICA :: (A) Hindu : Indian (B) wetback : Mexico (C) soil : land (D) magic : India (E) Hindu : India

56. WEALTH : MERCENARY :: (A) fame : soldier (B) love : mother (C) gold : South Africa (D) poverty : crime (E) gold : Midas

57. BOTTLE : BRITTLE :: (A) tire : elastic (B) rubber : opaque (C) glass : transparent (D) iron : strong (E) chair : comfortable

58. ELEPHANT : TUSK :: (A) camel : hump (B) leopard : skin (C) knight : spear (D) snake : fangs (E) desk : top

59. CAUSEWAY : BRIDGE :: (A) swamp : stream (B) viaduct : land (C) bridge : river (D) train : road (E) low : high

60. HACK : DRIVER :: (A) buggy : horse (B) army : captain (C) machine : operator (D) tug : pilot (E) school : teacher

61. CONVEX : CONCAVE :: (A) in : out (B) nose : mouth (C) hill : hole (D) round : square (E) myopia : astigmatism

62. PRISM : KALEIDOSCOPE :: (A) window : house (B) bottle : glass (C) tool : toy (D) gear : machine (E) sight : play

63. MARTINET : STOIC :: (A) soldier : bravery (B) general : philosopher (C) man : boy (D) sergeant : general (E) benefactor : kindness

64. CADAVER : ANIMAL :: (A) salad : greens (B) corpse : man (C) death : life (D) morgue : jungle (E) life : death

65. MORPHINE : PAIN :: (A) symptom : illness (B) doctor : relief (C) dope : addict (D) eraser : spot (E) hope : relief

66. POLYMER : CELL :: (A) chain : link (B) fibre : plastic (C) coin : money (D) chemistry : elements (E) food : wheat

67. MACAROON : ALMOND :: (A) cake : dough (B) mint : flavor (C) vanilla : bean (D) caramel : butter (E) bread : wheat

68. INTEGER : DECIMAL :: (A) 100 : 10 (B) 1 : 0 (C) decimal : fraction (D) whole number : fraction (E) 100 : per cent

69. PROPERTY : MORTGAGE :: (A) owner : lender (B) inventory : merchandise (C) word : promise (D) security : price (E) equity : interest

70. HYGROMETER : BAROMETER :: (A) water : mercury (B) snow : rain (C) humidity : pressure (D) temperature : weather (E) forecast : rain

71. NEGOTIABLE : CHECK :: (A) frozen : asset (B) inventory : merchandise (C) bank : money (D) trade : tariff (E) flowing : water

72. CAUCASIAN : SAXON :: (A) white : colored (B) Chinese : Indian (C) furniture : chair (D) carriage : horse (E) city : house

73. OCTAVO : BINDING :: (A) pica : printing (B) music : octave (C) day : week (D) pamphlet : book (E) ruler : artist

74. CLASSIC : GREECE :: (A) Empire : France (B) Roman : Italy (C) colonialism : India (D) Ionic : Rome (E) new : America

75. MARACAS : DANCER :: (A) xylophone : player
(B) metronome : pianist (C) tambourine : gypsy
(D) sample : salesman (E) wrench : plumber

76. BOTTLE : ALCOHOLISM :: (A) pill : dope (B)
tranquilizer : emotions (C) atomizer : sinusitis (D)
candy : overweight (E) perfume : smell

77. MACE : MAJESTY :: (A) king : crown (B) sword
: soldier (C) diploma : knowledge (D) book :
knowledge (E) house : security

78. COURT : JUSTICE :: (A) doctor : sickness (B)
chief : boss (C) machinist : product (D) police-
man : government (E) auditor : accuracy

79. PEDAGOGUE : LEARNING :: (A) teaching :
books (B) professor : erudition (C) Plato : pedant
(D) schoolmaster : ABC's (E) books : knowledge

X 80. STICK : DISCIPLINE :: (A) bat : ball (B) carrot
: incentive (C) hit : hurt (D) book : learning (E)
seat : rest

81. RESTRAIN : REPRESS :: (A) advance : capitulate (B) march : refrain (C) surround : surrender
(D) retire : battle (E) urge : spur

82. RUN : RACE :: (A) walk : pogo stick (B) swim
: boat (C) fly : kite (D) sink : bottle (E) operate :
automobile

83. ELIXIR : PILL :: (A) life : health (B) water :
ice (C) bottle : box (D) mystery : medicine (E)
nurse : doctor

84. SCHOOL : LEARN :: (A) book : read (B) wheel
: tire (C) knife : bread (D) press : print (E)
teacher : learn

85. PEOPLE : ELECT :: (A) statesman : govern (B) diplomat : argue (C) lawyer : debate (D) teach : teacher (E) journalist : news

86. CALIBRATOR : MEASURE :: (A) plumber : wrench (B) clamp : hold (C) measure : tolerance (D) ruler : line (E) thermometer : temperature

87. AUTHOR : NOVEL :: (A) teacher : student (B) reader : interest (C) hero : conquest (D) carpenter : cabinet (E) doctor : cure

88. CITIZEN : CONSTITUTION :: (A) alien : consul (B) emigrant : passport (C) resident : law (D) immigrant : visa (E) union : laborer

89. LAW : PROSECUTOR :: (A) constitution : Attorney General (B) Congress : President (C) legislation : governor (D) Bible : minister (E) athletics : boxer

90. PORT : SHIP :: (A) ship : storm (B) ground : plane (C) garage : automobile (D) home : sailor (E) safety : danger

91. BAY : PENINSULA :: (A) safety : danger (B) river : cape (C) mountain : hill (D) stand : sit (E) sea : land

92. HOTEL : SHELTER :: (A) bed : pillow (B) boat : transportation (C) restaurant : drink (D) train : ride (E) home : recuperation

93. REWARD : PUNISHMENT :: (A) money : laughter (B) medal : bravery (C) bravery : cowardice (D) North : South (E) have : give

94. VIBRATE : UNDULATE :: (A) sound : light (B) shudder : quiver (C) ripple : wave (D) flutter : waver (E) rattle : brandish

95. TRANSPARENT : TRANSLUCENT :: (A) water : milk (B) glass : water (C) translucent : opaque (D) clear : murky (E) angry : choleric

96. HEROISM : REWARD :: (A) wish : deed (B) civilian : criminal (C) misdemeanor : felony (D) trespassing : burglary (E) crime : punishment

97. REFORM : RECIDIVISM :: (A) crime : prison (B) dilettante : professional (C) connoisseur : judge (D) probation : parole (E) divorce : alimony

98. DISCRIMINATE : SEGREGATE :: (A) select : separate (B) good : best (C) sift : unravel (D) blend : fuse (E) convict : punish

99. EMULATE : MIMIC :: (A) slander : defame (B) praise : flatter (C) obituary : eulogy (D) complain : condemn (E) express : imply

100. ASSIST : SAVE :: (A) agree : oppose (B) rely : descry (C) request : command (D) declare : deny (E) help : aid

### Answer Key to Verbal Analogies Questions

| | | | | |
|---|---|---|---|---|
| 1. D | 7. D | 13. E | 19. E | 25. C |
| 2. B | 8. A | 14. E | 20. B | 26. D |
| 3. B | 9. B | 15. D | 21. A | 27. C |
| 4. C | 10. A | 16. E | 22. C | 28. B |
| 5. D | 11. C | 17. D | 23. A | 29. E |
| 6. D | 12. A | 18. C | 24. D | 30. D |

| | | | | |
|---|---|---|---|---|
| 31. E | 45. D | 59. A | 73. A | 87. D |
| 32. B | 46. A | 60. D | 74. A | 88. C |
| 33. C | 47. D | 61. C | 75. B | 89. A |
| 34. A | 48. E | 62. D | 76. D | 90. C |
| 35. C | 49. C | 63. E | 77. C | 91. E |
| 36. E | 50. C | 64. B | 78. E | 92. B |
| 37. A | 51. B | 65. D | 79. D | 93. C |
| 38. A | 52. A | 66. A | 80. B | 94. C |
| 39. D | 53. D | 67. D | 81. E | 95. C |
| 40. C | 54. C | 68. D | 82. C | 96. E |
| 41. D | 55. E | 69. A | 83. C | 97. B |
| 42. B | 56. E | 70. C | 84. D | 98. A |
| 43. E | 57. A | 71. E | 85. A | 99. B |
| 44. D | 58. D | 72. C | 86. B | 100. C |

*Note:* In the analogy practice tests which follow ("Analogy Tests by Levels"), we present another form of analogy question which you may get on the SAT. You will find that these exercises (in the succeeding pages) appear in either of the following two manners.

HEAR : SOUND—SEE :
   (A) movie (B) taste (C) picture (D) vision
or
HEAR is to SOUND as SEE is to
   (A) movie (B) taste (C) picture (D) vision

(Answer—C)

We are giving both forms of analogy questions so that you may be prepared for either analogy type. A number of the practice questions to follow (Level One—Easy Analogies) are quite similar to a few of the analogy questions you have just studied. This should help you to acquire a facility with both types.

# ANALOGY TESTS BY LEVELS

## Level One—Easy Analogies

*Directions:* In each of the questions below, the first two words are related to each other in some way. Find the relationship between the first two words, and then decide to which of the uncapitalized words the third word is related in the same way.

## TEST 1—EASY ANALOGIES

1. FATHER is to DAUGHTER as UNCLE is to
   (A) son (B) daughter (C) son-in-law (D) niece (E) aunt

2. PISTOL is to TRIGGER as MOTOR is to
   (A) wire (B) dynamo (C) amperes (D) barrel (E) switch

3. CUBE is to PYRAMID as SQUARE is to
   (A) box (B) Egypt (C) pentagon (D) triangle (E) cylinder

4. PROFIT is to SELLING as FAME is to
   (A) buying (B) cheating (C) bravery (D) praying (E) loving

5. BINDING is to BOOK as WELDING is to
   (A) box (B) tank (C) chair (D) wire (E) pencil

6. GYMNASIUM is to EXERCISE as LIBRARY is to
   (A) sick (B) study (C) books (D) knowledge (E) school

7. COKE is to COAL as BREAD is to
   (A) eat (B) money (C) dough (D) man (E) yeast

8. INDIAN is to AMERICA as HINDU is to
   (A) Indian (B) Mexico (C) soil (D) magic (E) India

9. WEALTH is to MERCENARY as GOLD is to
   (A) Midas (B) miner (C) fame (D) eleemosynary (E) South Africa

10. BOTTLE is to BRITTLE as TIRE is to
    (A) elastic (B) scarce (C) rubber (D) spheroid (E) automobile

### Answers Test 1

| | | | | |
|---|---|---|---|---|
| 1. D | 3. D | 5. B | 7. C | 9. A |
| 2. E | 4. C | 6. D | 8. E | 10. A |

## TEST 2—EASY ANALOGIES

1. PENINSULA : LAND—BAY :
   (A) boats (B) pay (C) ocean (D) Massachusetts

2. HOUR : MINUTE—MINUTE :
   (A) man (B) week (C) second (D) short

3. ABIDE : DEPART—STAY :
   (A) over (B) home (C) play (D) leave

4. JANUARY : FEBRUARY—JUNE :
   (A) July (B) May (C) month (D) year

5. BOLD : TIMID—ADVANCE :
   (A) proceed (B) retreat (C) campaign (D) soldiers

6. ABOVE : BELOW—TOP :
   (A) spin (B) bottom (C) surface (D) side

7. LION : ANIMAL—ROSE :
   (A) smell (B) leaf (C) plant (D) thorn

8. TIGER : CARNIVOROUS—HORSE :
   (A) cow (B) pony (C) buggy (D) herbivorous

9. SAILOR : NAVY—SOLDIER :
   (A) gun (B) cap (C) hill (D) army

10. PICTURE : SEE—SOUND :
    (A) noise (B) music (C) hear (D) bark

**Answers Test 2**

| 1. C | 3. D | 5. B | 7. C | 9. D |
|------|------|------|------|------|
| 2. C | 4. A | 6. B | 8. D | 10. C |

## TEST 3—EASY ANALOGIES

1. SUCCESS : JOY—FAILURE :
   (A) sadness (B) success (C) fail (D) work

2. HOPE : DESPAIR—HAPPINESS :
   (A) frolic (B) fun (C) joy (D) sadness

3. PRETTY : UGLY—ATTRACT :
   (A) fine (B) repel (C) nice (D) draw

4. PUPIL : TEACHER—CHILD :
   (A) parent (B) dolly (C) youngster (D) obey

5. CITY : MAYOR—ARMY :
   (A) navy (B) soldier (C) general (D) private

6. ESTABLISH : BEGIN—ABOLISH :
   (A) slavery (B) wrong (C) abolition (D) end

7. DECEMBER : JANUARY—LAST :
   (A) least (B) worst (C) month (D) first

8. GIANT : DWARF—LARGE :
   (A) big (B) monster (C) queer (D) small

9. ENGINE : CABOOSE—BEGINNING :
   (A) commence (B) cabin (C) end (D) train

10. DISMAL : CHEERFUL—DARK :
    (A) sad (B) stars (C) night (D) bright


**Answers Test 3**

| | | | | |
|---|---|---|---|---|
| 1. A | 3. B | 5. C | 7. D | 9. C |
| 2. D | 4. A | 6. D | 8. D | 10. D |


## TEST 4—EASY ANALOGIES

1. QUARREL : ENEMY—AGREE :
   (A) friend (B) disagree (C) agreeable (D) foe

2. RAZOR : SHARP—HOE :
   (A) bury (B) dull (C) cuts (D) tree

3. WINTER : SUMMER—COLD :
   (A) freeze (B) warm (C) wet (D) January

4. RUDDER : SHIP—TAIL :
   (A) sail (B) bird (C) dog (D) cat

5. GRANARY : WHEAT—LIBRARY :
   (A) desk (B) books (C) paper (D) librarian

6. INTELLIGENCE : UNDERSTANDING—STUPID-
ITY :
   (A) ignorance (B) pleasure (C) school (D) unhap-
piness

7. SAND : GLASS—CLAY :
   (A) stone (B) hay (C) bricks (D) dirt

8. DISLOYAL is to FAITHLESS as IMPERFECTION
is to
   (A) confirmation (B) depression (C) foible (D)
decrepitude

9. TEARS : SORROW—LAUGHTER :
   (A) comedy (B) smile (C) girls (D) grain

10. COLD : ICE—HEAT :
    (A) lightning (B) warm (C) steam (D) coat

**Answers Test 4**

1. A    3. B    5. B    7. C    9. A
2. B    4. B    6. A    8. C    10. C

**TEST 5—EASY ANALOGIES**

1. REMUNERATIVE is to PROFITABLE as FRAUD-
ULENT is to
   (A) lying (B) slander (C) fallacious (D) plausible
(E) reward

2. AX is to WOODSMAN as AWL is to
   (A) cut (B) hew (C) plumber (D) pierce (E)
cobbler

3. SURGEON is to SCAPEL as BUTCHER is to
   (A) mallet (B) cleaver (C) chisel (D) wrench (E) medicine

4. CAT is to FELINE as HORSE is to
   (A) equine (B) tiger (C) quadruped (D) carnivorous (E) vulpine

5. ADVERSITY is to HAPPINESS as VEHEMENCE is to
   (A) misfortune (B) gaiety (C) troublesome (D) petulance (E) serenity

6. CAMEO is to ADORNMENT as MEDAL is to
   (A) jewel (B) metal (C) bravery (D) bronze (E) decoration

7. GUN is to HOLSTER as SWORD is to
   (A) pistol (B) scabbard (C) warrior (D) slay (E) plunder

8. NECKLACE is to PEARLS as CHAIN is to
   (A) metal (B) prisoner (C) locket (D) silver (E) links

9. SHOE is to LEATHER as HIGHWAY is to
   (A) passage (B) road (C) asphalt (D) trail (E) journey

10. SERFDOM is to FEUDALISM as ENTREPRENEUR is to
    (A) laissez-faire (B) captain (C) radical (D) agriculture (E) capitalism

### Answers Test 5

| | | | | |
|---|---|---|---|---|
| 1. C | 3. B | 5. E | 7. B | 9. C |
| 2. E | 4. A | 6. E | 8. E | 10. E |

## TEST 6—EASY ANALOGIES

1. FIN is to FISH as PROPELLER is to
   (A) auto (B) airplane (C) grain elevator (D) water
   (E) bus

2. PULP is to PAPER as HEMP is to
   (A) rope (B) baskets (C) yarn (D) cotton (E) silk

3. SKIN is to MAN as HIDE is to
   (A) scales (B) fur (C) animal (D) hair (E) fish

4. RAIN is to DROP as SNOW is to
   (A) ice (B) cold (C) zero (D) flake (E) hail

5. RAISIN is to GRAPE as PRUNE is to
   (A) apricot (B) currant (C) plum (D) berry (E)
   peach

6. CONSTELLATION is to STAR as ARCHIPELAGO
   is to
   (A) continent (B) peninsula (C) country (D) island
   (E) mono

7. ACCOUNTANCY is to BOOKKEEPING as COURT
   REPORTING is to
   (A) law (B) judgment (C) stenography (D) lawyer
   (E) judge

8. RUBBER is to FLEXIBILITY as PIPE is to
   (A) iron (B) copper (C) pliability (D) elasticity
   (E) rigidity

9. ABSENCE is to PRESENCE as STABLE is to
   (A) steady (B) secure (C) safe (D) changeable
   (E) influential

10. SAFETY VALVE is to BOILER as FUSE is to
    (A) motor (B) house (C) wire (D) city (E) factory

**Answers Test 6**

| | | | | |
|---|---|---|---|---|
| 1. B | 3. C | 5. C | 7. C | 9. D |
| 2. A | 4. D | 6. D | 8. E | 10. A |

# TEST 7—EASY ANALOGIES

1. SCHOLARLY is to UNSCHOLARLY as LEARNED is to
   (A) ignorant (B) wise (C) skilled (D) scholarly (E) literary

2. IMMIGRANT is to ARRIVAL as EMIGRATION is to
   (A) leaving (B) alien (C) native (D) Italian (E) emigrant

3. GOVERNOR is to STATE as GENERAL is to
   (A) lieutenant (B) navy (C) army (D) captain (E) admiral

4. LETTER CARRIER is to MAIL as MESSENGER is to
   (A) value (B) dispatches (C) easy (D) complicated (E) fast

5. CLOTH is to COAT as GINGHAM is to
   (A) doll (B) cover (C) washable (D) dress (E) dressmaker

6. BOAT is to DOCK as AIRPLANE is to
   (A) wing (B) strut (C) engine (D) wind (E) hangar

7. OAT is to BUSHEL as DIAMOND is to
   (A) gram (B) hardness (C) usefulness (D) carat
   (E) ornament

8. PHYSIOLOGY is to SCIENCE as LAW is to
   (A) jurist (B) court (C) professor (D) contract
   (E) suit

9. HUNGER is to INSTINCT as IMAGINATION is to
   (A) ideal (B) mind (C) magic (D) image (E)
   development

10. CAPTAIN is to VESSEL as DIRECTOR is to
    (A) touring party (B) board (C) travel (D) orches-
    tra (E) musician

### Answers Test 7

| | | | | |
|---|---|---|---|---|
| 1. A | 3. C | 5. D | 7. D | 9. B |
| 2. A | 4. B | 6. E | 8. C | 10. D |

## Level Two—Difficult Analogies

*Directions:* Find the relationship between the first two capitalized words. The third capitalized word bears the same relationship to one of the remaining words.

### TEST 8—DIFFICULT ANALOGIES

1. ADUMBRATE is to FORESHADOW as DECLINE
   is to
   (A) increase (B) decrease (C) stultify (D) stupefy

2. APOGEE is to PERIGEE as APPOSITE is to
   (A) inappropriate (B) opposite (C) composite (D)
   pardoxical

3. FULMINATION is to TRINITROTOLUENE as DISSIPATION is to
   (A) tyranny (B) gluttony (C) concentration (D) desire

4. EDIFICATION is to AWARENESS as EXACERBATION is to
   (A) soreness (B) excitement (C) reduction (D) deliberation

5. GASTRONOMICAL is to GOURMET as GEOLOGICAL is to
   (A) raconteur (B) entomologist (C) etymologist (D) paleontologist

6. ECUMENICAL is to CHURCH as CULINARY is to
   (A) bedroom (B) closet (C) knife (D) kitchen

7. DICHOTOMY is to DIVISION as DISSEMBLE is to
   (A) feign (B) assemble (C) resemble (D) return

8. CREPUSCULAR is to INDISTINCT as CURSORY is to
   (A) profane (B) egregious (C) superficial (D) unique

9. VIXEN is to SEAMSTRESS as BACCHUS is to
   (A) Ceres (B) Neptune (C) Venus (D) Minerva

10. GLABROUS is to HIRSUTE as FACTITIOUS is to
    (A) authentic (B) fictional (C) fluent (D) replete

**Answers Test 8**

| | | | | |
|---|---|---|---|---|
| 1. B | 3. B | 5. D | 7. A | 9. B |
| 2. A | 4. A | 6. D | 8. C | 10. A |

## TEST 9—DIFFICULT ANALOGIES

1. CHOLERIC is to PLACID as BANAL is to
   (A) portly (B) flippant (C) reasonable (D) unique

2. CADENZA is to MUSIC as LOB is to
   (A) baseball (B) football (C) cricket (D) boxing

3. ARROGATE is to USURP as CLOY is to
   (A) collect (B) employ (C) glut (D) cut

4. DENIGRATE is to DEFAMER as MEDIATE is to
   (A) mathematician (B) arbitrator (C) employer
   (D) relaxed

5. INCHOATE is to TERMINAL as SATURNINE is to
   (A) mercurial (B) planetary (C) saturated (D)
   laborer

6. LITTORAL is to COAST as PECTORAL is to
   (A) throat (B) leg (C) skeleton (D) chest

7. BUCOLIC is to PEACEFUL as CIMMERIAN is to
   (A) warlike (B) tenebrous (C) doubtful (D) smirk-
   ing

8. LIMPID is to LUCID as TURBID is to
   (A) torpid (B) muddy (C) truculent (D) urban

9. PHYSIOGNOMY is to FACE as NECROLOGY
   is to
   (A) philosophy (B) magic (C) psychology (D)
   mortality

10. ARCHAEOLOGIST is to ANTIQUITY as ICH-
    THYOLOGIST is to
    (A) theology (B) marine life (C) horticulture (D)
    mysticism

**Answers Test 9**

| 1. D | 3. C | 5. A | 7. B | 9. D |
|------|------|------|------|------|
| 2. C | 4. B | 6. D | 8. B | 10. B |

## Level Three—Very Difficult Analogies

It is not likely (but is it possible) that the actual examination will have Analogy questions which include words of the difficulty exemplified in the following tests.

## TEST 10—VERY DIFFICULT ANALOGIES

1. ANNULAR is to RING as NUMMULAR is to
   (A) limb (B) sum (C) shell (D) coin

2. DOWSER is to ROD as GEOMANCER is to
   (A) stones (B) maps (C) plants (D) configurations

3. ETYMOLOGY is to WORDS as HAGIOLOGY is to
   (A) saints (B) senility (C) selling (D) writing

4. EUPEPTIC is to DIGESTION as EUPHEMISTIC is to
   (A) speech (B) race (C) sound (D) drug

5. LOGGIA is to GALLERY as JALOUSIE is to
   (A) lintel (B) dowel (C) jamb (D) louver

6. PHILIPPIC is to DEMOSTHENES as EUREKA is to
   (A) Aristotle (B) Phidias (C) Archimedes (D) Aristophanes

7. PROLOGUE is to EPILOGUE as PROTASIS is to
   (A) epitome (B) epigenesis (C) apodosis (D) apogee

8. SAUTÉEING is to COOKERY as FAGOTING is to
   (A) juggling (B) forestry (C) embroidery (D) medicine

9. ACOLYTE is to ALTAR as CAMPANOLOGIST is to
   (A) tours (B) bells (C) scouts (D) politicos

10. BRASS is to COPPER as PEWTER is to
    (A) lead (B) zinc (C) silver (D) bronze

**Answers Test 10**

| | | | | |
|---|---|---|---|---|
| 1. D | 3. A | 5. D | 7. C | 9. B |
| 2. D | 4. A | 6. C | 8. C | 10. A |

## TEST 11—VERY DIFFICULT ANALOGIES

1. CAPE is to PROMONTORY as WADI is to
   (A) river (B) waterfall (C) meadow (D) fen

2. CATALYST is to CHANGE as ACCELERATOR is to
   (A) cylinder (B) inertia (C) motion (D) exhaust

3. CATAMARAN is to RAFT as TERGMAGANT is to
   (A) grisette (B) benedict (C) spinster (D) shrew

4. CINCTURE is to WAIST as SPHINCTER is to
   (A) didoes (B) bone splint (C) blood clot (D) orifice

5. DEBIT is to CREDIT as DENOUEMENT is to
   (A) climax (B) outcome (C) complication (D) untying

6. OBSTRUCT is to IMPEDE as IMPENETRABLE is to
   (A) forebearing (B) hidden (C) impervious (D) merciful

7. FELICITY is to BLISS as CONGENIAL is to
   (A) clever (B) compatible (C) fierce (D) unfriendly

8. CAUTIOUS is to CIRCUMSPECT as PRECIPITOUS is to
   (A) deep (B) flat (C) high (D) steep

9. INQUISITIVE is to INCURIOUS as MANIFEST is to
   (A) latent (B) many-sided (C) obvious (D) manipulated

10. FETISH is to TALISMAN as FEALTY is to
    (A) allegiance (B) faithlessness (C) payment (D) real estate

**Answers Test 11**

| | | | | |
|---|---|---|---|---|
| 1. A | 3. D | 5. C | 7. B | 9. A |
| 2. C | 4. D | 6. C | 8. D | 10. A |

# READING COMPREHENSION

## Helpful Hints for the Reading Comprehension Part of the Examination

1. Do all of the reading comprehension exercises in this book. In these pages, you will find paragraphs of various types and of various levels of difficulty.

2. Use the following sources for getting additional practice in comprehending what you read:

   a. Editorial pages of various newspapers—you'll find many interesting editorials.
   b. Book reviews (also drama and movie reviews).
   c. Magazine articles.

For each selection that you read, do the following:

   a. Jot down the main idea of the article.
   b. Look up the meanings of words that you don't know or that you aren't sure of.

## Spot the Topic Sentence to Get the Main Thought

An analysis of paragraphs shows that they all have a unity of construction that is fundamental for all writing. There is a central idea in every paragraph, called a topic sentence from which all other sentences grow. The topic sentence may occur at the beginning, in the middle, or at the end of a paragraph. The development of the topic sentence may take the form of presenting details, of showing a comparison or a contrast, of listing examples, or of citing causes or results. Whatever the method used, you must remember that the topic sentence is the clue for the main idea or central thought of the whole paragraph. It is similar to the headline or lead in a newspaper article. It gives you at a glance the theme or subject matter of the article. The supporting ideas are merely a detailed development of the thought of the topic sentence.

When you get to the reading comprehension questions on the test, these hints may be helpful:

### A 10-Point Check List to Insure Success in Reading Comprehension

(1) Read over the entire paragraph carefully to get the general sense. Look for a topic sentence.

(2) Then look at the questions asked.

(3) Go back over the paragraph to get the exact answers. Sometimes the question cannot be answered on the basis of the stated facts. You may be required to make a deduction from the facts given, to interpret or analyze the facts, or to draw a conclusion regarding the facts or the author. If you understand what you read, you should have little difficulty with any reading comprehension question.

(4) Read rapidly.

(5) Underline words and phrases in the paragraph that seem important to you.

(6) Check for "false-impressions."

(7) Eliminate your personal opinions.

(8) Rule out subordinate ideas.

(9) Reread the paragraph several times if necessary.

(10) Beware of negatives and all-inclusive statements. Watch particularly words like always, never, all, only, every, absolutely, completely, none, entirely.

# READING COMPREHENSION TESTS

## READING COMPREHENSION TEST 1

The standardized educational or psychological tests, that are widely used to aid in selecting, classifying, assigning, or promoting students, employees, and military personnel have been the target of recent attacks in books, magazines, the daily press, and even in Congress. The target is wrong, for in attacking the tests, critics divert attention from the fault that lies with ill-informed or incompetent users. The tests themselves are merely tools, with characteristics that can be measured with reasonable precision under specified conditions. Whether the results will be valuable, meaningless, or even misleading depends partly upon the tool itself but largely upon the user.

All informed predictions of future performance are based upon some knowledge of relevant past performance: school grades, research productivity, sales records, batting averages, or whatever is appropriate. How well the predictions will be validated by later performance depends upon the amount, reliability, and appropriateness of the information used and on the skill and wisdom with which it is interpreted. Anyone who keeps careful score knows that the information available is always incomplete and that the predictions are always subject to error.

Standardized tests should be considered in this context. They provide a quick, objective method of getting some kinds of information about what a person has learned, the skills he has developed, or the kind of person he is. The information so obtained has, qualitatively, the same advantages and shortcomings as other kinds of information. Whether to use tests, other kinds of information, or both in a particular situation depends, therefore, upon the empirical evidence concerning comparative validity, and upon such factors as cost and availability.

In general, the tests work most effectively when the traits or qualities to be measured can be most precisely defined (for example, ability to do well in a particular course or training program) and least effectively when what is to be measured or predicted cannot be well defined (for example, personality or creativity). Properly used, they provide a rapid means of getting comparable information about many people. Sometimes they identify students whose high potential has not been previously recognized. But there are many things they do not do. For example, they do not compensate for gross social inequality, and thus do not tell how able an underprivileged youngster might have been had he grown up under more favorable circumstances.

Professionals in the business and the conscientious publishers know the limitations as well as the values. They write these things into test manuals and in critiques of available tests. But they have no jurisdiction over users; an educational test can be administered by almost anyone, whether he knows how to interpret it or not. Nor can the difficulty be controlled by limiting sales to qualified users; some attempts to do so have been countered by restraint-of-trade suits.

In the long run it may be possible to establish better controls or to require higher qualifications. But in the meantime, unhappily, the demonstrated value of these tests under many circumstances has given them a popularity that has led to considerable misuse. Also unhappily, justifiable criticism of the misuse now threatens to hamper proper use. Business and government can probably look after themselves. But school guidance and selection programs are being attacked for using a valuable tool, because some of the users are unskilled.

—by Watson Davis, Sc.D., Director of Science Service (reprinted with permission)

1. The essence of this article on educational tests is:
   (A) These tests do not test adequately what they set out to test.
   (B) Don't blame the test—blame the user.
   (C) When a student is nervous or ill, the test results are inaccurate.
   (D) Publishers of tests are without conscience.
   (E) Educators are gradually losing confidence in the value of the tests.

2. Tests like the College Entrance Scholastic Aptitude Test are, it would seem to the author,
   (A) generally unreliable
   (B) generally reliable
   (C) meaningless
   (D) misleading
   (E) neither good nor bad

3. The selection implies that, more often, the value of an educational test rests with
   (A) the interpretation of results
   (B) the test itself
   (C) the testee
   (D) emotional considerations
   (E) the directions

4. Which statement is not true, according to the passage, about educational tests?
   (A) Some students "shine" unexpectedly.
   (B) Predictions do not always hold true.
   (C) Personality tests often fail to measure the true personality.
   (D) The supervisor of the test must be very well trained.
   (E) Publishers cannot confine sales to highly skilled administrators.

5. According to the passage, the validity of a test requires, most of all,
   (A) cooperation on the part of the person tested
   (B) sufficient preparation on the part of the applicant
   (C) clearcut directions
   (D) one answer—and only one—for each question
   (E) specificity regarding what is to be tested

## READING COMPREHENSION TEST 2

When television is good, nothing—not the theatre, not the magazines, or newspapers—nothing is better. But when television is bad, nothing is worse. I invite you to sit down in front of your television set when your station goes on the air and stay there without a book, magazine, newspaper, or anything else to distract you and keep your eyes glued to that set until the station signs off. I can assure you that you will observe a vast wasteland. You will see a procession of game shows, violence, audience participation shows, formula comedies about totally unbelievable families, blood and thunder, mayhem, more violence, sadism, murder, Western badmen, Western goodmen, private eyes, gangsters, still more violence, and cartoons. And, endlessly, commercials that scream and cajole and offend. And most of all, boredom. True, you will see a few things you will enjoy. But they will be very, very few. And if you think I exaggerate, try it.

Is there no room on television to teach, to inform, to uplift, to stretch, to enlarge the capacities of our children? Is there no room for programs to deepen the children's understanding of children in other lands? Is there no room for a children's news show explaining something about the world for them at their level of understanding? Is there no room for reading the great literature of the past, teaching them the great traditions of freedom? There are some fine children's shows, but they are drowned out in the massive doses of cartoons, violence, and more violence. Must these be your trademarks? Search your conscience and see whether you cannot offer more to your young beneficiaries whose future you guard so many hours each and every day.

There are many people in this great country, and you must serve all of us. You will get no argument from me if you say that, given a choice between a Western and a symphony, more people will watch the Western. I like Westerns and private eyes, too—but a steady diet for the whole country is obviously not in the public interest. We all know that people would more often prefer to be entertained than stimulated or informed. But your obligations are not satisfied if you look only to popularity as a test of what to broadcast. You are not only in show business; you are free to communicate ideas as well as to give relaxation. You must provide a wider range of choices, more diversity, more alternatives. It is not enough to cater to the nation's whims—you must also serve the nation's needs. The people own the air. They own it as much in prime evening time as they do at

6 o'clock in the morning. For every hour that the people give you—you owe them something. I intend to see that your debt is paid with service.

—excerpt from speech by Newton N. Minow, chairman of the Federal Communications Commission, before the National Association of Broadcasters.

1. The wasteland referred to describes
   (A) Western badmen and Western goodmen
   (B) average television programs
   (C) the morning shows
   (D) television shows with desert locales
   (E) children's programs

2. The author's attitude toward television is one of
   (A) sullenness          (D) rage
   (B) reconciliation       (E) hopelessness
   (C) determination

3. The National Association of Broadcasters probably accepted Minow's remarks with
   (A) considerable enthusiasm
   (B) shocked wonderment
   (C) complete agreement
   (D) some disagreement
   (E) absolute rejection

4. The Federal Communications Commission chairman is, in effect, telling the broadcasters that
   (A) the listener, not the broadcaster, should make decisions about programs
   (B) children's shows are worthless
   (C) mystery programs should be banned
   (D) television instruction should be a substitute for classroom lessons
   (E) they had better mend their ways

granite block in order to produce a delicate curve or feature has labored more painstakingly than White in fashioning a short paragraph. Obviously we can't expect our schools to make every Johnny into a White or a Flaubert or a Mann, but it is not unreasonable to expect more of them to provide the conditions that promote clear, careful, competent expression. Certainly the cumulative effort of the school experience should not have to be undone in later years.

—by Norman Cousins, Editor of *Saturday Review* (reprinted with permission)

1. According to the passage, competence in writing is
   (A) an art that takes practice
   (B) a skill that requires dexterity
   (C) a technique that is easy to learn
   (D) a result of the spontaneous flow of words
   (E) an innate ability that few people have

2. The main purpose of the passage is to
   (A) present an original idea
   (B) describe a new process
   (C) argue against an established practice
   (D) comment on a skill and its techniques
   (E) urge the reader to action

3. Our schools, according to the passage,
   (A) are providing proper conditions for good writing
   (B) should not stress writing speed on a test
   (C) should give essay tests rather than multiple-choice tests
   (D) teach good writing primarily through reading
   (E) correlate art and music with writing instruction

4. In describing White as a "word-artist," the author
   means that White
   (A) was also a cartoonist
   (B) illustrated his stories
   (C) was colorful in his descriptions
   (D) had artistic background
   (E) was a great writer

5. It can be inferred from the passage that the author
   values good literature primarily for its ability to
   (A) relieve the boredom of everyday life
   (B) accurately describe events as they occur
   (C) prevent disorder in society
   (D) communicate ideas and experience
   (E) provide individuals with skills for success

## READING COMPREHENSION TEST 4

A vast health checkup is now being conducted in the
western Swedish province of Varmland with the use of
an automated apparatus for high-speed, multiple-blood
analyses. Developed by two brothers, the apparatus can
process more than 4,000 blood samples a day, subjecting
each to 10 or more tests. Automation has cut the cost of
the analyses by about 90 per cent.

The results so far have been astonishing, for hundreds
of Swedes have learned that they have silent symptoms
of disorders that neither they nor their physicians were
aware of. Among them were iron-deficiency anemia, hy-
percholesterolemia, hypertension, and even diabetes.

The automated blood analysis apparatus was developed by Dr. Gunnar Jungner, 49 year-old associate professor of clinical chemistry at Goteborg University, and
his brother, Ingmar, 39, the physician in charge of the

chemical central laboratory of Stockholm's Hospital for Infectious Diseases.

The idea was conceived 15 years ago when Dr. Gunnar Jungner was working as clinical chemist in northern Sweden and was asked by local physicians to devise a way of performing multiple analyses on a single blood sample. The design was ready in 1961.

Consisting of calorimeters, pumps and other components, many of them American-made, the Jungner apparatus was set up here in Stockholm. Samples from Varmland Province are drawn into the automated system at 90-second intervals.

The findings clatter forth in the form of numbers printed by an automatic typewriter.

The Jungners predict that advance knowledge about a person's potential ailments made possible by the chemical screening process will result in considerable savings in hospital and other medical costs. Thus, they point out, the blood analyses will actually turn out to cost nothing.

In the beginning, the automated blood analyses ran into considerable opposition from some physicians who had no faith in machines and saw no need for so many tests. Some laboratory technicians who saw their jobs threatened also protested. But the opposition is said to be waning.

1. Automation is viewed by the writer with
   (A) animosity
   (B) indecision
   (C) remorse
   (D) indifference
   (E) favor

2. The results of the use of the Jungner apparatus indicate that
   (A) a person may become aware of an ailment not previously detected
   (B) blood diseases can be cured very easily

(C) diabetes does not respond to the apparatus

(D) practically all Swedish physicians have welcomed the invention

(E) only one analysis may be made at a time

3. All of the following statements about automated blood analysis are true EXCEPT:

    (A) the analysis is recorded in a permanent form

    (B) the idea for the apparatus involved an international effort

    (C) the system has met opposition from physicians and technicians

    (D) the machine is more efficient than other types of analysis

    (E) the process is a means to save on hospital costs

4. The main purpose of the passage is to

    (A) predict the future of medical care

    (B) describe a health check-up system

    (C) show how Sweden has superior health care

    (D) warn about the dangers of undetected disease

    (E) describe in detail the workings of a new machine

5. The prediction process that the Jungners use is essentially

    (A) biological

    (B) physiological      (D) anatomical

    (C) chemical        (E) biophysical

## READING COMPREHENSION TEST 5

In discussing human competence in a world of change, I want to make it crystal-clear that I am not ready to accept all the changes that are being pressed on us. I am not at all prepared to suggest that we must blindly find

new competences in order to adjust to all the changes or
in order to make ourselves inconspicuous in the modern
habitat. Let me be specific. I see no reason in the world
why modern man should develop any competence what-
soever to pay high rents in order to be permitted to live
in buildings with walls that act as soundtracks rather
than sound-absorbers. Nor do I believe that this problem
can or should be overcome by developing such novel
engineering competences as "acoustical perfume"—artificial noise to drown out next-door noises. When I don't
wish to be a silent partner to the bedroom conversation
of the neighbors, I am not at all satisfied by having the
sound effects of a waterfall, the chirping of crickets, or
incidental music superimposed on the disturbance, just
to cover up the incompetence or greed of modern build-
ers.

The other day I found myself wandering through the
desolate destruction of Pennsylvania Station in New
York, thoroughly incompetent in my efforts to find a
ticket office. Instead I found a large poster which said
that "your new station" was being built and that this was
the reason for my temporary inconvenience. Nonsense!
my station was not being built at all. My station is being
destroyed, and I do not need the new competence of an
advertising copywriter or a public relations consultant to
obscure the facts. The competence that was needed—and
which I and great numbers of like-minded contempo-
raries lacked—was the competence to prevent an unde-
sirable change. In plain language—the competence to stop
the organized vandalism which, in the name of progress
and change, is tearing down good buildings to put up
flimsy ones; is dynamiting fine landmarks to replace
them with structures that can be ripped down again
twenty years later without a tear.

When the packaging industry finds it increasingly easy

to design containers that make reduced contents appear to be an enlarged value at a steeper price, the change does not call for the competence of a consumer psychologist to make the defrauded customer feel happy. The change calls simply for a tough public prosecutor.

Lest I be mistaken for a political or even a sentimental reactionary who wants to halt progress and change, let me add another example of modern life the improvement of which may call for radical public action rather than for any new competence. Commuter rail transportation has fallen into decline in many parts of the country. Persons dependent on it find themselves frustrated and inconvenienced. In reply to their plight, they are given explanations such as the economic difficulties facing the railroad. Explanations, however, are no substitute for remedies. The competence required here is not technological or mechanical. After all, it would be difficult to persuade any sane citizen that a technology able to dispatch men into space and return them on schedule is mechanically incapable of transporting commuters from the suburbs to the cities in comfort, in safety, and on time.

The competence lacking here is one of general intelligence of the kind that is willing to shed doctrinaire myths when they stand in the way of the facts of modern life. To make millions of commuters suffer (and I use this example only because it is readily familiar, not because it is unique today) merely because the doctrine of free, competitive enterprise must be upheld, even after competition has disappeared as a vital ingredient, is an example of ludicrous mental incompetence. So is the tendency to worry whether a public takeover of a public necessity that is no longer being adequately maintained by private enterprise constitutes socialism or merely the protection of citizens' interests.

We ought to place the stress of competence in such a fashion that we can use it to mold, control, and—in extreme instances—even to block change rather than merely to adjust or submit to it.

—by Fred M. Hechinger (reprinted with permission)

1. The attitude of the writer is
    (A) sardonic and uncompromising
    (B) critical and constructive
    (C) petulant and forbidding
    (D) maudlin and merciful
    (E) reflective and questioning

2. A "doctrinaire myth" (next to last paragraph) may be defined as a belief based on the false premises of
    (A) a deluded lexicographer
    (B) a public relations man
    (C) an insincere politician
    (D) a quack
    (E) an impractical theorist

3. In the article, the author urges us
    (A) to fight against unethical political deals
    (B) to disregard the claims of the advertiser
    (C) to be opposed to many of the changes going on in our society today
    (D) not to rent a luxury apartment
    (E) to avoid becoming a commuter

4. An appropriate title for this article would be
    (A) Antidotes for Incompetence
    (B) The Suffering Commuter
    (C) Unwarranted Destruction
    (D) Structured Vandalism
    (E) Progress and Change

5. The passage, in no way, states or implies that
   (A) much construction today is inferior to what it was in other years
   (B) the razing of the Pennsylvania Station was justifiable
   (C) consumers are often deceived
   (D) some engineering devices are not worth the trouble spent in contriving them
   (E) space scientists have made great progress

6. You would expect the author to say that
   (A) there is no reason for the United States to send nuclear-powered submarines to Japanese ports
   (B) a great deal of confusion reigns in credit card circles
   (C) a truly fundamental need in our society is honesty of thought and attitude
   (D) the damage done to our language by the structural linguists is not altogether irreparable
   (E) the world's population seems now to be increasing out of all proportion to the world's ability to provide food and education

## READING COMPREHENSION TEST 6

There is a time in every man's education when he arrives at the conviction that envy is ignorance; that imitation is suicide, that he must take himself for better or for worse as his portion; that though the wide universe is full of good, no kernel of nourishing corn can come to him but through his toil bestowed on that plot of ground which is given him to till. The power which resides in him is new in nature, and none but him knows what he can do, nor does he know until he has tried.

Society everywhere is in conspiracy against the manhood of every one of its members. Society is a joint-stock company, in which the members agree for the better securing of his bread to each shareholder, to surrender the liberty and culture of the eater. The virtue in most request is conformity. Self-reliance is its aversion. It loves not realities and creators, but names and customs.

Whoso would be a man, must be a nonconformist. He who would gather immortal palms must not be hindered by the name of goodness, but must explore if it be goodness. Nothing is at last sacred but the integrity of your own mind. Absolve you to yourself, and you shall have the suffrage of the world.

A foolish consistency is the hobgoblin of little minds, adored by little statemen and philosophers and divines. With consistency a great soul has simply nothing to do. He may as well concern himself with his shadow on the wall. Speak what you think now in hard words, and tomorrow speak what tomorrow thinks in hard words again, though it contradicts everything you said today. "Ah, so you shall be sure to be misunderstood." Is it so bad, then, to be misunderstood? Pythagoras was misunderstood, and Socrates, and Jesus, and Luther, and Copernicus, and Galileo, and Newton, and every pure and wise spirit that ever took flesh. To be great is to be misunderstood. . . .

1. According to the passage, the practice of adhering, at all times, to the regulations is
   (A) praiseworthy
   (B) characteristic of inadequate people
   (C) a matter of democratic choice
   (D) reserved only for the intelligent
   (E) not workable

2. The writer, in effect, is saying that one
   (A) must always change his opinions
   (B) who agrees with the findings of Newton may also agree with those of Copernicus, Pythagoras, Socrates, Jesus, Luther, and Galileo
   (C) must join a group to survive in our society
   (D) should continue to appraise the facts at the cost of changing a previous conclusion
   (E) can find solace only in a belief in the hereafter

3. You may infer that the author
   (A) was a philosopher-humorist
   (B) once remarked that Toil, Want, Truth, and Mutual Faith were the four angels of his home
   (C) was a leader of oyster pirates, a deck hand on a North Pacific sealer, a mill worker hobo, and college student for a time
   (D) achieved a reputation as a clever business entrepreneur
   (E) was a vivid personality who led a strenuous life and became President of the United States

4. Society, so the selection implies,
   (A) does not encourage an individual to be creative
   (B) wants its members to be self-starters
   (C) can thrive only under democratic rule
   (D) encourages investments in stocks and bonds
   (E) will not improve unless the quality of its leaders improve

## READING COMPREHENSION TEST 7

Shams and delusions are esteemed for soundest truths, while reality is fabulous. If men would steadily observe realities only, and not allow themselves to be deluded, life, to compare it with such things as we know, would be like a fairy tale and the Arabian Nights' Entertainments.

If we respected only what is inevitable and has a right to be, music and poetry would resound along the streets. When we are unhurried and wise, we perceive that only great and worthy things have any permanent and absolute existence,—that petty fears and petty pleasures are but the shadow of the reality. This is always exhilarating and sublime. By closing the eyes and slumbering, and consenting to be deceived by shows, men establish and confirm their daily life of routine and habit everywhere, which still is built on purely illusory foundations. Children, who play life, discern its true law and relations more clearly than men, who fail to live it worthily, but who think that they are wiser by experience, that is, by failure. I have read in a Hindoo book, that "there was a king's son, who, being expelled in infancy from his native city, was brought up by a forester, and, growing up to maturity in that state, imagined himself to belong to the barbarous race with which he lived. One of his father's ministers having discovered him, revealed to him what he was, and the misconception of his character was removed, and he knew himself to be a prince. So soul," continues the Hindoo philosopher, "from the circumstances in which it is placed, mistakes its own character, until the truth is revealed to it by some holy teacher, and then it knows itself to be *Brahme.*" We think that that *is* which *appears* to be. If a man should give us an account of the realities he beheld, we should not recognize the place in his description. Look at a meeting-house, or a court-house, or a jail, or a shop, or a dwelling-house, and say what that thing really is before a true gaze, and they would all go to pieces in your account of them. Men esteem truth remote, in the outskirts of the system, behind the farthest star, before Adam and after the last man. In eternity there is indeed something true and sublime. But all these times and places and occasions are now and here. God himself culminates in the present moment, and will never be more divine in the lapse of all ages. And we are enabled to apprehend at all what is sublime and noble only by the perpetual instilling and drenching of the reality that surrounds us. The universe constantly and obediently answers to our conceptions; whether we travel fast or slow, the track is laid for us. Let us spend our lives in conceiving then. The poet or the artist never yet had so fair and noble a design but some of his posterity at least could accomplish it.

1. The writer's attitude toward the arts is one of
   (A) indifference        (D) repulsion
   (B) suspicion           (E) flippancy
   (C) admiration

2. The author believes that a child
   (A) should practice what the Hindoos preach
   (B) frequently faces vital problems better than grown-ups do
   (C) prefers to be a barbarian than to be a prince
   (D) hardly ever knows his true origin
   (E) is incapable of appreciating the arts

3. The passage implies that human beings
   (A) cannot distinguish the true from the untrue
   (B) are immoral if they are lazy
   (C) should be bold and fearless
   (D) believe in fairy tales
   (E) have progressed culturally throughout history

4. The word "fabulous" in the second line means
   (A) wonderful
   (B) delicious
   (C) birdlike
   (D) incomprehensible
   (E) nonexistent

5. The author is primarily concerned with urging the reader to
   (A) meditate on the meaninglessness of the present
   (B) look to the future for enlightenment
   (C) appraise the present for its true value
   (D) honor the wisdom of past ages
   (E) spend more time in leisure activities

6. The passage is primarily concerned with problems of
   (A) history and economics
   (B) society and population
   (C) biology and physics
   (D) theology and philosophy
   (E) music and art

## READING COMPREHENSION TEST 8

Suppose you go into a fruiterer's shop, wanting an apple—you take up one, and, on biting it, you find it is sour; you look at it, and see that it is hard and green. You take up another one, and that too is hard, green, and sour. The shopman offers you a third; but, before biting it, you examine it, and find that it is hard and green, and you immediately say that you will not have it, as it must be sour, like those that you have already tried.

Nothing can be more simple than that, you think; but if you will take the trouble to analyse and trace out into its logical elements what has been done by the mind, you will be greatly surprised. In the first place you have performed the operation of induction. You found that, in two experiences, hardness and greenness in apples went together with sourness. It was so in the first case, and it was confirmed by the second. True, it is a very small basis, but still it is enough to make an induction from; you generalise the facts, and you expect to find sourness in apples where you get hardness and greenness. You found upon that a general law, that all hard and green apples are sour; and that, so far as it goes, is a perfect induction. Well, having got your natural law in this way, when you are offered another apple which you find is hard and green, you say, "All hard and green apples are sour; this apple is hard and green, therefore this apple is sour." That train of reasoning is what logicians call a syllogism, and has all its various parts and terms—its major premiss, its minor premiss, and its conclusion. And, by the help of further reasoning, which, if drawn out, would have to be exhibited in two or three other syllogisms, you arrive at your final determination, "I will not have that apple." So that, you see, you have, in the first place, established a law by induction, and upon that you have founded a deduction, and reasoned out the special particular case. Well now, suppose, having got your conclusion of the law, that at some times afterwards, you are discussing the qualities of apple with a friend; you will say to him, "It is a very curious thing, but I find that all hard and green apples are sour!" Your friend says to you, "But how do you know that?" You at once reply, "Oh, because I have tried them over and over again, and have always found them to be so." Well, if we were talking science instead of common sense, we should call that an experimental verification. And, if still opposed, you go further, and say, "I have heard from the people in Somersetshire and Devonshire, where a large number of apples are grown, that they have observed the same thing. It is also found to be the case in Normandy, and in North America. In short, I find it to be the universal experience of mankind wherever attention has been directed to the subject." Whereupon, your friend, unless he is a very unreasonable man, agrees with you, and is convinced that you are quite right in the conclusion you have drawn. He believes, although perhaps he does not know he believes it, that the more extensive verifications have been made, and results of the same kind arrived at—that the more varied the conditions under which the same results are attained, the more certain is the ultimate conclusion, and he disputes the question no further. He sees that the experiment has been tried under all sorts of conditions, as to time, place, and people, with the same result; and he says with you, therefore, that the law you have laid down must be a good one, and he must believe it.

1. The writer is probably
   (A) French
   (B) English          (D) Italian
   (C) American          (E) none of the above

2. "All men are mortal; Socrates was a man; Socrates was mortal."
   The foregoing represents reasoning that is
   (A) verification
   (B) inductive          (D) experimental
   (C) syllogistic          (E) developmental

3. Apples are used
   (A) in order to convince the reader that fruit has no intellect
   (B) as an analogy
   (C) to give color to the story
   (D) for sarcasm
   (E) to compare various types of persons

4. The word "premiss" as it appears is more commonly spelled
   (A) promise          (D) premise
   (B) permit          (E) in none of the
   (C) premit                above ways

5. The author has the approach of
   (A) a scientist
   (B) an artist                    (D) an economist
   (C) a novelist                   (E) a businessman

6. You would expect the following to be the writer of this article:
   (A) William Babington Macaulay
   (B) Henry Steele Commager
   (C) Sir Francis Bacon
   (D) Thomas Henry Huxley
   (E) John Steinbeck

## READING COMPREHENSION TEST 9

By volume of production as well as by value, the fisheries industries of the world broke all records in 1963, the last year for which complete statistics are available.

The part of the catch that entered international trade had a value of $1.7 billion, exceeding the preceding year's level by $89 million, the Food and Agriculture Organization reports in its newly published yearbook of fishery statistics.

The global catch reached 46.4 million metric tons of 2,204 pounds each, surpassing the 1962 total by 1.1 million tons.

Concurrently with the publication of the yearbook, the F.A.O. commented that the percentage of the world catch entering international commerce had climbed steeply since 1948, when the agency's compilations began. It was then only 19 per cent. In 1963, it had expanded to about 33 per cent.

One of the year's developments as reflected in the comparative figures on catches and landings, dating to 1938, is that Peru has displaced Japan as the champion fishing nation, in volume of catches and landings.

Revised figures indicate that in fact Peru overtook and passed Japan in 1962, with a total of 6,961,900 tons, against Japan's 6,864,900 tons.

Both countries registered minor reductions in their 1963 totals, Peru's figure having been 6,901,300 tons to Japan's 6,698,800.

1. It is true that
   (A) Peru broke a fishing record (for catches and landings) in 1963
   (B) Japan overtook Peru in 1962, but lost the "championship" in 1963
   (C) a fishing metric ton is 2,000 pounds
   (D) Japan shows every indication of leading the world in fishery income
   (E) F.A.O. stands for Food and Agriculture Organization

2. The world fish catch increased in 1963 over 1962 by
   (A) 10,000 tons
   (B) 100,000 tons
   (C) 1,000,000 tons
   (D) 1,000,000,000 tons
   (E) none of the above

3. The world catch entering international commerce in 1962 was worth approximately
   (A) $50 million
   (B) $90 million
   (C) $1.5 billion
   (D) $2 billion
   (E) $2.5 billion

4. The most recent year for which we have records for the fishery industry is
   (A) 1938
   (B) 1948
   (C) 1958
   (D) 1962
   (E) not the year listed above

5. The percentage of the catch that entered international trade in 1963 was closest to
   (A) 20%
   (B) 30%          (D) 50%
   (C) 40%          (E) 60%

### Answer Key to Reading Comprehension Tests

| Test 1 | Test 2 | Test 3 |
|--------|--------|--------|
| 1. B | 1. B | 1. A |
| 2. B | 2. C | 2. D |
| 3. A | 3. D | 3. B |
| 4. D | 4. E | 4. E |
| 5. E | 5. B | 5. D |
|      | 6. A |      |
|      | 7. D |      |

| Test 4 | Test 5 | Test 6 |
|--------|--------|--------|
| 1. E | 1. B | 1. B |
| 2. A | 2. E | 2. D |
| 3. B | 3. C | 3. B |
| 4. B | 4. A | 4. A |
| 5. C | 5. B |      |
|      | 6. C |      |

| Test 7 | Test 8 | Test 9 |
|--------|--------|--------|
| 1. C | 1. B | 1. E |
| 2. B | 2. C | 2. C |
| 3. A | 3. B | 3. C |
| 4. E | 4. D | 4. E |
| 5. C | 5. A | 5. B |
| 6. D | 6. D |      |

# MATHEMATICS PRACTICE

The tests to follow "mix" the types of questions—that is, each test includes a variety of areas. This treatment will give you a "feel" of the way in which the problems will be presented in the SAT.

If, after taking these tests, you require instruction in specific phases of mathematics (Profit and Loss, Fractions, Interest, etc.), we advise you to make good use of the "Mathematics Study Section." We also refer you to "Mathematics Simplified and Self-Taught."—$4.00 (Arco Publishing Co., Inc.)

## TEST 1

1. The distance run in a 100 meter race approximates most closely (a meter equals 39.37 inches)
   (A) 100 yards (B) 90 yards (C) 105 yards (D) 110 yards

2. The number of degrees through which the hour hand of a clock moves in 2 hours and 12 minutes is
   (A) 66 (B) 72 (C) 732 (D) none of these

3. All the faces of a four-inch cube have been painted. If this cube is cut into one-inch cubes the number of one-inch cubes that will have paint on none of their faces is
   (A) 27 (B) 16 (C) 8 (D) none of these

4. A cylindrical container has a diameter of 14 inches and a height of 6 inches. Since one gallon equals 231 cubic inches, the capacity of the tank is approximately (A) 2⅔ gallons (B) 4 gallons (C) 1⅐ gallons (D) none of these

5. A train running between two towns arrives at its destination 10 minutes late when it goes 40 miles per hour and 16 minutes late when it goes 30 miles per hour. The distance between the towns is
(A) 720 miles (B) 12 miles (C) 8⁶⁄₇ miles (D) none of these

6. If Paul can paint a fence in 2 hours and Fred can paint the same fence in 3 hours, Paul and Fred working together can paint the fence in
(A) 2.5 hours (B) 1.2 hours (C) 5 hours (D) 1 hour

7. An autoist drives 60 miles to his destination at an average speed of 40 miles per hour and makes the return trip at an average rate of 30 miles per hour. His average speed per hour for the entire trip is
(A) 35 miles (B) 34⅔ miles (C) 43⅓ miles (D) none of these

8. In the Fahrenheit scale, the temperature that is equivalent to 50° Centigrade is
(A) 122° (B) 90° (C) 106° (D) none of these

9. If the base of a rectangle is increased by 30% and the altitude is decreased by 20% the area is increased by
(A) 25% (B) 10% (C) 5% (D) 4%

10. Of the following sets of fractions, the set which is arranged in increasing order is
(A) ⁷⁄₁₂, ⁶⁄₁₁, ³⁄₅, ⅝ (B) ⁶⁄₁₁, ⁷⁄₁₂, ⅝, ³⁄₅ (C) ⁶⁄₁₁, ⁷⁄₁₂, ³⁄₅, ⅝ (D) none of these

### Answers Test 1

| | | | | |
|---|---|---|---|---|
| 1. D | 3. C | 5. B | 7. B | 9. D |
| 2. A | 4. B | 6. B | 8. A | 10. C |

## TEST 2

1. If the price of an automobile, including a 3% sales tax, is $2729.50, the amount of the sales tax is
(A) $79.50 (B) $129.50 (C) $81.89 (D) none of these

2. If the sum of the edges of a cube is 48 inches, the volume of the cube is
(A) 512 inches (B) 96 cubic inches (C) 64 cubic inches (D) none of these

3. The front wheels of a wagon are 7 ft. in circumference and the back wheels are 9 ft. in circumference. When the front wheels have made 10 more revolutions than the back wheels, the wagon has gone a distance of
(A) 126 ft. (B) 189 ft. (C) 315 ft. (D) none of these

4. In any square, the length of one side is
(A) one-half a diagonal of the square (B) the square root of the perimeter of the square (C) about .7 the length of a diagonal of the square (D) none of these

5. A rectangular flower bed whose dimensions are 16 yards by 12 yards is surrounded by a walk 3 yards wide. The area of the walk is
(A) 93 square yards (B) 396 square yards (C) 204 square yards (D) none of these

6. If the radius of a circle is diminished by 20%, the area is diminished by
(A) 20% (B) 400% (C) 40% (D) 36%

7. If a distance estimated at 150 feet is really 140 feet, the per cent of error in this estimate is
(A) 6⅔% (B) 7½% (C) 10% (D) none of these

8. The number of prime numbers between 50 and 75 is
(A) 6 (B) 7 (C) 8 (D) none of these

9. If an airplane flies 550 yards in 3 seconds, the speed of the airplane, expressed in miles per hour, is
(A) 125 (B) 375 (C) 300 (D) none of these

10. If the numerator and the denominator of a fraction are increased by the same quantity, the resulting fraction is
(A) always greater than the original fraction (B) always less than the original fraction (C) always equal to the original fraction (D) none of these

### Answers Test 2

| | | | | |
|---|---|---|---|---|
| 1. A | 3. C | 5. C | 7. B | 9. B |
| 2. C | 4. C | 6. D | 8. A | 10. A |

### TEST 3

1. A merchant sold two radios for $120 each. One was sold at a loss of 25% of the cost and the other was sold at a gain of 25% of the cost. On both transactions combined the merchant lost
(A) $64 (B) $36 (C) $16 (D) none of these

2. The number missing in the series 2, 6, 12, 20, ?, 42, 56, 72 is
(A) 30 (B) 40 (C) 36 (D) none of these

3. If two angles of a triangle are acute angles, the third angle
(A) is less than the sum of the two given angles (B) is an acute angle (C) is the largest angle of the triangle (D) may be an obtuse angle

4. The closest approximation to the value of $\sqrt{2/5}$ is
(A) .6 (B) ⅕ (C) .16 (D) .4

5. The best approximation for $\dfrac{1.300672 \times 2.00013}{0.05269873}$ is
(A) nearly but not quite 50 (B) somewhat more than 5 (C) somewhat more than 50 (D) none of these

6. The period of a pendulum is proportional to the square root of its length. Therefore, when the length of a pendulum is doubled, its period is
(A) doubled (B) decreased about 50% (C) increased about 40% (D) quadrupled

7. A wheel 24 inches in diameter is geared to another wheel 8 inches in diameter. When the larger wheel makes 30 revolutions per minute, the number of revolutions per minute made by the smaller circle is
(A) 90 (B) 30 (C) 10 (D) about 270

8. If one angle of a triangle equals the sum of the other two angles, the triangle must be
(A) scalene (B) obtuse-angled (C) acute-angled (D) right-angled

9. The rate for residential gas service (for bi-monthly periods) is in accordance with the following schedule:
For the first 1,000 cu. ft. or less $2.00
For the next 4,000 cu. ft.          12.5¢ per 100 cu. ft.
For the next 7,000 cu. ft.          10.0¢ per 100 cu. ft.
For the next 8,000 cu. ft.           9.0¢ per 100 cu. ft.
For excess over 20,000 cu. ft.       8.0¢ per 100 cu. ft.
The meter reading at the beginning of a given period was 5,000, and at the close 7,800. The charge for gas consumed (exclusive of sales tax) is
(A) $5.50 (B) $4.25 (C) $26.80 (D) $20.30

10. The sum of $8\frac{1}{8}$, $\frac{4}{5}$, $5\frac{1}{4}$, and $4\frac{3}{8}$ is
(A) $18\frac{91}{120}$ (B) $17\frac{91}{120}$ (C) $18\frac{17}{24}$ (D) $17\frac{5}{24}$

### Answers Test 3

| 1. D | 3. D | 5. C | 7. A | 9. B |
|------|------|------|------|------|
| 2. A | 4. A | 6. C | 8. D | 10. A |

## TEST 4

1. The difference in standard time between New York and San Francisco is 3 hours. When it is 12 o'clock noon, daylight saving time in New York, the standard time in San Francisco is
(A) 8 A.M. (B) 9 A.M. (C) 2 P.M. (D) 3 P.M.

2. A certain triangle has sides which are, respectively, 6 inches, 8 inches, and 10 inches long. A rectangle equal in area to that of the triangle has a width of 3 inches. The perimeter of the rectangle, expressed in inches, is
(A) 11 (B) 16 (C) 22 (D) 24

3. A room 27 feet by 32 feet is to be carpeted. The width of the carpet is 27 inches. The length, in yards, of the carpet needed for this floor is
(A) 1188 (B) 648 (C) 384 (D) 128

4. A bird flying 400 miles covers the first 100 at the rate of 100 miles an hour, the second 100 at the rate of 200 miles an hour, the third 100 at the rate of 300 miles an hour, and the last 100 at the rate of 400 miles an hour. The average speed was (in miles per hour)
(A) 192 (B) 212 (C) 250 (D) 150

5. The closest approximation to the correct answer for $5 - \sqrt{32.076} + (1.00017)^3$ is
(A) 1 (B) 2 (C) 5 (D) 9

6. The cube of $\frac{1}{3}$ is
(A) $\frac{3}{9}$ (B) $\frac{3}{27}$ (C) $\frac{1}{81}$ (D) $\frac{1}{27}$

7. One-fourth per cent of 360 is
(A) 0.09 (B) 0.9 (C) 9.0 (D) 90

8. In general, the sum of the squares of two numbers is greater than twice the product of the numbers. The pair of numbers for which this generalization is not valid is
(A) 8,9 (B) 9,9 (C) 9,10 (D) 8,10

9. A man spent exactly one dollar in the purchase of 3-cent stamps and 5-cent stamps. The number of 5-cent stamps which he could *not* have purchased under the circumstances, is
(A) 5 (B) 8 (C) 9 (D) 11

10. A bicycle was purchased for $50 payable in 60 days or at a discount of 5% for cash. If the purchaser pays in 60 days, he is paying interest per annum at an approximate rate of
(A) 5% (B) 10% (C) 15% (D) 30%

**Answers Test 4**

| | | | | |
|---|---|---|---|---|
| 1. A | 3. D | 5. A | 7. B | 9. C |
| 2. C | 4. A | 6. D | 8. B | 10. D |

## TEST 5

1. A piece of wire 132 inches long is bent successively in the shape of an equilateral triangle, a square, a regular hexagon, a circle. The plane surface of largest area is included when the wire is bent into the shape of a
(A) circle (B) square (C) hexagon (D) triangle

2. The number missing in the series 2, 5, 10, 17, _____, 37, 50, 65 is
(A) 22 (B) 24 (C) 26 (D) 27

3. Pieces of wire are soldered together so as to form the edges of a cube whose volume is 64 cubic inches. The number of inches of wire used is
(A) 24 (B) 48 (C) 64 (D) 96

4. Four quarts of a certain mixture of alcohol and water is at 50% strength. To it is added a quart of water. The alcoholic strength of the new mixture is
(A) 12.5% (B) 20% (C) 25% (D) 40%

5. A is older than B. With the passage of time
(A) the ratio of the ages of A and B remains unchanged (B) the ratio of the ages of A and B increases (C) the ratio of the ages of A and B decreases (D) the difference of their ages varies

6. An illustration in a dictionary is labeled: Scale ⅛. A measure of 1½ inches in the illustration corresponds to a real measure of
(A) ³⁄₁₆ inches (B) ⅜ inches (C) ⅜ foot (D) 1 foot

7. The diagonals of every rectangle
(A) are perpendicular to each other (B) bisect the angles (C) are equal (D) are oblique to each other

8. If the radius of a circle is increased by 100%, the per cent increase of its area is
(A) 100% (B) 200% (C) 300% (D) 400%

9. The distance from City A to City B is 150 miles; from City A to City C, 90 miles. Therefore it is necessarily true that
(A) the distance from B to C is 60 miles (B) six times the distance from A to B equals 10 times the distance from A to C (C) the distance from B to C is 240 miles (D) the distance from A to B exceeds by 30 miles twice the distance from A to C

10. A is 15 years old. B is one-third older. The number of years ago when B was twice as old as A is
(A) 3 (B) 5 (C) 7.5 (D) 10

**Answers Test 5**

| | | | | |
|---|---|---|---|---|
| 1. A | 3. B | 5. C | 7. C | 9. B |
| 2. C | 4. D | 6. D | 8. C | 10. D |

## TEST 6

1. A recent "educational bulletin" states that if you were
to eat each meal in a different restaurant in New York
City, it would take you more than 19 years to cover
all of New York City's eating places, assuming that
you eat three meals a day. On the basis of this information the best of the following choices is that the
number of restaurants in New York City:
(A) exceeds 20,500 (B) is closer to 21,000 than
22,000 (C) exceeds 21,000 (D) does not exceed
21,500

2. The cost of electricity for operating an 875 watt
toaster, an 1100 watt steam iron and four 75 watt
lamps, each for one hour, at 7.5 cents per kilowatt
hour (1 kilowatt equals 1000 watts) is:
(A) $.15 (B) $.17 (C) $1.54 (D) $1.71

3. If 4 typists can type 600 letters in 3 days, how many
letters can 2 typists complete in one day?
(A) 100 letters (B) 120 letters (C) 90 letters (D)
150 letters

4. The smaller angle, in degrees, between the directions
southeast and west is:
(A) 90 (B) 135 (C) 180 (D) 225

5. Assuming that the series will continue in the same
pattern, the next number in the series 3, 5, 11,
29 . . . is:
(A) 41 (B) 47 (C) 65 (D) 83

6. DCCXLIX in Roman numerals represents the
number:
(A) 749 (B) 764 (C) 1249 (D) 1264

7. In the total area of a picture measuring 10 inches by 12 inches plus a matting of uniform width surrounding the picture is 224 square inches, the width of the matting is:
(A) 2 inches (B) 2⁴⁄₁₁ inches (C) 3 inches (D) 4 inches

8. The net price of a $25 item after successive discounts of 20% and 30% is:
(A) $11.00 (B) $12.50 (C) $14.00 (D) $19.00

9. The cost of 63 inches of ribbon at $.12 per yard is:
(A) $.20 (B) $.21 (C) $.22 (D) $.23

10. If 1½ cups of cereal are used with 4½ cups of water, the amount of water needed with ¾ of a cup of cereal is:
(A) 2 cups (B) 2⅛ cups (C) 2¼ cups (D) 2½ cups

### Answers Test 6

| 1. A | 3. A | 5. D | 7. A | 9. B |
|------|------|------|------|------|
| 2. B | 4. B | 6. A | 8. C | 10. C |

### TEST 7

1. Under certain conditions, sound travels at about 1100 ft. per second. If 88 ft. per second is approximately equivalent to 60 miles per hour, the speed of sound, under the above conditions, is, of the following, closest to:
(A) 730 miles per hour (B) 740 miles per hour (C) 750 miles per hour (D) 760 miles per hour

2. Six quarts of a 20% solution of alcohol in water are mixed with 4 quarts of a 60% solution of alcohol in water. The alcoholic strength of the mixture is:
(A) 36% (B) 80% (C) 40% (D) none of these

3. The sum of an odd number and an even number is:
(A) sometimes an even number (B) always divisible by 3 or 5 or 7 (C) always an odd number (D) always a prime number

4. If one angle of a triangle is three times a second angle and the third angle is 20 degrees more than the second angle, the second angle is (in degrees):
(A) 32 (B) 34 (C) 40 (D) 50

5. Assuming that on a blueprint ¼ inch equals 12 inches, the actual length in feet of a steel bar represented on the blueprint by a line 3⅜ inches long is:
(A) 3⅜ (B) 6¾ (C) 12½ (D) 13½

6. A plane leaves Denver, Colo. (Mountain Standard Time Zone), on June 1 at 2 p.m. and arrives at New York City (Eastern Standard Time Zone) June 2 at 2 a.m. Eastern Standard is two hours later than Mountain Standard. The actual time of flight was:
(A) 10 hours (B) 11 hours (C) 12 hours (D) 13 hours

7. Of the following, the value closest to that of
$$\frac{42.10 \times .0003}{.002}$$ is:
(A) .063 (B) .63 (C) 6.3 (D) 63

8. If Mrs. Jones bought 3¾ yards of dacron at $1.16 per yard and 4⅔ yards of velvet at $3.87 per yard, the amount of change she receives from $25 is:
(A) $2.12 (B) $2.28 (C) $2.59 (D) $2.63

9. The water level of a swimming pool, 75 feet by 42 feet, is to be raised four inches. The number of gallons of water needed for this is (1 cu. ft. = 7.5 gal.):
(A) 140 (B) 7,875 (C) 31,500 (D) 94,500

10. The part of the total quantity represented by a 24 degree sector of a circle graph is:
    (A) 6⅔% (B) 12% (C) 13⅓% (D) 24%

**Answers Test 7**

| | | | | |
|---|---|---|---|---|
| 1. C | 3. C | 5. D | 7. C | 9. B |
| 2. A | 4. A | 6. A | 8. C | 10. A |

## TEST 8

1. If shipping charges to a certain point are 62 cents for the first five ounces and 8 cents for each additional ounce, the weight of a package for which the charges are $1.66 is:
   (A) 13 ounces (B) 1⅛ pounds (C) 1¼ pounds (D) 1½ pounds

2. If 15 cans of food are needed for seven men for two days, the number of cans needed for four men for seven days is:
   (A) 15 (B) 20 (C) 25 (D) 30

3. The total saving in purchasing 30 13-cent ice cream pops for a class party at a reduced rate of $1.38 per dozen is:
   (A) $.35 (B) $.40 (C) $.45 (D) $.50

4. Find the value of x in the equation $2x - .2x = 9$:
   (A) $x = 0$ (B) $x = 4.5$ (C) $x = 5$ (D) $x = 18$

5. An automobile traveled 6 hours at an average speed of 40 miles per hour. It averaged only 30 miles per hour on the return trip. What was the average speed per hour, to the nearest mile, for the round trip?
   (A) 34 mph (B) 35 mph (C) 36 mph (D) 37 mph

6. What is the value of the following fraction?

   $$\frac{3.2 \times .5 \times .25}{.08}$$

   (A) .05 (B) .50 (C) 5.0 (D) 50

7. A gallon of water is equal to 231 cubic inches. How many gallons of water are needed to fill a fish tank that measures 11″ high, 14″ long, and 9″ wide?

   (A) 6 gal. (B) 8 gal. (C) 9 gal. (D) 14 gal.

8. A savings and loan association pays 4% interest which is compounded quarterly. At this rate, what is the interest on $600 for one quarter?

   (A) $4 (B) $6 (C) $24 (D) $60

9. At an end-of-season sale, an air conditioner was sold at a 40% discount. If the sale price was $135.00, what was the list price?

   (A) $54 (B) $81 (C) $189 (D) $225

10. A motorist averaged 60 miles per hour in going a distance of 240 miles. He made the return trip over the same distance in 6 hours. What was his average speed for the entire trip?

    (A) 40 mph (B) 48 mph (C) 50 mph (D) 60 mph

### Answers Test 8

| | | | | |
|---|---|---|---|---|
| 1. B | 3. C | 5. A | 7. A | 9. D |
| 2. D | 4. C | 6. C | 8. B | 10. B |

### TEST 9

1. In a 4H Club, 8 boys earned 39 bushels of corn to use in feeding their pigs. Each boy's share was 4⅞ bushels. ⅞ in the answer 4⅞, represents

MATHEMATICS PRACTICE

291

(A) ⅞ of all the bushels to be divided (B) ⅞ of the bushels left over after dividing the bushels evenly (C) ⅛ of the 7 bushels left over after an even division (D) ⅞ of the 7 bushels left over after an even division

2. A invested $7000 in a business venture and his partner, B, invested $8000. They agreed to share the profit in the same ratio. What was A's share of the profit of $2250? (A) $1200.00 (B) $1050.00 (C) $1968.75 (D) none of these amounts

3. The relationship between .01% and .1 is
(A) 1 to 10 (B) 1 to 100 (C) 1 to 1000 (D) 1 to 10,000

4. If the volume of a rectangular solid is to be increased by 50% without changing its base, its altitude must be (A) cubed (B) increased by 50% (C) doubled (D) increased by 150%

5. The factors of $a^2 - b^2$ are
(A) $(a - b)$, $(a + b)$ (B) $(a - b)$, $(a - b)$ (C) $a^2 - b^2$ (D) $(a^2 - 1)$, $(1 - b^2)$

6. .125 written as a per cent is
(A) ⅛% (B) .125% (C) 12.5% (D) 125%

7. The smaller partial product in this example,
```
   789
 ×  67
 -----
  5523
 4734
 -----
 52863  is
```
(A) 67 (B) 5523 (C) 4734 (D) 789

8. A bank president received 8 times as much salary as one of the messenger boys. If the sum of their salaries is $13,500, the president's salary is
(A) $1,500 (B) $10,000 (C) $12,000 (D) $12,500

9. A bridge cable, 500 feet long when the temperature was 60 degrees Fahrenheit, expanded 0.3% when the temperature rose to 90 degrees Fahrenheit; it increased
(A) .15 ft. (B) 1.5 ft. (C) 15 ft. (D) 501.5 ft.

10. 8 divided by zero is equivalent to
(A) 8)$\overline{0}$ (B) 0 (C) 8 (D) none of these

### Answers Test 9

| | | | | |
|---|---|---|---|---|
| 1. C | 3. C | 5. A | 7. B | 9. B |
| 2. B | 4. B | 6. C | 8. C | 10. D |

## TEST 10

1. The scale on a map is ⅛ inch to 1 mile. To represent an actual distance of 2½ miles, the distance between the two points on a map must measure
(A) 20 inches (B) ⅝ inch (C) 2½ inches (D) ⁵⁄₁₆ inch

2. If $9x + 5 = 23$, the numerical value of $18x + 5$ is:
(A) 46 (B) 32 (C) 41 (D) $23 + 9x$

3. If there are 10 mills in a cent, a tax of 43.2 mills per dollar on property assessed at $12,500 is
(A) $5400 (B) $54 (C) $540 (D) none of these

4. If both numerator and denominator of a proper fraction are each decreased by the same quantity, the value of the original fraction is thereby

(A) unchanged (B) decreased (C) increased (D) decreased by 1

5. A single discount equivalent to two successive discounts of 12½% and 20% is
(A) 30% (B) 16¼% (C) 32½% (D) 22½%

6. The number of square tiles each 8 inches on a side needed to cover a rectangular area 12 feet by 16 feet is
(A) 36 (B) 3 (C) 432 (D) 864

7. An alloy is composed of 49.2% bismuth, 12.3% tin, 24.6% lead, and the remainder cadmium. In making a circle graph to show this composition the number of degrees in the sector for cadmium is approximately
(A) 31 (B) 25 (C) 14 (D) 50

8. The next term in the series 2, 7, 14, 23, _____, is
(A) 32 (B) 33 (C) 34 (D) 35

9. The speed of an object moving at 45 miles per hour is decreased by 22 feet per second. The reduced speed in miles per hour is
(A) 36 (B) 44 (C) 23 (D) 30

10. The size of a parcel post package is limited to a maximum of a combined length plus girth (perimeter of cross section) of 72 inches. The volume in cubic inches of the maximum package allowed having a length of 36 inches and a square cross section is
(A) 1296 (B) 648 (C) 1958 (D) 2916

### Answers Test 10

| | | | | |
|---|---|---|---|---|
| 1. D | 3. C | 5. A | 7. D | 9. D |
| 2. C | 4. B | 6. C | 8. C | 10. D |

# QUANTITATIVE COMPARISONS

**Common Information:** In each question, information concerning one or both of the quantities to be compared is given in the Item column. A symbol that appears in any column represents the same thing in Column A as it does in Column B.

**Numbers:** All numbers used are real numbers.

**Figures:** Assume that the position of points, angles, regions, and so forth, are in the order shown.

Assume that the lines shown as straight are indeed straight.

Figures are assumed to lie in a plane unless otherwise indicated.

Figures accompanying questions are intended to provide information you can use in answering the questions. However, unless a note states that a figure is drawn to scale, you should solve the problems by using your knowledge of mathematics, and NOT by estimating sizes by sight or by measurement.

*Directions:* For each of the following questions two quantities are given . . . one in Column A; and one in Column B. Compare the two quantities and mark your answer sheet with the correct, lettered conclusion. These are your options:

A: if the quantity in Column A is the greater;
B: if the quantity in Column B is the greater;
C: if the two quantities are equal;
D: if the relationship cannot be determined from the information given.

Explanations of the key points behind these questions appear with the answers at the end of this test. The explanatory answers provide the kind of background that will enable you to answer test questions with facility and confidence.

| Item | Column A | Column B |
|---|---|---|
| 1. $a > 0$<br>$x > 0$ | $a + x$ | $a - x$ |
| 2. | The average of 17, 19, 21, 23, 25 | The average of 16, 18, 20, 22, 24 |

3.

| | 2x | y |

| 4. $0 < a < 12$<br>$0 < b < 10$ | a | b |
| 5. $4a - 4b = 20$ | a | b |
| 6. | Angle A | Angle B |

| Item | Column A | Column B |
|---|---|---|

7.   $\dfrac{a}{9} = b^2$     a     b

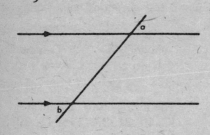

8.     a     b

9.     $3 + 24(3 - 2)$     $27 + 5(0)(5)$

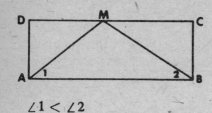

$\angle 1 < \angle 2$

10.     AM     BM

11.     Angle A +     Angle ACD
            Angle B

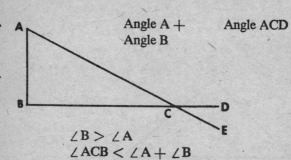

$\angle B > \angle A$
$\angle ACB < \angle A + \angle B$

12.     $(\tfrac{2}{3})^2(3)^3$     $(3)^2(\tfrac{2}{3})^3$

**Explanatory Answers**

1. (A)
   The statement a > 0 and x > 0 implies both a and x are positive. The sum of two positive numbers is always greater than their difference.

2. (A)
   The averages of Column A and Column B are 21 and 20 respectively.

3. (B)
   Angle ABC = x (all vertical angles are equal). Since $\angle C = 90°$, $\angle A + \angle ABC = 90°$ (180° in a $\triangle$). Therefore, 2x = 90°, and x = 45°. Angle ABC and $\angle y$ are supplementary; hence y = 135°. Therefore, y > 2x.

4. (D)
   Impossible to determine because a and b could be any integer from 1 to 11.

5. (A)
   4a − 4b = 20
   a − b = 5
   For all values of a and b, a > b.

6. (C)
   $\triangle$ ABC is an isosceles $\triangle$ and $\angle A = \angle B$.

7. (D)
   Impossible to determine because b could be a positive or negative integer.

8. (C)
   If two parallel lines are cut by a transversal, the alternate exterior angles are equal.

9. **(C)**
Column A and Column B both equal 27.

10. **(B)**
If 2 angles of a $\triangle$ are unequal, the greater side lies opposite the greater angle.

11. **(C)**
The exterior angle of a triangle is equal in degrees to the two interior nonadjacent angles.

12. **(A)**
The value of Column A is 12 and the value of Column B is $2\frac{3}{4}$. Therefore, A > B.

# QUANTITATIVE COMPARISONS
## PRACTICE TESTS

## Quantitative Comparisons Practice Test 1

*Directions:* For each of the following questions two quantities are given . . . one in Column A; and one in Column B. Compare the two quantities and mark your answer sheet with the correct, lettered conclusion. These are your options:

A: if the quantity in Column A is the greater;
B: if the quantity in Column B is the greater;
C: if the two quantities are equal;
D: if the relationship cannot be determined from the information given.

| Item | Column A | Column B |
|------|----------|----------|
| 1. | 5% of 34 | The number 34 is 5% of |
| 2. | $9^2$ | $\sqrt[3]{721}$ |
| 3. S = 1<br> T = 3<br> A = −2 | $[5A(4T)]^3$ | $[4A(5S)]^2$ |

1 < 2

| | | |
|------|----------|----------|
| 4. | IR | IT |

| Item | Column A | Column B |
|------|----------|----------|
| 5. $4 > x > -3$ | $x/3$ | $3/x$ |

6.

$$\frac{2}{8} + \frac{3}{7} \qquad\qquad \frac{16}{21} - \frac{3}{7}$$

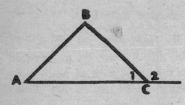

$\angle A > \angle B$

$\angle 1 < \angle A + \angle B$

| 7. | $\angle A + \angle B$ | $\angle 2$ |
|----|------------------------|------------|
| 8. $Y =$ an odd integer | The numerical value of $Y^2$ | The numerical value of $Y^3$ |

9.

| | $8 + 6 \div 3 - 7(2)$ | $6 + 8 \div 2 - 7(3)$ |

10. $N * A = 1/N^2 + A/2$

$$\frac{2}{8} * \frac{1}{3} \qquad\qquad \frac{1}{5} * \frac{3}{5}$$

11.

$$\frac{3}{4} \text{ of } \frac{9}{9} \qquad\qquad \frac{9}{9} \cdot \frac{3}{4}$$

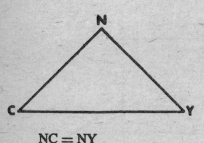

$NC = NY$

$\angle N > \angle C$

| 12. | NC | CY |

| Item | Column A | Column B |
|---|---|---|

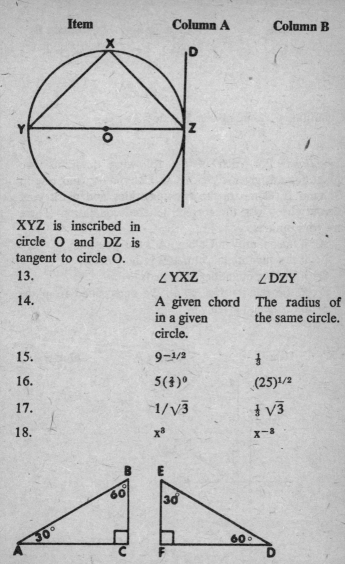

XYZ is inscribed in
circle O and DZ is
tangent to circle O.

| 13. | $\angle YXZ$ | $\angle DZY$ |
|---|---|---|
| 14. | A given chord in a given circle. | The radius of the same circle. |
| 15. | $9^{-1/2}$ | $\frac{1}{3}$ |
| 16. | $5(\frac{4}{3})^0$ | $(25)^{1/2}$ |
| 17. | $1/\sqrt{3}$ | $\frac{1}{3}\sqrt{3}$ |
| 18. | $x^3$ | $x^{-3}$ |

| 19. | BC | FD |
|---|---|---|

| Item | Column A | Column B |
|------|----------|----------|
| 20. | $4 + 3 \times 2 - 7$ | $8 \div 2 + 3 - 1$ |

## Quantitative Comparisons Practice Test 2

*Directions:* For each of the following questions two quantities are given . . . one in Column A; and one in Column B. Compare the two quantities and mark your answer sheet with the correct, lettered conclusion. These are your options:

A: if the quantity in Column A is the greater;
B: if the quantity in Column B is the greater;
C: if the two quantities are equal;
D: if the relationship cannot be determined from the information given.

| Item | Column A | Column B |
|------|----------|----------|

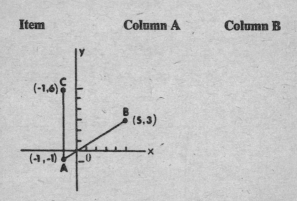

| | Column A | Column B |
|------|----------|----------|
| 1. | The length of AB | The length of AC |

| Item | Column A | Column B |
|---|---|---|

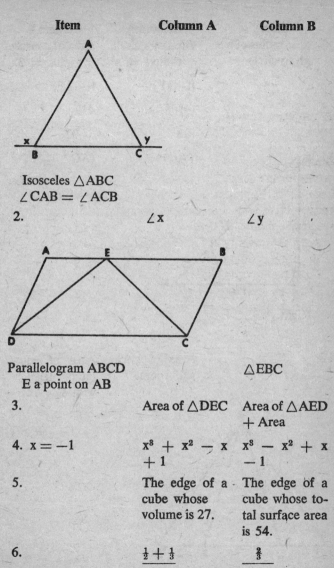

Isosceles △ABC
∠CAB = ∠ACB

2.           ∠x         ∠y

Parallelogram ABCD      △EBC
  E a point on AB

3.      Area of △DEC     Area of △AED + Area

4. $x = -1$    $x^3 + x^2 - x + 1$    $x^3 - x^2 + x - 1$

5.      The edge of a cube whose volume is 27.    The edge of a cube whose total surface area is 54.

6.      $\dfrac{\frac{1}{2} + \frac{1}{3}}{\frac{2}{3}}$      $\dfrac{\frac{2}{3}}{\frac{1}{2} + \frac{1}{3}}$

| Item | Column A | Column B |
|------|----------|----------|
| 7. $x$ = radius of a given circle. | Area of a circle radius = $x^3$ | Area of a circle radius = $3x$ |
| 8. | $[(-\frac{1}{2})^2]^3$ | $[(-\frac{1}{2})^3]^2$ |
| 9. | $(\frac{1}{4})^{-2}$ | $4^2$ |
| 10. | $.02$ | $\sqrt{.02}$ |
| 11. | $(AB)^2$ | $(AC)^2 + 5CB$ |

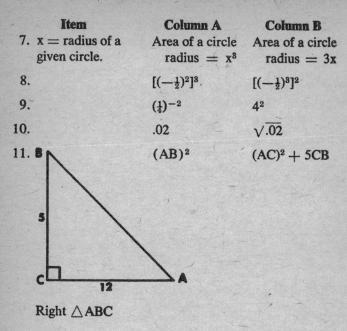

Right $\triangle ABC$

| | | |
|------|----------|----------|
| 12. | Area of circle with radius 7. | Area of equilateral triangle with side 14. |
| 13. | $\angle B$ | $\angle C$ |

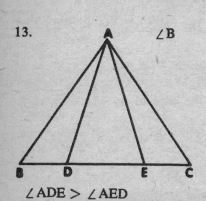

$\angle ADE > \angle AED$

| Item | Column A | Column B |
|------|----------|----------|
| 14. | Area of shaded portion. | Area of small circle. |

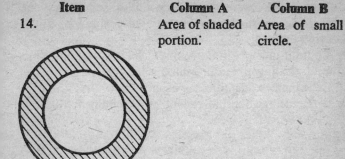

Radius of large
circle = 10
Radius of small
circle = 7

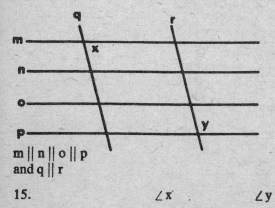

$m \parallel n \parallel o \parallel p$
and $q \parallel r$

| 15. | $\angle x$ | $\angle y$ |
|-----|------------|------------|

## Quantitative Comparisons Practice Test 3

*Directions:* For each of the following questions two quantities are given . . . one in Column A; and one in

Column B. Compare the two quantities and mark your answer sheet with the correct, lettered conclusion. These are your options:

A: if the quantity in Column A is the greater;
B: if the quantity in Column B is the greater;
C: if the two quantities are equal;
D: if the relationship cannot be determined from the information given.

| Item | Column A | Column B |
|------|----------|----------|
| 1. a < 0 < b | $a^2$ | b/2 |
| 2. t < 0 < r | $t^2$ | r |

(Diagram for problems 3 to 7)

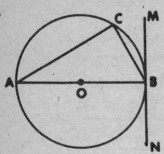

MN tangent to circle
O at point B and
∠A = 30°

| | | |
|---|---|---|
| 3. | m ∠ACB | m ∠NBO |
| 4. | CB | AC |
| 5. | m ∠CBM | m ∠CAB |
| 6. | m ∠CBA | m ∠CBM |
| 7. | $\overline{AO} + \overline{AC}$ | $\overline{BO} + \overline{BC}$ |

| Item | Column A | Column B |
|---|---|---|

(Diagram for problems 8 to 12)

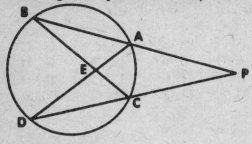

$\overline{AB} = \overline{CD}$
BD = 160°
AC = 40°

| | Column A | Column B |
|---|---|---|
| 8. | m ∠APC | m ∠ABC |
| 9. | m ∠BED | m ∠BEA |
| 10. | m ∠BAD | m ∠DCB |
| 11. | m ∠BCP | m ∠AEC + m ∠ADC |
| 12. | DC + AC | BD |
| 13. | 75% of ¾ | .09 × 6 |
| 14. | 4% of .003 | 3% of .004 |

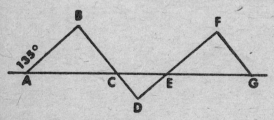

Intersecting straight lines
AB | CB, CD = ED

| | | |
|---|---|---|
| 15. | ∠BCA | ∠FEG |

## Answer Key to Quantitative Comparisons Tests

### Test 1

| | | | | |
|---|---|---|---|---|
| 1. B | 5. D | 9. A | 13. C | 17. C |
| 2. A | 6. A | 10. B | 14. D | 18. D |
| 3. B | 7. D | 11. C | 15. C | 19. D |
| 4. A | 8. D | 12. B | 16. C | 20. B |

### Test 2

| | | | | |
|---|---|---|---|---|
| 1. A | 4. A | 7. D | 10. B | 13. D |
| 2. D | 5. C | 8. C | 11. C | 14. A |
| 3. C | 6. A | 9. C | 12. A | 15. D |

### Test 3

| | | | | |
|---|---|---|---|---|
| 1. D | 4. B | 7. A | 10. C | 13. A |
| 2. D | 5. C | 8. A | 11. B | 14. C |
| 3. C | 6. A | 9. A | 12. B | 15. C |

## MATHEMATICS STUDY SECTION

Ten kinds of problems are explained and solved in this section. Samples of each of the ten "basic" kinds of problems are solved in step-by-step fashion. Most of the problems you will face on actual SAT are quite like these problems, or variations of these. The principles they apply encompass a vast number and variety of problems.

### PROFIT AND LOSS

1. Hammers are bought for $18.00 a dozen. In order to gain 40%, what must the selling price per hammer be?
   (A) $2.10 (B) $2.00 (C) $2.50 (D) $3.00

*SOLUTION:* To find the selling price we must multiply the cost by the rate of profit or loss.

In this case the cost $18.00 divided by 12; $18.00 being the cost of an entire dozen. Since there is a profit of 40% we must multiply the cost by 1.40 or 140%. (If we sold something at 100% of its cost, we should be getting what we paid for it.)

$$\frac{18}{12} \times 1.40 = \begin{array}{r} 18 \\ \times 1.40 \\ \hline 720 \\ 18 \\ \hline 25.20 \end{array}$$

$$\begin{array}{r} 2.10 \quad \text{Answer} \\ 12)\overline{25.20} \end{array}$$

To find the rate of profit or loss, we first find the actual profit or loss and then find what per cent of the COST this is.

2. Hammers are bought for $30.00 a dozen and sold at $3.50 each. The rate of profit on the transaction is:
(A) 30% (B) 40% (C) 50% (D) 45%

*SOLUTION:* Multiplying $3.50 by 12 to find the cost of a dozen hammers:

$$\$3.50 \times 12 = \$42.00$$

Subtracting the cost from the selling price to find the actual profit:

$$
\begin{array}{r}
\$42.00 \\
-\ 30.00 \\
\hline
\$12.00
\end{array}
$$

Finding what per cent of the cost the profit is involves converting a fraction into a per cent. We multiply the fraction by 100 and perform the indicated divisions:

$$\frac{\$12}{\$30} \times 100 =$$

$$
\begin{array}{r}
40\% \quad \text{Answer} \\
\overline{30)\ 1200}
\end{array}
$$

## ADDITION OF FRACTIONS

3. If we add $8\frac{1}{5}$, $45\frac{5}{8}$, $2\frac{17}{20}$, $14\frac{1}{2}$, and $1\frac{21}{40}$ the answer will be
(A) $70\frac{8}{10}$ (B) $72\frac{7}{10}$ (C) $72\frac{1}{5}$ (D) $70\frac{7}{10}$

*SOLUTION:* In adding mixed numbers like these, we perform three additions: The addition of the whole numbers, the addition of the fractions, and combination of the added whole numbers and fractions. Adding the whole numbers presents no difficulty. Our sum is 70.

To add the fractions we must first find the least common denominator. In this case it is 40.

Then for each separate fraction we divide the denominator into the common denominator and multiply the resulting quotient by the numerator.

We add all these products and divide by the common denominator. Here are the actual calculations:

$$
\begin{array}{r}
\dfrac{40}{} \\
8\frac{1}{5} \qquad 8 \\
45\frac{5}{8} \qquad 25 \\
2\frac{17}{20} \qquad 34 \\
14\frac{1}{2} \qquad 20 \\
12\frac{1}{40} \qquad 21 \\
\hline
\dfrac{108}{40} = 2\frac{28}{40} = 2\frac{7}{10}
\end{array}
$$

$$
\begin{array}{r}
70 \\
+\,2\dfrac{7}{10} \\
\hline
72\dfrac{7}{10} \text{ Answer}
\end{array}
$$

## INTEREST

4. $1,850 is invested for 50 days at a rate of 5%. The interest return is
   (A) $12.00 (B) $10.00 (C) $12.67 (D) $13.00

*SOLUTION:* While there are many short cuts used by banks and commercial houses in computing interest, the best plan for the candidate is to understand thoroughly all the steps involved in this computation and to use them all intelligently.

If we multiply the principal by the rate of interest, and the length of time the money draws interest, we have the amount of interest due.

If the money were to bear interest for a year we would merely have to multiply $1,850 by 5% ($\frac{5}{100}$) in this example. However, the money bears interest for only 50 days or $\frac{50}{365}$ of a year. The rest is done by simple cancellation.

$$\frac{\$925 \quad 1 \quad 1}{\$1850 \times 5 \times 50} = \frac{925}{73} = \$12.67 \text{ Answer}$$
$$\frac{100 \quad 365}{2 \quad 73}$$
$$1$$

Expressed as a formula, interest may be computed thus: $P \times R \times T = I$. If we are given interest, principal, and time, and asked to find the Rate, the operation may be expressed thus:

$$R = \frac{I}{P \times T}$$

And if we are given R, T, and I, and asked to find the Principal, this is the formula:

$$P = \frac{I}{R \times T}$$

5. What amount of money yields $40.00 per month if invested at an annual rate of 5%?
   (A) $9,000 (B) $9,500 (C) $9,600 (D) $9,400

*SOLUTION:* To find the principal we must divide interest by the product of rate and time.

If we multiply $40.00 per month by twelve we find the interest yield for a year. $40 × 12 = $480.00. The Time factor in this problem is now one year.

For the rest we have only to follow out our formula:

$$P = \frac{I}{R \times T} = P = \frac{\$480}{\frac{5}{100} \times 1}$$

**DIVISION OF FRACTIONS:** At this point an interesting difficulty presents itself: the division of fractions. To divide $480 by $\frac{5}{100}$ we have simply to invert the fraction and multiply thus:

$$\$480 \div \frac{5}{100} = \$\overset{96}{\cancel{480}} \times \frac{100}{\cancel{5}} = \$9,600 \text{ Answer}$$

6. A woman invested $4,000 in a speculative venture for 9 months. A second woman invested $6,000 in the same business for 6 months. The net gain was $720.00. What was the second woman's return on her investment if all the profits were divided between the two women?

   (A) $360 (B) $700 (C) $400 (D) $350

*SOLUTION:* In the matter of dividends, the investment of $6,000 for 6 months is the same as the investment of $36,000 for 1 month. The same statement can be made regarding $4,000 for 9 months.

| | |
|---|---|
| First Woman | — $4,000 for 9 months = $36,000 for 1 month. |
| Second Woman | — $6,000 for 6 months = $36,000 for 1 month. |
| Both | $72,000 for 1 month. |

It is a coincidence that the shares of the two women in this example are the same. However, the procedure here is exactly the same as though they had different shares.

We find what part the second woman's share bears to the total. We then take this proportion of the total income and our result is the second woman's share.

$$\frac{\overset{1}{\cancel{36,000}}}{\underset{2}{\cancel{72,000}}} \times 720 = \$360 \text{ Answer}$$

7. The rate of interest on a principal of \$10,000 that will yield \$80.00 in 65 days is
   (A) 4% (B) 5.5% (C) 4.49% (D) 6%
   *SOLUTION:* The formula here is

$$R = \frac{I}{P \times T}$$

Substituting, we have:

$$R = \frac{\$80}{10,000 \times \dfrac{65}{365}} = \frac{\$80}{\dfrac{650,000}{365}} =$$

$$\$80 \times \frac{365}{650,000} = \frac{29,200}{650,000}$$

CONVERTING A FRACTION INTO A PERCENT: This is a simple operation if the proper steps be known and taken. We must convert the fraction $\dfrac{29,200}{650,000}$ into a per cent so that we may properly express the rate of interest.

To change a fraction into a per cent we must multiply

the fraction by 100 and then carry through the indicated division.

$$\frac{29,200}{650,000} \times 100 = \frac{2,920,000}{650,000} =$$

$$\overline{650,000 ) \,\, 2,920,000} \quad 4.49\% \quad \text{Answer}$$

## ASSESSMENT

8. If a piece of property is assessed at $45,700 and the tax rate on real property is $2.40 per $1,000, the amount of tax that must be paid on this property is
   (A) $110 (B) $112 (C) $109.68 (D) $109

*SOLUTION:* Since the tax rate is $2.40 per $1,000, we must determine how many thousands of dollars are involved. To do this, we divide $45,700 by $1,000. And the result is 45.7.

When we multiply 45.7 by $2.40,
we learn the amount of the tax—$109.68.

9. $60,000 worth of land is assessed at 120% of its value. If the tax rate is $2.56 per $1,000 the amount of tax to be paid is
   (A) $190 (B) $195 (C) $184.32 (D) $180

*SOLUTION:* To find how much the land has been assessed:

$$60,000 \times \frac{120}{100} = \frac{720,000}{10} = \$72,000$$

If tax is $2.56 per $1,000, multiply:

$$\begin{array}{r} 2.56 \\ \times\ 72 \\ \hline 512 \\ 1792 \\ \hline \$184.32 \quad \text{Answer} \end{array}$$

## CUBIC VOLUME

10. A bin measures 14 feet by 9 feet by 7½ feet. Allowing ⅘ bushel of grain per cubic foot, how many bushels will the bin hold?

*SOLUTION:* Length × Width × Height = Cubic Area.

$$14 \times 9 \times 7\tfrac{1}{2} = \cancel{14}^{\,7} \times 9 \times \frac{15}{\cancel{2}} = 945 \text{ cubic ft.}$$

Since each cubic foot of space holds ⅘ bushel of grain:

$$\cancel{945}^{\,189} \times \frac{4}{\cancel{5}} = 756 \text{ Bushels.}$$

## LITERAL PROBLEMS

11. If L explosions occur during a given month and result in Q dollars of loss, the average loss per explosion in dollars is:

(A) $L \times Q$ (B) $\dfrac{Q}{L}$ (C) $\dfrac{L}{A}$ (D) $\dfrac{12K}{2P}$ (E) none

*SOLUTION:* This is a simple problem in determining an average. The presence of letters rather than numbers makes it slightly more difficult by imposing upon us the burden of using fundamental principles rather than habitual modes of action.

The average loss per explosion is the total loss divided by the number of explosions, or the average loss per explosion equals

$$\frac{\text{Total amount of loss}}{\text{Number of explosions}}$$

Since the total loss in a given month is Q and the number of explosions is L we may say that the average loss per explosion is $\dfrac{Q}{L}$.

12. If there is a total of J garbage trucks in operation in New York City, covering a total street mileage of N miles at an average speed of E miles per hour, we can find the average street mileage per truck from the above data, without considering

   (A) the number of cars
   (B) the total street mileage
   (C) the average speed
   (D) any of these values
   (E) any further data besides the above.

*SOLUTION:* The average street mileage per truck is the total street mileage divided by the total number of trucks, that is, the average street mileage per truck = $\dfrac{\text{Total street mileage}}{\text{Total No. of trucks}}$ (if we had 20 trucks covering a total street mileage of 300 miles then the average mileage covered by each truck is 15 miles or

$$\frac{300}{20} = 15 \text{ miles.})$$

From this it is clear that the average speed of the trucks does not come into the consideration of the average mileage per truck and therefore answer C is correct.

13. During 1938, T families took out insurance policies, representing an increase of M families over the number taking them in 1936. In 1937, however, the number taking out insurance was P less than in 1936. If there were R insurance agents in each of these 3 years, the average number of policies written per insurance agent in 1937 was:

(A) $\dfrac{T - M}{P + R}$    (B) $\dfrac{T - M - P}{R}$

(C) $\dfrac{M + T - R}{R}$    (D) $\dfrac{T + M + P}{R}$

*SOLUTION:* We must first determine how many people took out insurance in 1937 and get this quantity in terms of T, M, and P.

in 1938—T families took out insurance

in 1936—T — M families took out insurance (since 1938 is an increase of M over 1936.)

in 1937—(no. in 1936) — P (since it was P less than 1936) = T — M — P — Total number of Policies in 1937.

Now the average number of policies per insurance agent:

$$\frac{\text{Total number of policies in 1937}}{\text{Total number of insurance agents in 1937}} =$$

$$\frac{T - M - P}{R} \quad \text{Answer}$$

14. Clerk A sorts B letters per hour; clerk C sorts D letters per hour. The D letters which clerk C sorts exceeds those which clerk A sorts by 10 letters per hour. Measured in number sorted per 8-hour day, clerk C exceeds A by:

(A) $D - B \times 10$ (B) $(D - B) \times 8$ (C) $D + C - A + B$ (D) $C + D - A + B$

SOLUTION: The D letters sorted per hour by clerk C exceeds (is greater than) the B letters sorted per hour by clerk A, by an amount of 10 letters per hour, or D is 10 more than B. In symbols: $D = B + 10$.

In 8 hours, clerk C will have sorted 8 D letters while clerk A will have sorted 8 B letters and since the difference in one hour is 10 letters, in 8 hours, the difference will be $8 \times 10$. $8D = 8B + 80$ or by bringing 8B to the other side, we have $8D - 8B = 80$. By factoring out the 8 on the left, we have $8(D - B) = 80$ which is the amount of letters by which clerk C's output exceeds clerk A's output and hence answer B above is correct.

15. The annual salary of a machinist is R dollars more than that of his assistant. His assistant earns V dollars annually. The amount in monthly salary, by which the machinist exceeds his assistant is given by:

(A) $\dfrac{V - R}{13}$     (B) $\dfrac{RV}{12}$

(C) $R - V$     (D) $12V - R$

(E) $\dfrac{R}{12}$

SOLUTION: The annual salary of the machinist is $V + R$ dollars. The annual salary of his assistant is V dollars.

The monthly salary of the machinist is $\dfrac{V}{12} + \dfrac{R}{12}$ dollars. (Since in a year the machinist receives 12 times as much as he receives in a month, we divide the yearly salary by 12 to find the amount earned in one month.) Similarly, the monthly salary of his assistant is $\dfrac{V}{12}$ dollars. Therefore the machinist's monthly salary exceeds his assistant's salary, monthly, by $\dfrac{R}{12}$ dollars.

16. A family of 5 has two employed members earning L dollars a month. The family receives a total semimonthly relief allowance of M dollars. If the rent allowance is N dollars, and the amount spent for food is twice that for rent, the amount spent monthly for all items other than food and rent is

(A) $L + 2M - 3N$  (B) $\dfrac{N + L + M}{5}$

(C) $L + M - 2N$

SOLUTION: The amount spent monthly for all items other than food and rent is the total income for one month minus the total expenditure for food and rent.

Total income $= L + 2M$ (since M is a semi-monthly allowance, the monthly allowance is 2M or M multiplied by 2.)

Total expenditure for food and rent per month $= N$ (for rent) $+ 2N$ (for food). Since the total income per month $= L + 2M$, if we subtract the expenditure for food and rent, we will have the amount spent for other items: $L + 2M - (N + 2N) = L + 2M - 3N$. Answer.

17. If psychological studies of college students show K per cent to be emotionally unstable, the number of college students not emotionally unstable per one hundred college students is:

(A) 100 minus K (B) 100 times (K minus) (C) K minus 1

*SOLUTION:* Since K per cent $= \dfrac{K}{100}$ in 100 students,

K% of 100 are emotionally unstable then $\dfrac{K}{100} \times 100 =$ K students who are unstable. Therefore the remaining students are emotionally stable and they number 100 — K.

## RATE, TIME, AND DISTANCE PROBLEMS

In all these problems the formula to be followed is very simple:

$$\text{Rate (speed)} \times \text{Time} = \text{Distance.}$$

If you are given the RATE and DISTANCE and are asked to find time, then you simply make the obvious modification in the formula:

$$\text{Time} = \frac{\text{Distance}}{\text{Rate}}$$

To find rate given distance and time:

$$\frac{\text{Distance}}{\text{Time}} = \text{Rate}$$

There are many variations that can be introduced but if these fundamental ideas can be kept clearly in view, few difficulties will be encountered.

18. Two hikers start walking from the city line at different times. The second hiker whose speed is 4 miles per hour starts 2 hours after the first hiker whose speed is 3 miles per hour. Determine the amount of time and distance that will be consumed before the second hiker catches up with the first.

*SOLUTION:* Since the first man has a 2 hour head-start and is walking at the 3 miles per hour, he is 6 miles from the city line when the second hiker starts.

$$\text{Rate} \times \text{Time} = \text{Distance}.$$

Subtracting 3 miles per hour from 4 miles per hour gives us 1 mile per hour or the difference in the rates of speed of the two men. In other words, the second hiker gains one mile on the first hiker in every hour.

Since there is a 6 mile difference to cut down and it is cut down one mile every hour, it is clear that the second hiker will need 6 hours to overtake his companion.

In this time he will have traveled $4 \times 6 = 24$ or 24 miles. The first hiker will have been walking 8 hours since he had a 2 hour headstart $8 \times 3 = 24$.

19. The same two hikers start walking toward each other along a road connecting two cities which are 60 miles apart. Their speeds are the same as in the preceding problem, 3 and 4 miles per hour. How much time will elapse before they meet?

*SOLUTION:* In each hour of travel toward each other the men will cut down a distance equal to the sum of their speeds. $3 + 4 = 7$ miles per hour. To meet they must cut down 60 miles, and at 7 miles per hour this would be

$$T = \frac{D}{R} = \frac{60}{7} = 8\frac{4}{7}\text{hours.}$$

20. The problem might also have asked: "How much distance must the slower man cover before the two hikers meet?" In such case we should have gone through the same steps plus one additional step:

The time consumed before meeting was $8\frac{4}{7}$ hours. To find the distance covered by the slower hiker we merely multiply his rate by the time elapsed.

$$R \times T = D \qquad 3 \times 8\frac{4}{7} = 25\frac{5}{7} \text{ Answer.}$$

## TIME AND WORK PROBLEMS

21. If A does a job in 6 days, and B does the same job in 3 days, how long will it take the two of them, working together, to do the job?

*SOLUTION:* Almost any problem of this type can be solved quite simply by fractions, without resorting to higher mathematics.

A. If A does the whole job in 6 days, he will do ⅙ of the job in one day.
   If B does the whole job in 3 days, he will do ⅓ of the job in one day.

B. ⅓ + ⅙ = ½

C. ½ of the job will be finished in one day if the two men work together.

D. The whole job will be finished in two days.

## EXPLANATION OF SOLUTION:

A. If you are given the time that a job takes you have merely to find the reciprocal of that time in order to find how much of the work would be done in one day. Finding the reciprocal simply means inverting the figure.

If you do a job in $2\frac{1}{2}$ days, you would do $\frac{2}{5}$ of the job in one day.

$$2\frac{1}{2} = \frac{5}{2}$$

Finding the reciprocal or inverting:

$$\frac{5}{2} \rightarrow \frac{2}{5}$$

Another way of looking at the same operation:

All of the work is done in $\frac{5}{2}$ days. In other words it takes 5 half-days to finish the job. In one-half day $\frac{1}{5}$ of the job would be completed, and consequently in one day ($\frac{2}{2}$) $\frac{2}{5}$ of the job would be completed.

CAUTION: If the total time for the job is given in HOURS you will, by getting the reciprocal, find what fraction of the work is done in one HOUR. The procedure for the rest of the problem, of course, is the same as above, except that the answer is in hours.

B. The total time must be reduced to a fraction of the total job because it would not do to simply add the time consumed by each man. 3 days and 6 days added together yield nine days, which is merely TIME and tells us nothing of the AMOUNT OF WORK. But $\frac{1}{3}$ and $\frac{1}{6}$ do represent amounts of work.

C. Adding these two factors together we discover the part of the job that would be completed in one day.

D. If we are told that a certain fraction represents the amount of work done in one day and if we wish to find how long the entire job would take, we find the reciprocal of the fraction.

½ in 1 day        $\dfrac{2}{2}$ (or all) in $\dfrac{2}{1}$ days.

Two principles should be kept in mind.

1. To find the part, invert the time.
2. To find the time, invert the part.

22. A and B working together do a job in 4½ days. B, working alone, is able to do the job in 10 days. How long would it take A, working alone, to do the job?

*SOLUTION:* All of the job in 9/2 days; $\dfrac{2}{9}$ of the job in 1 day.

If B takes 10 days to do the job alone he will do $\frac{1}{10}$ of the job in one day.

To find the work done by A in one day we subtract B's work from the amount of work done by the two men together in one day.

$$\text{2/9} - \text{1/10} = \frac{20 - 9}{90} = \frac{11}{90}$$

$\frac{11}{90}$ represents the portion of the total job done by A in one day.

Inverting, we find how long it would take him to do the entire job.

$$\frac{90}{11} = 8 \frac{2}{11} \text{ Days.}$$

23. If A can do a job in 6 days which B can do in 5½ days, and C can do in 2⅕ days, how long would the job take if A, B, and C were working together?

*SOLUTION:*

A  Does the job in 6 days: 1/6 of the job in 1 day.

B  Does the job in 5½ days: 2/11 of the job in 1 day.

C  Does the job in 2⅕ days: 5/11 of the job in 1 day.

Add the work done by A, B, and C in one day to find the work done by all three in one day:

$$\frac{1}{6} + \frac{2}{11} + \frac{5}{11} = \frac{11 + 12 + 30}{66} = \frac{53}{66}.$$

Find the reciprocal of $\frac{53}{66}$ in order to find how long the

total job would take:

$$\frac{66}{53} = 1\frac{13}{53}\text{Days.}$$

24. One pipe fills a pool in 20 minutes, a second can fill the pool in 30 minutes, and a third can fill it in 10 minutes. How long would it take the three together to fill the pool?

*SOLUTION:* First pipe—fills in 20 minutes—fills 1/20 of pool in 1 minute.

Second pipe—fills in 30 minutes—fills 1/30 of pool in 1 minute.

Third pipe—fills in 10 minutes—fills 1/10 of pool in 1 minute.

B. Add the three fractions together to determine what part of the pool will be filled in one minute when the three pipes are working together:

$$\frac{1}{20} + \frac{1}{30} + \frac{1}{10} = \frac{3 + 2 + 6}{60} = \frac{11}{60}.$$

C. If $^{11}/_{60}$ of the pool is filled in one minute the reciprocal of the fraction will tell us how many minutes will be required to fill the whole pool:

$$\frac{60}{11} = 5\frac{5}{11} \text{ minutes. Answer.}$$

## PROBLEMS IN PROPORTIONS

25. If 5 men can build 6 miles of railroad track in 40 days, how many miles of track can be built by 3 men in 15 days?

*SOLUTION:* One of the best methods of solving such problems is by directly making the necessary cancellations, divisions, and multiplications.

In this example, we wish to find how many miles of track will be built if both the number of workers and the working time are reduced. It is easily seen that the amount of track constructed will be less than under the old conditions. But how much less?

Since we now have 3 men where before there were 5, we may assume that so far as man power is concerned, production will be $^3/_5$ as high as when 5 men were working. Consequently:

$$6 \times 3\frac{3}{5} \text{ miles of track.}$$

Thus we know that if 3 men worked 40 days they would build $3\frac{3}{5}$ miles of track.

But another factor serves to lessen production. And that is the decrease in time. Only 15 days are expended, or $^{15}/_{40}$ of the time that was expended before. Consequently:

$$3\frac{3}{5} \times \frac{15}{40} = \frac{18}{5} \times \frac{15}{40}$$

$$= \frac{27\cancel{0}}{20\cancel{0}} = 1\frac{7}{20} \text{ Miles of track.}$$

The two arithmetical operations just shown can, of course, be combined into one. Thus:

$$6 \times \frac{3}{5} \times \frac{15}{40} = 1\frac{7}{20} \text{ Miles of track.}$$

26. If 5 men build 6 miles of railroad track in 40 days, how many miles of track can be built by 8 men working 90 days?

*SOLUTION:* Here we have a problem which is similar to the previous one, with this exception: more men are working a longer period of time and consequently the the answer will yield not a reduced but an increased number of miles of track.

If we multiply a number by a fraction whose value is less than one, we are reducing the value of that number. If, however, we multiply the number by a fraction whose value is more than one, we are increasing the value of that number. In solving this problem, then, we would not multiply $6 \times \frac{40}{90} \times \frac{5}{8}$. That would produce a number

less than 6 and we know that our answer should be more than 6 since we have more men working a longer time than were required to produce 6 miles of track. The proper way of expressing the facts given in the example is:

$$6 \times \frac{90}{40} \times \frac{8}{5} = \frac{43\cancel{2}0}{20\cancel{0}} = 21\frac{12}{20} \text{ Miles of track.}$$

Some examples indicate an increase in one factor and a decrease in another.

27. If 10 men earn $500 in 12 days, how much will 6 men earn in 15 days?

*SOLUTION:* The number of men involved decreases and consequently the fraction will be less than one. The smaller number will therefore be the numerator.

$$\$500 \times \frac{6}{10}$$

The number of days worked increases and so the fraction will be more than one. The larger number will therefore be the numerator.

$$\$500 \times \frac{6}{10} \times \frac{15}{12} = \frac{45,000}{120} = \$375$$

## MIXTURE PROBLEMS

28. A wine merchant has 32 gallons of wine worth $1.50 a gallon. If he wishes to reduce the price to $1.20 a gallon, how many gallons of water must he add?
   (A) 10 (B) 9 (C) 8 (D) 7

*SOLUTION:* First let us find the cost of the 32 gallons of undiluted wine at the old price.

$$32 \times \$1.50 = \$48.00.$$

$48, then, is the value of the wine that is ultimately to be mixed with water. By the conditions of the problem, $48 will be the price realized from the sale of the wine at the new price of $1.20.

To find how many gallons of wine we shall have at the

new price let us divide $48 by $1.20, the new price. The answer, of course, is 40. We see then that we must have 40 gallons of the $1.20 wine.

This is 8 gallons more than the undiluted wine. And that difference of 8 gallons is made up by water.

29. A bakery shop sold 3 kinds of cake. The prices of these three kinds were 25¢, 30¢, and 35¢ per pound. The income from these sales was $36. If the number of pounds of each kind of cake sold was the same, how many pounds were sold?

*SOLUTION:* To buy all three kinds of cake would cost 25¢ + 30¢ + 35¢ = 90¢.

If we divide $36, the total income, by 90¢, the total price of the three kinds of cake, we will know how many times each kind of cake was sold in order to realize the $36. $\frac{\$36.00}{\$ \ .90} = 40$. Since there were just as many of each kind of cake sold, the total number of pounds sold = 40 × 3 = 120.

30. The number of dimes in a cash register was equal to the number of quarters. There were five times as many nickles as quarters. All these coins together totalled $120. How many of each were there?

*SOLUTION:* Let us again make groups, this time of coins. A group will consist of five nickles + 1 quarter + 1 dime which equals 60¢. If we divide $120 by 60¢ we find that there are 200 such 60¢ groups contained in $120. Since there are 5 nickles in every one of the 200 groups we multiply 200 by 5 to find the number of nickles—1,000. There are 200 dimes and 200 quarters.